Meaning, Madness and Political Subjectivity

D1726484

This book explores the relationship between subjective experience and the cultural, political, and historical paradigms in which the individual is embedded. Providing a deep analysis of three compelling case studies of schizophrenia in Turkey, the book considers the ways in which private experience is shaped by collective structures, offering insights into issues surrounding religion, national and ethnic identity and tensions, modernity and tradition, madness, gender, and individuality.

Chapters draw from cultural psychiatry, medical anthropology, and political theory to produce a model for understanding the inseparability of private experience and collective processes. The book offers those studying political theory a way for conceptualizing the subjective within the political, it offers mental health clinicians and researchers a model for including political and historical realities in their psychological assessments and treatments, and it provides anthropologists with a model for theorizing culture in which psychological experience and political facts become understandable and explainable in terms of, rather than despite each other.

Meaning, Madness, and Political Subjectivity provides an original interpretative methodology for analyzing culture and psychosis, offering compelling evidence that not only 'normal' human experiences but also extremely 'abnormal' experiences such as psychosis are anchored in and shaped by local cultural and political realities.

Sadeq Rahimi is an assistant professor of Medical Anthropology and an associate faculty member in Psychiatry at the University of Saskatchewan, Canada. He received his training in cultural psychiatry from McGill University and in child and adult psychoanalytic psychotherapy from the Montreal Children's Hospital and the Boston Institute for Psychotherapy.

The International Society for Psychological and Social Approaches to Psychosis Book Series
Series editors: Alison Summers and Nigel Bunker

ISPS (The International Society for Psychological and Social Approaches to Psychosis) has a history stretching back more than fifty years during which it has witnessed the relentless pursuit of biological explanations for psychosis. The tide has been turning in recent years and there is a welcome international resurgence of interest in a range of psychological factors that have considerable explanatory power and therapeutic possibilities. Governments, professional groups, people with personal experience of psychosis and family members are increasingly expecting interventions that involve more talking and listening. Many now regard practitioners skilled in psychological therapies as an essential component of the care of people with psychosis.

ISPS is a global society. It aims to promote psychological and social approaches both to understanding and to treating psychosis. It also aims to bring together different perspectives on these issues. ISPS is composed of individuals, networks, and institutional members from a wide range of backgrounds and is especially concerned that those with personal experience of psychosis and their family members are fully involved in our activities alongside practitioners and researchers, and that all benefit from this. Our members recognise the potential humanitarian and therapeutic potential of skilled psychological understanding and therapy in the field of psychosis, and ISPS embraces a wide spectrum of approaches from psychodynamic, systemic, cognitive, and arts therapies to the need-adapted approaches, family and group therapies, and residential therapeutic communities.

We are also most interested in establishing meaningful dialogue with those practitioners and researchers who are more familiar with biological-based approaches. There is increasing empirical evidence for the interaction of genes and biology with the emotional and social environment, and there are important examples of such interactions in the fields of trauma, attachment relationships in the family and in social settings and with professionals.

ISPS activities include regular international and national conferences, newsletters and email discussion groups. Routledge has recognised the importance of our field in publishing both the book series and the ISPS journal: *Psychosis – Psychological, Social and Integrative Approaches* with the two complementing one another. The book series started in 2004 and by 2012 had 13 volumes with several more in preparation. A wide range of topics are covered and we hope this reflects some success in our aim of bringing together a rich range of perspectives.

The book series is intended as a resource for a broad range of mental health professionals as well as those developing and implementing policy and people whose interest in psychosis is at a personal level. We aim for rigorous academic standards and at the same time accessibility to a wide range of readers, and for the books to promote the ideas of clinicians and researchers who may be well known in some countries but not so familiar in others. Our overall intention is to encourage the dissemination of existing knowledge and ideas, promote productive debate, and encourage more research in a most important field whose secrets certainly do not all reside in the neurosciences.

For more information about ISPS, e-mail isps@isps.org or visit our website, www.isps.org.

For more information about the journal *Psychosis* visit www.isps.org/index.php/publications/journal

Meaning, Madness and Political Subjectivity: A study of schizophrenia and culture in Turkey
Sadeq Rahimi

Models of Madness: Psychological, social and biological approaches to schizophrenia 1st edition
Edited by John Read,
Loren R. Mosher & Richard P. Bentall

Psychoses: An integrative perspective
Edited by Johan Cullberg

Evolving Psychosis: Different stages, different treatments
Edited by Jan Olav Johanessen,
Brian V. Martindale &
Johan Cullberg

Family and Multi-Family Work with Psychosis
Gerd-Ragna Block Thorsen,
Trond Gronnestad &
Anne Lise Oxenvad

Experiences of Mental Health In-Patient Care: Narratives from service users, carers and professionals
Edited by Mark Hardcastle, David Kennard,
Sheila Grandison & Leonard Fagin

Psychotherapies for the Psychoses: Theoretical, cultural, and clinical integration
Edited by John Gleeson,
Eión Killackey & Helen Krstev

Therapeutic Communities for Psychosis: Philosophy, history and clinical practice
Edited by John Gale, Alba Realpe &
Enrico Pedriali

Making Sense of Madness: Contesting the meaning of schizophrenia
Jim Geekie and John Read

Psychotherapeutic Approaches to Schizophrenia Psychosis
Edited by Yrjö O. Alanen,
Manuel González de Chávez,
Ann-Louise S. Silver &
Brian Martindale

Beyond Medication: Therapeutic engagement and the recovery from psychosis
Edited by David Garfield and
Daniel Mackler

Meaning, Madness and Political Subjectivity

A study of schizophrenia and culture in Turkey

Sadeq Rahimi

Routledge
Taylor & Francis Group

LONDON AND NEW YORK

First published 2015
by Routledge
2 Park Square, Milton Park, Abingdon, Oxfordshire OX14 4RN

and by Routledge
711 Third Avenue, New York, NY 10017

First issued in paperback 2016

*Routledge is an imprint of the Taylor & Francis Group,
an informa business*

© 2015 Sadeq Rahimi

The right of Sadeq Rahimi to be identified as author of this work has
been asserted by him in accordance with sections 77 and 78 of the
Copyright, Designs and Patents Act 1988.

All rights reserved. No part of this book may be reprinted or
reproduced or utilised in any form or by any electronic, mechanical,
or other means, now known or hereafter invented, including
photocopying and recording, or in any information storage or
retrieval system, without permission in writing from the publishers.

Trademark notice: Product or corporate names may be trademarks
or registered trademarks, and are used only for identification and
explanation without intent to infringe.

British Library Cataloguing in Publication Data
A catalogue record for this book is available from the British Library

Library of Congress Cataloging-in-Publication Data
Rahimi, Sadeq, author.
    Meaning, madness, and political subjectivity : a study of
schizophrenia and culture in Turkey / Sadeq Rahimi.
       p. ; cm.
    Includes bibliographical references.
    RC514
    616.89'80094961 – dc23
    2014037783

ISBN 13: 978-1-138-23556-4 (pbk)
ISBN 13: 978-1-138-84082-9 (hbk)

Typeset in Sabon
by Apex CoVantage, LLC

To my father and my mother whose love has shown me here and to my sons Aatash-Reza and Kianoush whose love will lead me forward.

'The case studies – Emel, Senem, Ahmet – are a tour de force of cultural interpretation.'

– **Arthur Kleinman**, *Esther and Sidney Rabb Professor,*
Department of Anthropology, Harvard University, and
Professor of Psychiatry, Harvard Medical School, USA.

'Psychiatry has stripped phenomenology down to its barest bones, counting symptoms and signs with little attention to context and meaning. In this creative ethnography, Sadeq Rahimi makes a bold counter-move, locating psychotic experience in the social, cultural and historical contexts of contemporary Turkey. Through gripping case studies, he shows how psychosis is deeply imbricated in local forms of life. Above all, he guides us toward a new politics of experience, grounded in understanding the interplay of power and meaning in subjectivity. The semiotics of political subjectivity that Rahimi develops advances our understanding of psychosis but it also has much to teach us about the ordinary madness of everyday life.'

– **Laurence J. Kirmayer**, *MD, James McGill Professor and*
Director of the Division of Social and
Transcultural Psychiatry, McGill University, Canada.

'Sadeq Rahimi's book takes us along a fascinating journey traversing disciplinary boundaries and conventional categories of knowledge. It introduces readers into an innovative, rigorous and sophisticated approach to transcultural psychiatry; it equally introduces a larger approach to the notion of political subjectivity that reflects the solidarity between meaning and power. Building on an intelligent and sensible analysis of personal and collective associative chains inhabiting schizophrenic patients' narratives, the author demonstrates the degree to which private associations are embedded within semiotic landscapes and illustrates the necessity to be attentive to historical references colouring words and expressions.'

– **Ellen Corin**, *Associate Professor, Departments of*
Anthropology and Psychiatry,
McGill University, Canada.

'An uncommon work that provides powerful narrative materials to demonstrate that persons living with serious mental illness are every bit as 'cultural' and 'political' as their unafflicted counterparts. A forceful contribution to the study of schizophrenia as a paradigm case for the understanding of fundamental human processes'

– **Janis H. Jenkins**, *Professor of Anthropology and*
Adjunct Professor of Psychiatry,
University of California, San Diego, USA.

Contents

Preface

This book opens with a paradox. In the first sentence of the Introduction, the author announces, "This is a book about political subjectivity." A moment later, the author tells us, "Yet, what follows is also a study of culture and schizophrenia in Turkey." These two fields – studies of "political subjectivity" and those of "culture and schizophrenia" – seldom speak to or about each other, and neither is likely to see the other as relevant, or certainly central, to its field. It is paradoxical therefore that a book would be 'about' political subjectivity as well as culture and schizophrenia. Those interested in culture and schizophrenia often write about the subjective experience of schizophrenia and its being embedded in local systems of meaning and culture. But with the exception of those who see the category 'schizophrenia' to imply the politically persecuted 'other,' a position not taken in this book, students of culture and schizophrenia are unlikely to approach their 'subject' as fundamentally political. Does it make sense to claim that a person living with schizophrenia, often stigmatized and shorn of basic rights of citizenship, be considered essentially a political subject, as this book argues? And what might be learned about political subjectivity more generally by analyzing in great detail conversations with persons living with schizophrenia? On the other hand, although scholars of political subjectivity might accept the book's claim that an important starting point for their field includes the study of 'power and meaning,' it is almost unthinkable that such scholars would consider entering this field through a study of discourse of persons living with schizophrenia in Turkey. What indeed can be learned about the 'political subject' by close readings of conversations with persons in Turkey who live with schizophrenia?

The heart of this book is a set of case studies of individuals living with schizophrenia in Turkey, each of which focuses on attempting to make sense of a limited number of conversations between the author and the 'patients' (interviews were held in several hospital settings), as well as with their family members and clinicians. The analytic approach is rooted in semantics or semiotics. Students of schizophrenia might reasonably be suspicious: what is being assumed about the coherence of this discourse and what is thus assumed about the nature of the subjectivity of the individual living with psychotic illness? The experience of talking with an individual who is actively psychotic is often one of bafflement, of constantly struggling to make sense of what is being said. Indeed, incoherence of speech and narrative, as well as strange and unexpected associative patterns, are often considered hallmarks of psychotic speech. So what is being assumed by the author in a study that makes culture, power, and meaning the heart of the analysis?

It is one of the great strengths of this book that the author constantly shares with us the experience of puzzlement, of utter confusion and inability to understand what is being said, as he enters a conversation with those interlocutors who are the central figures in this text:

Patient (P)   My name is Emel . . . I was born, I came to the world 2 months to the first day of the first month. I was 7 months old when I came to this world. . . . . I get fits. I get fevers all the time. I had meningitis. They took some liquid from my back. I have hernia in my back.

P   My problem [*sorun*: question, illness, issue, case] is . . . I have a brother . . . in the army. He is supposed to be coming back today. So . . . And I smoke cigarettes.

I   Pardon me . . . you have a brother . . . ?

P   My brother was both my mother and my father.

I   How is that?

P   Both mother ...both *mommy* and *daddy* [italics signify original language].

I   Both mother, and . . . ?

P   I am here because of sorrow. I do *panic attack*. I cannot distinguish fantasy from reality . . .

It is not until the conclusion of the book that the author gives us a vivid metaphor for the breakdown of coherent meaning that lies at the heart of the experience of schizophrenia, for both sufferers and those who engage them:

A difficult yet unfortunately relevant metaphor in understanding the impact of schizophrenia on subjective experience would be a city ravaged by an earthquake. I think of the difficulties and challenges faced by a schizophrenia patient somewhat similar to those of a person thrown into the aftermath of a terrible quake who now has to make sense of what is going on there, or perhaps to rebuild a whole town. It is a terrifying task, even to simply make sense of the blocks and pieces and the structural foundations of buildings and to try to comprehend what things may have looked like. Similar challenges are faced by both the person who is struck by psychotic illness and the clinician or the anthropologist who is trying to help or relate to the patient's experience.

This metaphor takes us to the heart of this book. It provides an entrée both to the author's understanding of conversations he held with persons suffering psychotic illness as well as to his analytic methods. The conversations are strewn with 'blocks and pieces,' which the individuals, whom we come to know with increasing depth as the analysis of each progresses, are attempting to use 'to make sense of what is going on there' and 'rebuild a whole town,' which turns out to be their lives. The analysis therefore tacks back and forth between careful cultural analyses of these 'blocks and pieces' and their use by individuals to construct meaningful lives. The author refers to these as "building blocks of meaning systems," which however are related to critical psychological realities of the individuals as well as to social and historical realities – linked as *points de capiton*, or 'quilting points,' which he takes from Lacan. What is critical is that the author does not simply find the discourse of these struggling individuals as meaningful because he, as an analyst, can show that they link to an underlying cultural system. Instead, the analysis turns on moving back and forth between personal meanings or efforts to piece together a life amid the chaotic blocks and pieces and using these efforts to find increasingly rich access to deep cultural, historical, and religious structures of meaning and power.

It is the content of this analysis that makes this book such a remarkable text. Sadeq Rahimi is himself a member of the extended religious and historical traditions that one must understand to explore with real richness and depth how these individuals with psychotic illness are struggling to construct meaningful lives. He was born and grew up in Shiraz, Iran; was displaced by the Iranian Revolution; spent time in Turkey; and was allowed to immigrate to Canada, where he took up residence and studied cultural psychiatry. He conducted extended anthropological field research in Turkey, before returning to take up residence in Canada. Rahimi's historical and ethnographic analysis of Turkish cultural and political history, particularly of Ataturk's efforts to construct a modern, secular nation and the continued conflicts these have generated, makes sense of critical aspects of the struggles of the individuals he studies. His tacking back and forth between understandings of Turkey's national ambivalence in its relations to its European Western and its Islamic Eastern identities is shown to be present precisely in the experiences of psychotic individuals such as Emel. But perhaps what makes this text so very special is Rahimi's demonstration of the relevance of deep Sufi structures to his efforts to understand both the individual lives and the historical, political, and civilizational struggles in which they are embedded. Sadeq does not read classic Sufi texts as simply cultural artifacts or aesthetic works but as religious texts. Deep religious structures – of separation from the Divine and the desire for unification with the Beloved, of love and madness being ultimately related to identification with Allah, of the conspiratorial character of jinns or Şeytan in dividing humans from God – are shown to be present not only as cultural and religious themes but as deep structures drawn on by even those who are psychotic in their efforts to elaborate meaningful lives as well.

I am only hinting here at what makes this such a powerful text. Over the course of reading these case studies we find ourselves immersed more and more deeply in the lives of these complex individuals. But we find ourselves also more and more drawn into rich understandings of political history and complex Islamic themes and how these provide the very bedrock of individual and social lives. Scholars of Islam and Middle Eastern civilizations will find as much in these case studies of persons who are psychotic – probably to their surprise – as will those interested in cultural psychiatry. Cultural anthropologists will find a rich form of cultural exegesis that rejects interpretations leading to closure in favor of those that are multilayered and multidimensional, showing culture at 'work' in "fluid and non-static ebbs and flows, taking place in multiple simultaneous layers of meanings and associations." For those interested in political subjectivity, the case studies demonstrate that cultural forms are always and at once meaningful in the present, related to contemporary struggles for power while at the same time represent never resolved historical struggles for national identity, cultural authority, and overt political power that haunt the present.

What emerges is not only a powerful set of cultural analyses elaborated through efforts to understand the lives of the individuals whose stories we enter into. But in the end the book represents a deeply humanistic claim: that persons with schizophrenia are indeed political subjects 'all the way down,' despite the shattering experience of the earthquake which has so dramatically altered their lives. The book demonstrates the significance for clinicians and students of cultural psychiatry how important it is to attend deeply to what those who live with schizophrenia say. It is easy to dismiss the discourse of people living with psychosis as evidence of hallucinations and delusions, as essentially meaningless. While not coherent, this 'speech' is shown in this book to be profoundly meaningful in complex and often enigmatic ways. Much of this speech is highly 'private': "the way concepts, events, and characters of [this individual's] life – real or fantasized – are put together leads to a unique and personal narrative, so unique to be considered psychotic by people around him." At the same time it is grounded in the bedrock of culture – which for Rahimi is itself always political, embedded in power and meaning. The book offers a challenge to all interested in psychosis to struggle ever more intensely to understand what is being said – not to find easy coherence amid apparent meaningless talk but to struggle to make sense of very special ways of being human.

Byron J. Good
Harvard University

Acknowledgments

Just as this book brings home the undeniable presence of the collective in the private, so has the real-life experience of writing it over a number of years made obvious to me that this final product is far from being the fruit of a single tree. I have many a person to be grateful to for each and every aspect of this work from inception to fruition, and what follows is only a basic attempt at acknowledging the help and support I have received.

First and foremost, my gratitude belongs to Ellen Corin, my mentor, supporter and friend to whom I owe the courage of peering into the frightening abyss of psychosis, the creative impetus that inspired me to study psychosis and culture, and the means with which to approach subjectivity and culture through the labyrinths of madness. I am grateful also to my friend and mentor, Laurence J. Kirmayer, without whose support and presence, mental and material, this project would not have taken the rich path that it did. I am truly grateful and deeply indebted to my mentor and dear friend, Byron J. Good, the scope of whose presence, support, and influence on me goes well beyond this book, or words. If Byron's mentorship has offered me the inexpressible fortune of learning from one of the greatest minds in this domain of thought, his caring has given me the chance to experience and know the generativity that is born of deeply humane modesty coupled with the brilliance of liberated intellectuality. I owe much also to Mary-Jo DelVecchio Good, a caring mentor and colleague and a very dear friend to me and who was, together with Byron, instrumental in the development of this book as it evolved from the original manuscript to its current shape.

To Cécile Rousseau I owe much of my clinical courage and the skills to navigate extraordinary mazes of psychotic encounters with grace and a human touch. Perhaps more importantly, I owe to Cécile an awareness of not only the possibility but indeed the imperative necessity of merging together the urge to understand the world and its inhabitants with the resistance to that same world's and its inhabitants' violence and rigidities of thought and action; all in the frame of an overwhelming sense of caring, sympathy and responsibility. I am greatly indebted to Gilles Bibeau, Michael M. J. Fischer, and Arthur Kleinman, who gave me great encouragement and invaluable feedback as I worked my way through the analyses and writing, and who at times gave me the wonderful benefit of understanding what I meant to say better than I did myself. I owe much also to the genuine and generous support, advice and friendship of Ken Vickery, who read and reread my text and gave me tremendous editorial help but who, above all, believed in me, stood beside me through the most difficult moments of this journey, and made sure I walked when I was most likely to fall.

I did the original fieldwork for this project and later worked on the manuscript while supported by Doctoral and Postdoctoral Awards from the Canadian Institute of Health Research (CIHR). I would like to express my gratitude for their generous and timely support.

This book owes its existence to so many people and their generosities that any attempt at detailing would remain cursory at best. First and foremost, I am most sincerely grateful to the nameless patients, their families and the clinicians who so generously and openly allowed me into their worlds and shared with me their pains, thoughts, challenges, hopes, and fears. My dear friend Kemal Sayar, psychiatrist, Sufi, poet, intellectual, cultural specialist, and a man of extensive social skills and connections, has been the source of immeasurable assistance, insight, ideas, advice, leads, and access throughout this project. Without his rich presence and his sincere interest it would have taken me years to accomplish what I did in 1 year of fieldwork in Turkey. Above all else, Kemal has been a dear friend to me, there for me at the hardest moments of my work, assuring that my project, and I, survived all obstacles. I owe much to him, to his wonderful family who made me think of Istanbul as my second home, and to his warm and welcoming friends for many memorable evenings of *çay* and *sohbet*.

I owe much to the many clinicians and mental health workers in Istanbul hospitals who so kindly let me into their world, gave me access to their work and confidence to go on with mine. I am infinitely indebted to the kind, warm and welcoming assistance I have received from Doç. Dr. Esat Göktepe at the Marmara University Hospital; Doç. Dr. Şahap Erkoç and Doç. Dr. Serhat Çitak at Bakirkoy Psychiatric Hospital; Doç. Dr. Alp Uçok at ÇAPA, the Istanbul University Hospital; Prof. Dr. Özkan Pektaş, Balikli Rum Hospital; and Doç. Dr. Kerem Doksat at Cerrahpasa Medical Faculty and Hospital. This of course is only a cursory list of all who helped make my research possible in Istanbul. To this list must also be added Mr. Cahit Köytak at Kanal 7 TV station for finding me audio and visual documents that I could not have otherwise and for his deep and moving poetry; Dr. Nuri Sağlam, professor and researcher of Turkish literature at Istanbul University, for so many intelligent and inspiring conversations and insights; Ms. Mine Karagözoğlu, psychologist at the Balıklı Rum Hospital, for her great interest and help with interviews and access and for so much information and advice on how things work; Ayşe Şasa (1941–2014), writer, thinker, Sufi, and schizophrenia patient, may her soul rest in peace, for so many hours of wisdom, for introducing me to Ibn Arabi, and for opening on me the doors to her impressive world of memories and ideas; Mehmet Ali and Mehmet

Şeker, Sakina and Bhattin Çiftçi from *Ruzgarli Bahçe*, Çiğdem Yazici, and so many others, for so many ideas, advice and insight into the Turkish ways of being, living and thinking.

Here on this side of the waters I have received no less help and insightful assistance from so many people, Turkish and non-Turkish, toward putting together my thoughts and my work. I am grateful to Rachel Genesis for much support and inspiration. Many thanks to Raissa Graumans and Leslie Cutler for reading various parts of the manuscript and giving me valuable feedback. I owe gratitude to Sarah Darghouth for the many hours that she tolerated me as I inched my way through the oceans of readings and ideas. I owe much to Janet Dixon for her wonderful editorial help and advice and for giving me the courage to cut where I would not have dared otherwise. I remain grateful to all those who played the role of research assistants, formally or informally, and who offered me their points of view and advice on processing and understanding my data. My gratitude goes to these wonderful people: Emre Unlucayaklı, Gaye Soley, Uğraş Oğuz, Nurhak Yorulmaz, Uğurgul Tunç, Asligül Erman, Dinç Alnyak, Su Donovaro, Amanda Aitken, Emily Bodenberg, and Blanca Thibaut, whose names I have listed here in no specific order and whose help and generosity deserves recognition far beyond being recounted in a simple list like this. I owe to them much of what I have done with the collected data: they have transcribed, translated, traced, associated, explained, and helped interpret content for me.

Introduction

This is a book about political subjectivity. At the heart of what follows lies an investigation of the relationship between subjective human experience and the political paradigm in which the individual is embedded. Current theories of human subjectivity converge on an important idea: that human subjectivity is fundamentally context-dependent – a cultural context, woven out of political and historical threads. This book takes the idea to the field and examines its relevance to real-life experiences of real-life people. The pages that follow will single out one of the most idiosyncratic modalities of subjective experience, namely, schizophrenia, and show that even such a highly 'private' experience is in fact fundamentally shaped by culture, politics, and history. I have selected Turkey as the stage for this purpose and, even though the detailed analyses provide ample details of that cultural context, I have also decided to include a chapter dedicated to additional historical and political details on Turkey as the context in which the lives in question are lived. The analytic approach theorized, developed, and employed in this book lends strong support to the understanding of culture and subjectivity as products and manifestations of a common organizational system that functions in terms of power and meaning. Psychotic utterances in this sense can be understood as deviations from a local discourse of normalcy, yet traceable nonetheless within the same cultural logic that sustains that local discourse of normalcy. The so-called common organizational system in question here is where the twin concepts of meaning and power enter the story and where the notion of political subjectivity finds its strongest and clearest expression.

The outline of this book is straightforward. The general purpose is to study the idea that human subjective experience is constructed fundamentally of cultural fabrics woven of warps and wefts of power and meaning by the hands of politics and through the process of history. I do so by attempting to 'unpack' an assortment of such experiences, using a specific methodology, which I explain in detail. As the 'unpacking' continues, we encounter the inherent affinities of the subjective and the political, a finding that can, of course, be explained through the same basic ideas: Power and meaning constitute the warps and wefts not just of the cultural fabric but also of the political. And then, through the additional insight and perspective afforded by the diachronic analysis of systems of meaning and signification, it becomes apparent that just as the subjective coincides with the political synchronically through the cultural system, it is also anchored in local history and shaped by the historical through diachronic mechanisms integral to the internal workings of systems of signification.

As abstract and theoretical as this all may sound so far, the main strength of the upcoming pages lies in the fact that they will demonstrate all that through simple, concrete, and highly accessible real-life examples. The material used here comes from interviews with men and women afflicted by psychotic illness, hospitalized in psychiatric wards, and officially diagnosed with schizophrenia. I have decided to select examples from patients with schizophrenia because psychosis is a domain typically least related to such collective processes as common sense, history, or politics. If, however, we arrive to identify continuities of the cultural, political, and historical context within such 'aberrant' domains as schizophrenic experience and delusional content, the more basic argument concerning nonpsychotic experience as embedded in those same processes (culture, politics, and history) would seem only rudimentary.

The interviews with patients, their family members, and their clinicians were all conducted on location at three different hospitals in Istanbul. All patients had manifested psychotic behavior for varying lengths of time prior to the interviews, they had all encountered religious healers (hojas) because of those experiences, and with the exception of one (Senem), they had also had encounters with psychiatrists before. Invariably, however, this was the first time they were diagnosed with schizophrenia. By sheer coincidence, the year I spent in Istanbul for conducting this study also offered me the opportunity of witnessing an event that history has already started to recognize as an important turning point: when for the first time in the Turkish Republic (i.e., in about a century) a pro-Islamic party (Adalet ve Kalkınma Partisi, AKP) was elected and has remained in power without a military intervention against it. This was also a turning point in Turkey's foreign relations, when United States invaded Iraq and the new Turkish government made the unusual decision of refusing direct assistance. During this year I immersed myself intensely in the Turkish cultural milieu. Apart from my ongoing visits to different hospitals, I spent hours following TV shows, news and commercials; I read magazines, newspapers, comics, novels, poetry, schoolbooks; watched movies; saw plays and operas; and listened to concerts. I spent time chatting with people in parks, markets, and coffeehouses. I conducted countless hours of interviews with local healers, Sufi elders, housewives from back alleys of old Constantinople, young students from rich and highly Westernized private schools, construction workers from the slums of Istanbul, writers, doctors, psychiatrists, university professors, shopkeepers, and more. This chance to develop a robust base of data and ethnographic observation enabled me to produce thick cultural analyses while remaining focused on individual patient interviews.

In the broad sense, this book is about the relationship between subjective experience and the cultural logic and the political paradigm in which the individual is embedded. Yet, what follows is also a study of culture and schizophrenia in Turkey. I investigate the Turkish cultural content, heritage, and patterns, and I observe and analyze cases of schizophrenia to explore the relationships between culture and mental illness. From the point of view of cultural psychiatry – which happens to be my main area of expertise and training – the three case analyses in this book offer a unique treasure for clinical purposes, not only in terms of work with patients from Turkey and Islamic Middle East but also in terms of a general framework for analysis of narratives in a deeply culture-conscious way.

Due to the extensive output produced by thick analyses, only a limited number of the cases that I interviewed have made their way to his book, and given the extraordinary richness of every single case, the decision of which stories to exclude has been a challenging one. My original interviews included 15 (8 female, 7 male) patients along with their families and clinicians. The participants' age range criterion was set between 20 and 40, in conformity with a common practice in schizophrenia studies. I decided to interview patients from different hospitals, in order to avoid a client population bias, to have access to different socioeconomic groups, and to include patients from different care provision environments. Indeed, the location of hospitalization is significant in the patients' stories. The stories finally selected to be included here belong to three patients – two females and one male – each from a different hospital and each representing a different social, cultural, political, and economic niche within Turkish society. Each included interview shares important commonalities with those interviews that do not appear here but offered support in my research for the arguments I make.

The first chapter of this book expands the discussion of political subjectivity in terms of the practical question of an analytic methodology. I establish in that chapter the fundamental argument of this book, namely, that culture and psychosis and indeed, subjective experience as such can be analyzed as phenomena intertwined via a common matrix of associative patterns and logical attributions that can in turn be analytically unpacked in terms of local histories and politics. Based on that theoretical discussion, I then outline a methodological framework for analysis based on four principles derived from marrying the 'Russian' semiotics of Jakobson, Lotman, and Bakhtin with the meaning-oriented anthropologies of Geertz, Turner, and Good, on one hand, and with French psychoanalytic theories of Lacan and Kristeva, on the other. The four principles are (1) the inseparability of the notions of subject, culture, and meaning systems, which establishes the need for examination of subjectivity within the realms of culture and language; (2) the simultaneous synchronicity and diachronicity of sign systems, which confirms the need for a multidimensional analysis that examines not only the synchronic references and associative patterns but also those patterns of connections that no longer play an explicit role in the cultural and linguistic system and that become accessible only by analyzing archaic denotations and associations, obsolete etymologies, and historic references; (3) the heteroglossic nature of private associative networks, which provides the conceptual platform for liberating the act of interpretation from the limits of individually ascribed meaning by allowing to recognize traces of diverse and even contradictory discourses in various levels of meaning, starting from the level of signification to the level of organization of signifiers into constellations and patterns of meaning; and, finally, (4) the conglomerate composition of self-identificatory narratives, which recognizes, in addition to the broader implications of the idea of heteroglossia, the aggregate nature of narratives of identity as assemblages of partial narratives borrowed from diverse (and possibly contradictory) narratives.

Chapter 2 is intended for those readers who would like to read further about the cultural and political history of Turkey as it relates to the context of the study. While the idea of studying the relationship among culture, psychosis, and subjectivity rarely seems to evoke a strong reaction in people, "Why Turkey?" has been a common question whenever I have spoken of this work. A detailed response to that question has taken the form of that chapter, in which I discuss Turkey and Turkish identity as the context for demonstration of the ways in which subjective experience of psychosis is rooted in local politics and history. Chapter 2 illustrates the fact that Turkey made an ideal site for studying culture and identity for many reasons, such as the current psycho-geopolitical positioning of Turkey as a bridge between East and West, on one hand, and between Islam and Christianity, on the other, with the attendant dilemmas of identity and, above all, the complex and powerful array of social and cultural interventions made by Ataturk[1] at the turn of the 20th century and the aftermath of his social engineering project throughout the century. Turkey was not selected because it is a different culture, because it is a Muslim country, or even because of my personal familiarity with its history and its language. I selected Turkey as a place to study the relationship among culture, politics, history, and a state of identity crisis because Turkey itself is a state defined by a protracted identity crisis and is where the problematics of "identity" continues to be topical.

Chapters 3, 4, and 5 present the case analyses: concrete and detailed instances of data collected and analyzed according to the background information and theoretical discussions provided earlier. The three analytical chapters may be thought of as both occasions to examine the notion of 'political subjectivity' in its living manifestation and opportunities to test the accuracy and relevance of the analytical methodology developed in earlier chapters.

Finally, in Chapter 6, I examine the applicability of the basic ideas endorsed throughout the book and seek to synthesize into a basic conclusion the various trends and threads developed in this study. This is where I come back to the question with which I begin, trying to address what the relationship between culture and subjectivity is, and in what fashion we may most fruitfully analyze and understand that relationship.

As I sat down yesterday to make the final touchups to this introduction, I received a brief sad e-mail from my Turkish friend and colleague, Kemal Sayar, saying simply, "Dear Sadeq, I sadly inform that Ayşe hanım has passed away this morning. May she rest in peace." It is a strange coincidence in my mind, as I have grown to greatly associate this book and my ties to Turkey with Ayşe Şasa, our common friend we call Ayşe hanım. Kemal introduced me to Ayşe, and she soon became my main point of reference throughout the year I was collecting data for this book. Ayşe had grown to a legendary level of fame in Turkey. Today Prime Minister Erdoğan started his speech with regrets of Ayşe's death, and quoted her – "a society that does not come to peace with its roots, cannot decide its future"[2] – and all of Turkey's main newspapers covered her death. *Sabah Daily* wrote that "one of the most respected figures in Turkish cinema, scriptwriter and thinker Ayse Sasa, passed away early yesterday."[3]

I interviewed Ayşe as a schizophrenia patient, but a very special one: one who, after two harrowing decades of struggle with psychosis and extensive social and personal losses, had returned not only to boast recovery from the illness and reclaim her social status as an author and a screenplay writer but in fact to claim a newly gained spiritual status as a Sufi guru as well. Despite the intensive set of more than 25 interviews I had with her, despite the fundamental role of political events in the course and content of her psychosis, and while I briefly addressed her extraordinary story in a journal article (Rahimi, 2007), you will soon notice that there is no mention of her in this book. Ayşe's own life story would have indeed been a prime example of 'political subjectivity,' deserving of a whole book to its own. But, shortly after I had submitted the article to the *Journal of Religion and Health*, she contacted me and requested that I do not publish anything about her interviews so long as she lives, because she was afraid that might have political consequences for her. Because the journal article had already been accepted and in preparation for publication, and because it was very brief and used a pseudonym for her, she agreed to let that go ahead, but I promised that I would not discuss her in this book or other publications.

It is indeed with a great, if sad, sense of irony that I end the introduction to this book by speaking of my good friend Ayşe Şasa and by repeating the prime minister's reference to her as someone who managed to overcome the "schizo" of her private and collective identities through an intricate trope of integrating the opposites and, most important, integrating a history and a future that stood in stark opposition to each other in Turkish cultural and political context throughout the 20th century. She was truly a living example of the fact that neither societies nor individuals can construct their future until they identify themselves in a narrative capable of incorporating their imagined pasts and futures into a cogent present.

Notes

1 Mustafa Kemal Ataturk (1881–1938), founder and the first president of the Turkish Republic.
2 "Başbakan'dan Ayşe Şasa mesajı" [Message from Prime Minister about Ayşe Şasa], Aktif Medya, June 17, 2014. Available online: http://www.aktifmedya.com/politika/basbakandan-ayse-sasa-mesaji-h89112.html.
3 "Master of Cinema Dies from Cancer," *Daily Sabah*, June 16, 2014. Available online: http://www.dailysabah.com/cinema/2014/06/17/master-of-cinema-dies-from-cancer.

1 Culture, schizophrenia, and the political subject

Meaning, power, and the politicality of the subject

One could think of 'political subjectivity' through the interaction of meaning and power in at least two respects: the fundamental role of that interaction in the work of culture and the constitutive role of that relationship in the development of what we consider human subjectivity. In either case, however, the discussion starts with the very notion of 'structure.' There are a number of traditions of thinking about and conceptualizing a structure, a systematic process that presumably shapes our thoughts and guides our behavior unbeknownst to ourselves. There is Freud's psychological notion of an individual unconscious, for example, or Jung's metaphysical collective unconscious, or Durkheim's sociological notion of collective conscience, not to mention Levi Strauss and his notion of a grand universal "structure." Then there are the Marxist notions of class structure as formative of human consciousness, complete with the concepts of ideology and false consciousness, or the Hegelian idea of the Spirit. There is also the more recent idea of a political unconscious, addressed by people such as Fredric Jameson, and the cognitive psychologists' notion of implicit knowledge – which in many ways could be understood as a rediscovery of psychoanalysis by behaviorism's grandchild. One can certainly find many more ideas that theorize human mind and behavior in terms of implicit structures. In fact the discovery of the idea that some invisible structures are at work, fully unbeknownst to us, to shape and direct our thought and behavior deserves to be recognized as one of the greatest discoveries of social and human sciences over the recent centuries. It is something of an unfortunate fact that, rather than converging on the truly amazing notion of structure as such, each theory and school of thought has chosen its own interpretation of that phenomenon, understanding and describing it in terms of its own limited scope of interest and vision – not unlike Rumi's famous fable of the elephant in the dark room – or its translated version, the blind men and the elephant. Insofar as this book is concerned, however, without denying the value of the models I have just mentioned, and in fact building on a synthesis of much from those, I base the discussions primarily on contemporary theories of the subject developed in the wake of the so-called linguistic turn in social and psychological theories. The most basic common idea drawn from these theories might be that the human psyche is fundamentally structured, and that the structure is informed by a 'symbolic order,' a system of symbols the units of which always function as signifiers, and the organization of which is closely tied to the organization of another grand instance of symbolic systems: language. It is within this tradition that I discuss, investigate, and analyze the topic of human subjectivity, culture and politics, most importantly because this model allows on the one hand to develop a model of simultaneous analysis for notions typically taken as distinct by earlier theories, and on the other to incorporate temporality and memory in a broad sense connecting collective notions of history and historic memory to psychology and personal memory.

It might be worth mentioning here that while in some sense the Marxist-psychoanalytic formulation of the political unconscious developed by Fredric Jameson (1983) may appear similar to the idea of political subjectivity that I formulate here, significant differences distinguish the two. In short, Jameson's political unconscious is a way of approaching certain aspects of the human psyche as politically motivated. More specifically, Jameson's interest is primarily oriented toward depicting and "liberating" repressed notions of resistance in terms of class struggle, which, he suggests, are historically encrypted within texts in ways similar to the Freudian process of repression. In other words, political unconscious as a concept primarily serves the ideological objective of Marxism, namely, resistance to capitalism and awakening a class-based sense of struggle. Text, in Jameson's account, has buried in it an "interrupted" narrative of struggle that should be exhumed: The "function and necessity" of the "doctrine of a political unconscious," he says, lies in "detecting the traces of that uninterrupted narrative" and "restoring to the surface of the text the repressed and buried reality of this fundamental history" (p. 20).

The notion of political subjectivity, however, dramatically widens the scope of 'politicality' to understand the subject itself as a political event. In other words, here the subject is conceived of as political in its very subjectivity – both in the sense that it engages in an ongoing act of subjugating and conjugating the world into meaningful patterns and in the sense that the subject is continuously subjugated or conjugated by the local meaning system. Politicality, in this sense, is not an added aspect of the subject, but indeed the mode of being of the subject, that is, precisely what the subject *is*. And in contradistinction to the Marxist project of Jameson, the politicality of the subject (or the text, for that matter) is not limited to a struggle to decrypt hidden traces of class struggle. In fact the politicality of the subject is not limited to the concept of struggle or resistance but covers all aspects of subjectivity insofar as it recognizes the human social subject as the subject of language, or better put, the subject of the symbolic order.

The deepest sense in which the human subject is political is that 'the subject' comes to 'be' through acts of interpretation and being interpreted, or what I referred to earlier in terms of conjugation and subjugation. The moment of transformation of human infant into the social subject is therefore the political moment – and that moment is indeed the same as the developmental 'moment' of the formation of a sense of self/ego, according to a broad range of theories of intersubjectivity. The location of the political in this sense is therefore within the apparatus of meaning making, the process through which one makes sense and is made sense of by the other. Meaning, on the other hand, is always already political: it is fundamentally imbued with power because it is always the representation of a specific 'interest.' This does not have to be the interest of a specific class, as in the Marxist notion of class interests, but it is always an interest and always the interest commonly shared by a group of people – meaning is always a collective product after all.

All meaning is political in the sense that the very fundamental function of meaning is a preferential legitimization of certain associations of signifiers, or putting forward certain patterns of associations of concepts as more accurate or more truth bearing and thus more legitimate or more desirable than others. Needless to say, the combined network of signifiers as units of meaning, the broader discourses that emerge, or the broadest sense of such networks, which we would call 'systems of meaning,' are therefore coterminous with systems of legitimacy and power. This process is central to the general process of assignment of power. Consider the simple fact, for instance, that no societies would either give rise to and cultivate, or tolerate and sustain, a political system that does not make local sense, that does not comply with local meaning systems or the local 'cultural logic.' And finally another fundamental role of meaning systems manifest in culture and language is that they preserve and transfer across individuals and generations information encrypted with codes of power relations, not only in the form of implicit logical systems of legitimacy but also by molding collective memories, narratives, and fantasies such as histories, myths, folk beliefs, and other collective products.

At least three dimensions of meaning are significantly relevant in this account: (1) that, as de Saussure (1959) has taught us, meaning always exists within a network of configurations as a system of differences or negations, (2) that meaning is always vested with a kind of group interest, and, finally, (3) that, as with any good system, meaning always defends itself against alterations, innovations, and processes other to it. In turn, several interrelated conclusions may be drawn from these features. For instance, that meaning, along with power, is seated simultaneously within the individual and the group, or that the interaction between power and meaning is embedded within the work of culture, or that the relationship of power and meaning is vital to the development of human subjectivity. In a most elemental sense of the word then, meaning sustains power and translates that into 'reality' by making possible or allowing to 'exist' within the symbolic realm certain logical configurations that in turn justify certain thoughts, expressions and actions, and exclude certain others. Within such a system the individual subject gets trapped by cultural domains, by being 'forged' into certain possible sets of meanings and configurations of ideas – groups of associations locally permitted and available for the child to grow into. I provide a more detailed theoretic discussion of these ideas in the following and then a concrete demonstration of what this all means in real life, throughout the case analyses.

Once it is understood that meaning is basically the seat of and, as such, is always the manifestation of power, and once that premise is integrated with contemporary theories of subjectivity (such as Lacan's) that conceive of the subject as fundamentally embedded in, sustained by, and a manifestation of the orders of law and meaning, a number of consequences follow. It follows, for instance, that the process of subjectivity is always already political, and that in order to examine subjectivity one needs to engage an analysis of the local structures of meaning – a semiotic approach, in other words. These conclusions promise new analytic methods capable of incorporating hitherto divergent lines of inquiry concerning power, meaning, desire, and memory. It is precisely toward the development of such an intricate model of subjectivity in its social contexts that I have written this book.

Meaning as method in studying psychosis

My attention to the delusional networks of psychotic discourse builds on the insights of researchers of subjectivity in general and of schizophrenia in specific, such as Ellen Corin, Byron Good, Louis Sass, and Janis Jenkins. Sass and Corin, for example, speak of the interest of European phenomenological psychiatrists in what has been termed 'natural evidence' and its loss in psychosis (see, e.g., Corin, 1990, 2004; Sass, 1994, 2004). "Close observation of a certain number of psychiatric patients," wrote Corin and Lauzon (1994), "led clinicians, such as Binswanger and Blankenburg, to conclude that these patients live in a world different than ours" (p. 6). The case studies I describe here have in fact allowed me to ask whether in their delusional associations the basic ideas psychotic individuals fall back on and hold on to might not be those same building blocks as used by their society at large, albeit arranged in unfamiliar forms.

In the pursuit of similar questions scholars have begun to call on interactional models to refine and promote a meaning-oriented 'cultural psychiatry' that would further challenge the traditional psychiatric view of the subject as limited to the individual (Jenkins, 2004; Kirmayer, 2001). Corin and her colleagues (2004) outline an essentially meaning-oriented approach to the study of psychosis and culture, in which the researcher's task is to "identify the range of possible signifiers available in particular cultures" and then to determine the "relative weight" of those signifiers within the culture and within the subject's discourse, and finally "to bring out the interplays of cultural signifiers, by observing their use in concrete cases" (p. 141).

More recent literature in cultural psychiatry, medical anthropology, and social medicine is in fact rich with ideas and findings that support such a decentered view of the person and meaning-oriented interpretation of narratives and behavior in mental illness (e.g., Corin, 1990, 1998, 2012; Corin and Lauzon 1992; Corin et al., 2004; Good, 1994, 2012; Good and DelVecchio Good, 1981; Good and Subandi, 2004; Jenkins, 2004; Kleinman 1995, 1999; and Obeyesekere, 1985, 1990, among others). Beyond the general agreement on the theoretical basics of the approach, however, the question that has persisted is how best that theoretical stance can be translated into a methodology for analytic interpretation. Developing a clear and theory-driven analytic methodology for examining the relationship among culture, politics, and subjective experience of psychotic illness from a meaning-oriented point of view is therefore an important secondary goal – and hopefully an achievement – of this book.

Jacques Lacan (1993) speaks of a psychotic patient of his to whom "everything has become a sign." To the extent, he describes, that "not only is he spied upon, observed, watched over, not only do people speak to, point, look, and wink at him, but all this [also] invades the field of real, inanimate, nonhuman objects" (p. 9). Not only does this patient attribute specific intentions to other subjects' actions and speeches, but objects as well have now developed nonconsensual properties: "[I]f he encounters a red car in the street . . . it's not for nothing, he will say, that it went past at that very moment" (p. 9). One may argue that what is problematic in this patient's reality system is not simply that 'everything has become a sign,' because everything *is* already a sign before it can be a 'thing.' The difficulty for this patient is that the system that gives sense to his reality does not sufficiently coincide with the consensual one. He interprets the red car visual data according to an idiosyncratic system of associations and significations that does not coincide exactly with the dominant sign system. This same notion is also reflected in the far less sophisticated ideology of Benjamin Rush (1948), the founding figure of North American psychiatry, when he defines madness as "departure" from the "aptitude to judge things like other men" (p. 350). One such 'departure' is what happens in schizophrenia psychosis. From the phenomenological point of view, this is the process that leads to what can be understood as structural differences between the lifeworld of the psychotic and the nonpsychotic, who, while living in ultimately continuous worlds, become almost inaccessible to each other due to differences in basic "orientations" of the subject in time and space.

The fact is, however, that despite our common understanding that in the event of psychosis something happens to the way things mean what they mean, we do not seem to know why exactly such semiotic transformation takes place. One may well imagine, for example, that certain biological changes in the brain may lead to disturbances of learned structural functions of culture by reformatting associative patterns. Whatever explanatory model one might opt for in the current absence of a convincing scientific alternative, the 'transformation' itself remains largely indisputable. Schizophrenia psychosis, in other words, is generally identified with an alteration of associative patterns and meaning systems – an alteration of such depth that it affects not simply the individual's interpretation of the external world but indeed his or her very sense of selfhood and being in the world. Such 'associative' level of impact can be observed in the fact, for instance, that in schizophrenia two basic and intensely related aspects of the 'mind' are commonly altered: the sense of self and self-identity and the sense of meaning or 'reality' that we normally conceive to lie 'outside' the self. That is why Fabrega (1989), for example, describes schizophrenia as a disease of the self, one that "erodes and undermines the organization and functioning of the self" (p. 277), or why Estroff (1989) calls it "an *I am* illness" (p. 189). It is that systemic shift that has made schizophrenia famed as the illness that renders its victims perplexing and incomprehensible, a shift already considered essential to the diagnosis of schizophrenia by Bleuler (1924), who described it in terms of a deterioration of associative processes (e.g., p. 373). For Bleuler, the problem of inaccessibility was produced by the "fact" that the new state of associations was basically a nonsystem, so that the nonpsychotic observer would not find any 'meaningful' links between the chain of utterances of a psychotic subject. "The normal associative connections suffer in strength," he explained, "so that the links of association following one another in sequence may lack all relation to one another so that thinking becomes disconnected" (Bleuler, 1924, p. 373). The argument of meaning and non-meaning in psychosis is an old debate, and my interest at this point is not to argue whether schizophrenia psychosis is or is not intelligible. I want to point out, however, that what most parties in this debate have in common is a concern with 'meaning' and a notion of a system or systems of meaning with which the psychotic subject appears to be squarely at odds once he or she 'crosses' a presumed threshold.

Once one consents to the idea that the psychotic subject has crossed a boundary, exiting a realm to enter one 'other' to that of the nonpsychotic, then what begs the question is what exactly leads these patients to switch worlds, and how exactly such a 'departure' takes place. As I hinted earlier, there are no final answers to either question: the question of why is, more often than not, deferred to biology in today's scientific discourse, and here I have opted to bypass that question altogether. It is for an examination of the how of that departure, however, that I propose to draw on the notion of sign systems and their transformation within the tradition of meaning-oriented, culturally informed theories of psychosis and subjectivity. This, of course, is not a novel idea. The concept has long been around and debated, with proponents ranging from those who consider psychotic discourse "empty speech acts whose informational content refer to neither self nor world" (Berrios, 1991) to those who consider the major distinction between psychotic and nonpsychotic discourse in terms of "cognitive biases" (Bentall, 1996) and others who attribute deep or even universal meanings to psychotic discourse and symptoms (as in Jungian psychoanalytic traditions, for instance).

In early works addressing "the meaning of symptoms" (e.g., Good, 1977; Good and DelVecchio Good, 1981), Byron Good and Mary-Jo DelVecchio Good (1981) made a strong case for reconsideration of the place of 'meaning' in culturally informed assessments of mental health issues. Their discussion of semantic networks of associations and the significant role of these networks in the construction of clinical accounts made concrete a powerful contemporary trend of investigation in culture and mental health. Corin (1980, 1990) in developing such a method further raises two concerns, however, that are relevant here: that "this could be difficult with schizophrenia patients who may be unable, or reluctant to give such an analytical account of their experience," and that "[their] experience often appears as fractured, contradictory, difficult to face in a verbal account, if one is not engaged in a clinical encounter" (Corin, 1990, p. 158). In what follows I examine the theoretic contours of an analytic model that can address and accommodate these challenges.

The Russian connection: salvaging temporality

In pursuit of a method capable of addressing the delusional narrative of schizophrenia patients in its semiotic and temporal context, I would like to present here intellectual developments that originated and evolved, in dialogue with de Saussure's theory of signs and meaning, most coherently in some of the 20th-century Russian schools of literary criticism and semiotic analysis. This particular trend of semiotic analysis and criticism corresponds to the interests of this project in a number of significant respects, including but not limited to the following three. First, having flourished into a rich tradition of "cultural semiotics" associated with such figures as Yuri (Juri) Lotman, this approach conceptualizes the subject as indistinguishable from the cultural and semiotic flows and dynamics within which a person has come to existence. The subject of this discourse is conceived in precisely the terms I have chosen to follow here, as a product of the meeting of a force of agency and culturally formed patterns of signification. A second important characteristic of this line of thought, derived directly from its culture- and meaning-based model of the subject, is a conception of the subject as a conglomerate, dialogic, and ever-shifting assemblage of discursive tropes and semiotic constellations that can include varying and indeed discrepant parts and pieces. Third, a more concrete aspect of this school, namely, its defense of a diachronic analysis of semiotic systems, has deep implications for my analytic methodology, specifically by giving it a fundamental capacity for inclusion of social, historical, and political facts in its understanding of culture, of meaning, and of the subject.

To simplify, one could plot the trajectory as starting with people such as Yuri Tynianov (1894–1943) and Roman Jakobson (1896–1982) and culminating in the theories of Mikhail Bakhtin (1895–1975) and Yuri Lotman (1922–1993). I limit my scope to one issue within this trajectory here, namely, the different treatments of temporality of sign systems in the theories of de Saussure and his Russian critics and the implications of that difference for a theory of political subjectivity and a semiotic approach to analyzing culture and psychosis. Saussure's formulation is an emphatically 'atemporal' approach to semiotic analysis concentrating on the 'present' status of the sign system (see, e.g., de Saussure, 1959, as well as Bennington, 2004; Hutchings, 2004; or Thibault, 1997). De Saussure (1959) divided the study of signs and meaning systems into two 'points of view': one *diachronic* analysis, which concerns "relations that bind together successive terms not perceived by the collective mind but substituted for each other without forming a system" (p. 100), and another, *synchronic* analysis, which is "concerned with the logical and psychological relations that bind together coexisting terms and form a system in the collective mind of speakers" (pp. 99–100). In Saussure's ideal analytic construction of the human subject the "logical and psychological relations" and the "system in the collective mind of speakers" is a *flat* and time- or history-independent system of relations. As he clearly asserts, the researcher studying a system of signs must "discard all knowledge of everything that produced it, and ignore diachrony" (de Saussure, 1959, p. 81).

In a joint text originally published in 1928, Tynianov and Jakobson (1971) presented their criticism of Saussure's advocacy of an atemporal analysis of synchronic systems through the suggestion that diachronic evolution needs also be understood as a 'system' which affects final 'meaning,' logically and psychologically, by the terms it imposes on the synchronic system. "The history of a system," they wrote, "is in turn a system." And they went on to conclude that "pure synchrony now proves to be an illusion: every synchronic system has its past and its future as inseparable structural elements" (p. 80).

Expanding on this notion elsewhere, Jakobson (1990) used the analogy of a motion picture to problematize Saussure's simple binary opposition of synchronic as static versus diachronic states of a system of signification. He suggested that if at any specific moment the viewer of a motion picture is asked to report what she sees, she will give a response such as 'horses running' or 'a clown turning somersaults.' Even though the visual experience might be called a synchronically produced event, the obvious fact is that the reported experience is produced through a nonstatic, diachronic process (p. 165).

Starting in 1929, two other Russian theorists, Voloshinov and Bakhtin (e.g., Morris, 1994), developed their own criticism of an atemporal study of sign systems by distinguishing two approaches to semiotics, namely, an 'individual subjectivism' and an 'abstract objectivism.' Whereas individual subjectivism locates the source of meaning and change in sign systems within the individual subject as the wellspring of creativity, abstract objectivism attributes that role to a normative and closed system of linguistic signs above and beyond the subject. Saussure's conception of *la langue* was then categorized under the abstract objectivist camp. "Abstract objectivism," wrote Voloshinov (1994), "finds its most striking expression at the present time in the so-called Geneva school of Ferdinand de Saussure" (p. 29), because it takes into account neither ideological parameters nor the internal world of the subject in its account of the process whereby a sign becomes meaningful. Voloshinov addressed Saussure's notion of synchrony in terms similar to those of Jakobson. "From the standpoint of observing a language objectively, from above," he wrote,

> there is no real moment in time when a synchronic system of language could be constructed. Thus *a synchronic system, from the objective point of view, does not correspond to any real moment in the historical process of becoming.* And indeed, to the historian of language, with his diachronic point of view, a synchronic system is not a real entity; it merely serves as a conventional scale on which to register the deviations occurring at every real instant in time.
>
> (p. 32, original emphasis)

But Voloshinov then went further to pose fundamental questions about the relationship between the speaking subject and the signifying system. He wrote,

> Now we must ask: Does language really exist for the speaker's subjective consciousness as an objective system of incontestable, normatively identical forms? Has abstract objectivism [read "Saussure's semiotics"] correctly understood the point of view of the speaker's subjective consciousness? Or, to put it another way: Is the mode of being of language in the subjective speech consciousness really what abstract objectivism says it is?
>
> We must answer this question in the negative. The speaker's subjective consciousness does not in the least operate with language as a system of normatively identical forms. That system is merely an abstraction arrived at with a good deal of trouble and with a definite cognitive and practical focus of attention. The system of language is the product of deliberation on language, and deliberation of a kind by no means carried out by the consciousness of the native speaker himself and by no means carried out for the immediate purposes of speaking. . . . What the speaker values is not that aspect of the form which is invariably identical in all instances of its usage, despite the nature of those instances, but that aspect of the linguistic form because of which it can figure in the given, concrete context, because of which it becomes a sign adequate to the conditions of the given, concrete situation. We can express it in this way: *what is important for the speaker about a linguistic form is*

> *not that it is a stable and always self-equivalent signal, but that it is an*
> *always changeable and adaptable sign.*
>
> (pp. 32–33, original emphasis)

Important for my purposes is the two-sided treatment of the sign system as one which is simultaneously a 'system' in place before and independent of the subject, yet a system capable of being adapted, challenged, and changed by the force of agency of the subject in order to express the momentary experiences of the world. And more significantly, this becomes possible only in a point of view that goes beyond the flat atemporal and apolitical view of meaning systems and the subject within them. "For Voloshinov," writes Hutchings (2004), "we never encounter words in a reified form divorced from the living context of the ideological moment in which they are exchanged" (p. 152). Voloshinov and Bakhtin in effect refute both the abstract objectivist and the individual subjectivist points of view, because, they suggest, both these assumptions fail to address the fundamentally intersubjective nature of the process of subjectivity and signification, the process whereby 'meaning' is produced at each instance within the interaction of subjects.

The Voloshinov/Bakhtin paper became a seminal work marking the further 'dialogic' theories of selfhood and subjectivity as semiotic constructs, advocated specifically by Bakhtin and Lotman. This was to become the powerful cultural semiotic tradition that, to quote Pam Morris (1994), "rejecting subjective psychologism's false division between the individual and the social, brings these two levels together in the 'sign'" (p. 49) – a terminology that signified the arrival of a new generation of semiotics. This was a new semiotic interpretation of a broad range of notions including (and certainly not limited to) subjectivity, language, power, and the production of meaning. Hutchings (2004), for example, claims that "Bakhtin developed the dialogism articulated by Voloshinov into a radical reconception of the grounding of all the human sciences" (p. 153).

Typically treated under the rubric of dialogism, the concept of heteroglossia is one of the more significant concepts introduced by Bakhtin and Voloshinov, and of great relevance and utility to working with both psychotic content and political subjectivity. Heteroglossia is understood as the idea that every signifier contains within it the trace of other signifiers, "both in the past and in the future" (G. Roberts, 1994, p. 249). "Any word," asserted Bakhtin, exists in three dimensions: "as a neutral word belonging to no one, as another's word full of the echoes of other peoples' utterances, and as my own word" (quoted in Hutchings, 2004, p. 153). This concept is articulated more eloquently by Bakhtin himself writing elsewhere:

> As a living, socio-ideological concrete thing, as heteroglot opinion, language, for the individual consciousness, lies on the borderline between oneself and the other. The word in language is half someone else's. It becomes 'one's own' only when the speaker populates it with his own

intention, his own accent, when he appropriates the word, adapting it to his own semantic and expressive intention. Prior to this moment of appropriation, the word does not exist in a neutral and impersonal language, but rather it exists in other people's mouths, in other people's contexts, serving other people's intentions: it is from there that one must take the word and make it one's own . . . Language is not a neutral medium that passes freely and easily into the private property of the speaker's intentions; it is populated – over populated – with the intentions of others.

(1994, p. 77)

The notion of heteroglossia introduces a fundamentally liberating understanding of discourse as multilayered, multitemporal, and multidimensional and as containing of various and even contradicting aspects or 'meanings.' This concept is of direct relevance to my work here, not only because it introduces the idea that meaning is produced dialogically and in the interface of the subject and the symbolic system (or, in other words, in the margin of tension between the centripetal force of the symbolic system, as in language and law, and the centrifugal pull of creativity, madness, or chaos), but because it also supports the multilayered analysis of discourses in which a single line of utterance can contain simultaneous semiotic references resonating with a number of culturally provided patterns and themes, including those from the past. Let us now examine the way in which these developments in semiotics and the notions of meaning, power, and subjectivity can be utilized toward a more concrete set of guidelines for an analytic study of culture, subjectivity, and psychosis.

Analytic method

The previously presented theoretical models provide a sufficiently well-defined platform on which to outline a more pragmatic description of the methodological approach put to work in the following chapters. Keep in mind that schizophrenia psychosis is generally identified with an alteration of associative patterns, an alteration of such depth in fact that it affects not simply the individual's interpretation of the external world but indeed his or her very sense of selfhood and being in the world. The case studies that follow contain detailed analyses of narratives about such psychotic processes, produced by psychotic subjects about their experiences or by non-psychotic subjects about their conceptions of psychosis and its nature. While it would not be a wise objective to try to produce a 'manual' of step-by-step interpretational methods in a qualitative study of this nature, the fact remains that the interpretations produced in the coming chapters are informed by a number of specific analytic operations derived from some basic theoretical principles. The case study chapters in this book, in other words, are the grounds where the theoretic perspective developed here, and

the methodological approach derived from that perspective is operational-
ized. In what remains of this chapter I first present an overview of these
principles and analytical guidelines, and building on these guidelines, I then
outline the basic framework of a semiotically informed model of cultural
analysis for studying psychosis as a subjective mode. While the actual analyses may at first appear more free form than systematic, you will notice on
closer examination that they are fundamentally drawn from the following
methodological framework.

In general, four basic principles inform the analytic process. The principles, which have already been detailed in my discussions, can be summarized
as follows:

1   Inseparability of the notions of subject, culture, and meaning system,
    and thus continuity of private and collective domains of meaning
2   Simultaneous synchronicity and diachronicity of symbolic systems, and
    hence language, culture and the subject therein
3   Heteroglossic nature of private associative networks and narratives
4   Conglomerate composition of self-identificatory and autobiographic
    narratives

Let us now consider a basic analytic framework based on these principles. Such a framework would have three zones or dimensions, and an
analytic act might therefore be categorized according to its modality on each
of these dimensions. The three dimensions can be distinguished according
to the collective/private nature of analytic content, on one hand, and the
synchronic/diachronic and associative/thematic scope of the analytic act, on
the other. There are different possibilities for organizing these dimensions to
form a basic framework. Running across the distinctions made here between
collective *versus* private narratives and synchronic *versus* diachronic points
of view, for instance, the basic modes of analysis may be classified under the
two groups of associative, and pattern recognition (thematic). Associative
inquiries attempt to trace semantic and semiotic networks of associations
such as physical, logical, symbolic, metonymic, metaphoric, indexical, or
iconic relations produced in texts and narratives, collectively or privately,
and synchronically or diachronically. Pattern recognition or thematic inquiries, on the other hand, carry the task of identifying structural similarities
embedded within both privately produced associative networks and collectively produced patterns of associations. Pattern recognition inquiries, in
other words, are secondary to associative analyses in that they investigate the
similarities between patterns of associations (i.e., constellations) extracted
from private discourse and collectively produced meaning networks.

Associative inquiries are relatively straightforward, insofar as they seek
to explore and investigate various associative connections of a specific
concept or signifier. The 'pattern recognition' method of inquiry, however,
needs to be understood more closely perhaps, specifically in the context

of the distinction between the notions of heteroglossity and conglomerate composition. 'Conglomerate composition' refers to the idea that fragments and partial narratives and associative patterns can be borrowed from various available cultural texts (culturally endorsed associative networks) and put together in unique ways to produce a private narrative that would correspond to a subject's unique set of experiences. For example, a subject may put together partial associative patterns 'borrowed' from a religious story, local Nationalist political narratives, and a TV soap opera and make a story about what has happened to her and her infant, a 'psychotic' story, but a story nonetheless – *her* story.

The notion of heteroglossity, by contrast, is used here to describe the more subtle notion that 'traces' of simultaneously present layers of meanings from multiple domains of cultural environment, including contents of collective memory, can be detected both at the level of single signifiers, and throughout thematic patterns and constellations of signifiers in a patient's idiosyncratically produced narratives. A patient's story of unrequited love, for example, may integrate elements from local legends and folktales, from a romantic movie, and from his neighbor's divorce story to produce a single account. This is the conglomerate feature. But then, the story in its grand scheme or plot may also resonate with such culturally dominant themes as the love of God for man, the interference of the Devil, and the ensuing struggle, on one hand, and the historic love of 'Turkey' for Europe and the apparent unattainability of a union, on the other, both of which themes then also coincide with the culturally endorsed theme of madness as a result of unrequited love. It is this second set of multiple resonations of the overall meaning/plot that I refer to as heteroglossity. In practice, however, both these aspects are addressed by a common set of analytic tools, namely, systemic or associative pattern recognition.

Breaking the process down to a number of analytic modules may provide a more accessible frame of reference in which to classify specific acts of analysis. It is important to be aware of the fundamentally overlapping nature of these modules as we think of such classifications, however, because, as you will soon notice in the following chapters, in practice acts of analysis are almost always multidimensional, as are their subjects of analysis. Also worth noting is that across all these groupings association remains the basic analytic tool: either in the sense of 'network analysis,' where specific associations are investigated across culture or history, or in the sense of 'pattern analysis,' where sets of such associations are compared to other sets across time or cultural domains. The basic dimensions of these modules may be represented in Figure 1.1.

From the preceding classification, four analytical modalities can then be extracted as follows.

1. *Synchronic associative network analysis.* This consists of investigations of semiotic continuities by identifying associative and logical pathways within and across private (individually produced) and collective

	Synchronic Analysis	Diachronic Analysis
Network Analysis	interactions, discourses, family, semantic pathways, politics, media, etc.	personal history, genealogy, mythology, collective history, semantic and semiotic etymologies, etc.
Pattern Recognition	social models and locally dominant metanarratives (e.g., political, religious, sociocultural, ethical, and logical systems)	historic and traditional models, local archetypes (typically from mythology, religion, literary, or historic sources)

Collective Discourse; Shared Domain Of Meaning
Private Discourse; Subjective Domain Of Meaning
COLLECTIVE   PRIVATE

Figure 1.1 A Dimensional Representation of Analytic Modalities

(sociocultural) content from a synchronic point of view. Relevant data include collective productions such as artistic, political, or religious texts and private self-identificatory and autobiographical narratives. Synchronic network analysis typically starts from associative patterns organized around a concept or term in private discourse and work outward to explore the fashion in which these networks may be linked to or juxtaposed with current collectively shared networks of meaning. This analytic approach is useful in investigating the way an individual's specific array of associative pathways indicate or correspond with a specific 'subjective strategy,' a specific style of being-in-the-culture by the speaking subject. Examples for this type of analysis include investigation of the relationship between notions of love, loss, and madness so commonly found in psychotic patients' private narratives of their illness as well as investigation of similar relationships in contemporary cultural and literary contexts, such as movies or novels where strong associations often link notions of love and madness.

2. *Diachronic associative network analysis*. This strategy aims to search and identify semiotic patterns and logical and associative continuities as temporally informed dynamic processes in both individual and collective domains of meaning. Using this approach one investigates associative patterns and temporal developments of meaning networks in a range of contexts including personal histories and life events, familial, generational, and genealogical histories, as well as local mythologies, political histories, or semantic and semiotic etymologies of words and ideas. These associative networks may also be traceable across individual narratives and such shared collective experiences as historical, social, and political events, as well as potentially found in linguistically embedded traces of etymological developments of terms and concepts. Diachronic network analyses expand the two dimensionality of synchronic analysis of signs and sign constellations and their relationship to one another into a three dimensional model in which the structural movement of constellations of meanings through time is traced and given analytic significance wherever mappings are possible. Like synchronic investigations, diachronic investigations also target the way the

(private) subject and the (collective) culture interface in a 'meaning system,' with the exception that this coincidence is treated as an event in time that represents the crosscut of a trajectory. A simple example for this type of investigation would be studying the apparently inexplicable semantic association held in Turkey between the terms *kimya* (chemistry) and the concept of 'an extremely valuable or rare object.' Although puzzling synchronically, a diachronic study of this term demonstrates the semantic relationship through the old Ottoman Turkish the use of *kimya* to denote 'alchemy,' a science dedicated to finding the highly valuable and rare object, *elixir*. In modern Turkish, alchemy is called *alşimi* (pronounced al-*shimi*). A synchronically conceived model of that linguistic system fails to see any reason for connection between *kimya* and *alşimi* or between the term *kimya* and its common 'sense.'

3. *Synchronic pattern recognition and thematic analysis.* Addressing the third and fourth principles (heteroglossic and conglomerate narratives), and building on the output from the first module, this approach seeks to identify 'private' associative networks and patterns of logical connections with recurrent structural patterns of association within private discourse and any existing parallel discursive and semiotic patterns, themes, and groupings available in the subjects' cultural landscape of meanings. These configurations can often be traced back to basic 'blocks' of associations contained in dominant social narratives, current political discourses, religious practices and other contemporary collective narratives. A single story presented by a patient, for instance, may be broken down into a number of smaller or partial stories that can, in turn, be recognized as borrowed from other locally available narratives. Such analysis can bring to light, for example, that a specific set of associations in a segment of a patient's story follows the same logical or associative pathways as a certain political, social, or religious event or story, even though the stories are not necessarily tied explicitly to each other in the patient's narrative. Furthermore, thematic analyses may also show that the partial network is 'patched' in the patient's narrative with other partial themes that are sometimes borrowed from other domains and discourses. The resulting narrative is thus what I have termed a 'conglomerate' and can be partially elucidated in the approach discussed here. On the other hand, that so-called conglomerate story in its final form may also reproduce or 'resonate with' a culturally legitimized theme, such as the theme of madness as a result of unrequited love, while simultaneously also reproducing another culturally available theme, such as the religious theme of the love between Allah and Mankind, and then also resonating with a third local theme, of the unrequited love of Turkey for Europe. It is that presence of simultaneous multiple interpretative possibilities and cultural resonations that I have tried to convey by borrowing the term heteroglossia, the other quality of concern in this module. For example, once the specific logical and semantic pathways that associate love and madness in private narratives have been identified, a pattern recognition investigation addresses

the possible similarities between the overall structure of these privately produced networks and any existing cultural models that might similarly associate love with madness. The structural parallelism across domains is not always explicit. In some instances the relationship may be reduced to metaphoric or general thematic similarities. A young Anatolian man's recurrent theme of unrequited love for a Swiss woman, for example, may be found in patterns structurally similar to the current account of Turkey's unreciprocated interest in joining the European Union.

4. *Diachronic pattern recognition and thematic analysis*. This set of analyses is designed to target heteroglossic and conglomerate qualities of associative patterns in private narratives, with the distinction of extending the analytic inquiry beyond the synchronicity of current meaning systems. Queries are meant to identify recurrent structural patterns of association within private discourses and to further identify similarities between those associative patterns and collectively shared themes from noncontemporary contexts. Such contexts can include historic events and stories, fables and folktales, behavioral and psychological blueprints, and archetypes present in mythic, religious, or literary sources, and so on. Consider a young psychotic woman whose discourse associates repeated references of pollution and purification, death, and revival to the signifiers of fire, water, fish, the city of Urfa, and a contemporary pop singer by the name of Ibrahim Tatlıses. A diachronic pattern recognition analysis highlights thematic and structural similarities between that specific associative network and the ancient religious and mythological stories of the prophet Abraham, which are similarly constructed around the themes of pollution and purification, death, and survival through signifiers of fire, fish, and water and, according to local fables, take place in the city of Urfa.

Analysis of the color red might also take the direction of a third or fourth module analysis as one investigates specific associative patterns of such patterns within privately produced content that resonates with collective content, present and past, explicit and implicit. Imagine the case of a psychotic subject, for instance, whose discourse yields a number of distinct associative constellations around the color red and consider the progression of analysis toward a realization that indeed some of these patterns converge in a different layer of associations to produce a thematic story where, for instance, this patient's life events resonate with a certain reading of the Turkish political stage and/or the messianic stories of a specific religious group, or a certain reading of the Turkish history of modernity. This last group of findings includes those associated with the third and fourth analytic modules, whose specialty is to identify patterns across collective and individual realms of action and meaning.

I would like to emphasize once again the importance of remaining conscious of the overlapping nature of what has been presented here in the form of distinct modules. A basic analytic investigation such as 'the significance of color red in the discourse of a psychotic patient,' for example, can (and should) be analyzed under multiple modules because of the multiplicity of dimensions invoked in a close analysis. The investigation of the significance of the color red could be pursued through a module 1 analysis insofar as one traces the significance of color red in the patient's current thought system and in local social and political systems of references and associations. At the same time, however, a module 2 analysis would allow exploration of the role and associative significance of this specific color in that specific patient's past, memory, and life history, as well as in etymological, mythical, historical, religious, historic, or other 'past' frameworks where color red may be interwoven with the local social and political history. The point to keep to mind is that as 'meaning' is always diachronic, multilayered, and complex, so any method of approaching it must be similarly multivalent in order to reveal subjects and their worlds for what they are.

I should also address an important caveat as I begin to take you through deep analyses of a few cases of psychosis. Even though throughout this book I advocate a meaning-oriented analysis of psychotic discourse, and even though an analysis of 'associative relations' lies at the core of that approach, the resultant accounts are not intended to produce final 'interpretations' of the patients' accounts. These case analyses should be distinguished from traditional psychoanalytic interpretations, for instance, in the sense that the analyses here are intended to provide not a meta-network or state of associations, but to capture the *process* of a patient's experience of psychosis and his or her use of certain, often partial, associative patterns. Put in other words, the objective of the analyses is first and foremost the analysis itself, that is, the possibility of applying this analytic model to a hypothesized common ground of psychosis, culture, and subjectivity. My goal is simply to demonstrate how a multilayered and multidimensional reading of a case of psychosis can reveal history and politics and "culture" busy with their "work" (Obeyesekere, 1990) in extremely fluid and non-static ebbs and flows, while occupying multiple simultaneous layers of meaning, time, and dynamic associations.

In sum this project is a meaning-oriented study of political subjectivity that aims to unpack the processes of subjectivity within culture, history, and politics through a study of schizophrenia in Turkey. Schizophrenia psychosis has been selected as the site of investigation of subjectivity, because psychosis is the moment of crisis when the individual is struggling to use the most elemental tools available to him or her to organize, or reorganize a sense of meaningfulness and selfhood. The basic conceptualization of the relationship between subjectivity, psychosis, and culture here deems inevitable the inclusion of history, meaning, and power (or, to put it in other words, temporality, semiotics, and politics). In a sense this is the hypothesis put to the test in the case studies that will follow, where the analytic approach just articulated is employed to investigate three cases of psychosis in some depth. The overarching project requires subjectivity to be conceived as an interpretive process wherein experience emerges through interpretation and re-formulation of available patterns of association or 'meaning.' A central objective then is to provide an analytic matrix within which this process of interpretive subjectivity is highlighted and caught in action as psychotic subjects struggle to (re)organize their sense of selfhood by using basic semiotic instruments and material derived from their cultural and historic environment.

2 Old peoples, new identities

The story of Turkey

In what follows I sketch a general image of the story of the Turkish nation as it is known today, intended to serve as a basic backdrop against which to locate and better understand the private worlds of the 'Turkish' subject, psychotic or not. Like other nations, the Turkish nation is an imagined totality. Like any other culture, the Turkish culture is an imagined system of shared ideas, and like any other history, the Turkish history is an imagined trajectory that can be depicted in different ways. In addition to those challenges, however, writing about Turkey and 'Turkish identity' is an especially formidable task, for there seems to be no final consensus regarding what constitutes Turkishness and who exactly a 'Turk' is or even what an accurate Turkish history might be.

The Republican People's Party[1] that initiated in 1923 what we know today as the Republic of Turkey found the question of Turkish identity quite simple. "The Fatherland," the party's program in 1935 said, "is the sacred country within our present political boundaries, where the Turkish nation lives with its ancient and illustrious history, and with its past glories still living in the depths of its soil."[2] The new republic was constructed around the central scenario of an ancient Turkish Nation whose identity and autonomy was saved from annihilation by the heroic presence of a young soldier, thence titled Atatürk, the 'Father Turk' (*ata*: father). The hero himself conceived of his mission as a struggle to build a radically new national framework based on Western science, Western democracy, and Western civilization at large. The account of the change, according to Ataturk, was that "a great people, whose national course was considered as ended," rose and "created a national and modern State founded on the latest results of science" (1929, p. 723).

Reality, however, is hardly as self-evident as the official story has it. For one thing, the revolution that changed Turkey at the turn of the 20th century had deeply paradoxical characteristics and outcomes: while it claimed to have saved and ensured the continuity of the Turkish national identity, it featured a radical attempt to erase political, religious, and cultural traditions from collective memory. The fez, for example, a traditional hat worn by Turkish men,[3] became a banned cultural object precisely for that reason.

Ataturk (1929) personally explained his decision to ban the fez in these words:

> Gentlemen, it was necessary to abolish the fez, which sat on our heads as a sign of ignorance, of fanaticism, of hatred to progress and civilization; and to adopt in its place the hat, the customary head-dress of the whole civilized world, thus showing, among other things, that no difference existed in the manner of thought between the Turkish nation and the whole family of civilized mankind.
>
> (p. 722)[4]

In other words, the Turkish nation imagined and enforced by this ideology was simultaneously a distinct Islamic nation with its 'ancient and illustrious history' and yet was something new, something indistinguishable from "the civilized world" (read: the Christian Europe). As Mears (1924) testified, "in an effort to forget even the recent past, the leaders of the Turkish Republic have tabooed the word 'Ottoman.' 'The Ottoman Empire is dead,' they cry, 'long live Turkey!'" (p. 2).

Over about a century of real-life experience, the official discourse has undergone significant transformations. The Ottoman past is no longer as vigorously disowned and rejected. As a matter of fact, the changes have recently led to the coming to power of an altogether new breed of Turkish politicians whose outlook is called neo-Ottomanist by some. Many of the cultural objects and traditions initially banned are now allowed once again. I encountered an interesting "sign" for such reversals on the streets of old Istanbul. Not long after the currently ruling AK Party came to power through a landslide victory in 2002, finding large numbers of city workers painstakingly scraping thick layers of asphalt off the streets in Old Istanbul neighborhoods became a common scene. Their mission: rediscovering Ottoman-era cobblestone roads that have been covered through the 20th century with 'modern' asphalt to produce a more Western look.

An intriguing fact also remains as powerfully relevant today as Lewis (1975) described decades ago when he asserted the seemingly simple proposition that "Turks are a people who speak Turkish and live in Turkey," did not develop "naturally," but was "introduced and propagated" in what is known as Turkey, no earlier than late 19th century. Not only is this notion a modern idea, claimed Lewis, but it represents "a radical and violent break with the social, cultural, and political traditions of the past" in the Anatolian peninsula (p. 1). Writing at the time of that "introduction and propagation," Mears (1924) observed, "in the Turkish language there is no word equivalent to 'Turkey'. . . Formerly the official title of the Empire was the 'Exalted State' although the Arabic term for the 'Ottoman Lands' was frequently used" (p. 2).

In what follows, I introduce a number of examples in which paradox and a coexistence of seemingly incongruent models of meaning are defining features of modern Turkish identity. Such examples would also serve as useful material for unpacking the cultural and semiotic mixing and matching commonly identifiable in psychotic narratives. Let us not forget that the process of semiotic conglomeration is emphasized in this book as the modus operandi of subjectivity, and that the cultural landscape consisting of historic memories and systems of meaning and power is the primary resource from which the basic elements of such conglomeration are drawn. What seems to make the Turkish cultural content specifically unique is the degree to which such conglomeration is accommodated within the formal dominant discourse, and the ease with which this quality can be observed in various aspects of the country's social, political, and cultural domains, including its historic past. To begin, a history of Turkey has to be sketched as having two originally separate 'roots' that converge over time to form a single entity. While the 'ethnic' root of the nation was taking shape, mythically and genealogically, in the steppes of Central Asia, the land itself, Anatolia, was experiencing a separate history of its own, and these two trajectories merged not before the 10th or 11th centuries when the Seljuk Turks moved into Anatolia.

An abridged timeline

A peculiarity of the official identity discourse in Turkey is the merger of Anatolia, the peninsula and Turkish, the ethnicity. Despite the fact that Turkic tribal peoples started to migrate and occupy the peninsula no earlier than the 10th century, local Anatolian history and earlier Turkic tribal prehistory have been connected emphatically within the official account of the Turkish nation's heritage and identity. For practical reasons, the following timeline is constructed with the Anatolian Peninsula, rather than Turkic peoples, as the point of reference. The notion of 'Turkic peoples' is often used to refer to a great and complex network of tribes and ancestral groups that live primarily in eastern, central, and western Asia of which traces generally lead back to the steppes of Central Asia, and whose languages are rooted in the (somewhat controversial) Altaic family.

BC

2nd/1st millenniums	Hittite kingdom in Anatolia
750–600	Phrygian state in central Anatolia,
	Urartu kingdom in eastern Anatolia
550–334	Anatolia part of Persian Empire
334–333	Anatolia occupied by Alexander

AD

| 333 BC–AD 312 | Anatolia Hellenized under the Greeks and then ruled under the Roman (ca. 30–330) Empire. |
| 314/330 | Roman emperor Constantine converted to Christianity; Byzantine era begins. |

Turkish migrations

| 10th Century | Nomads convert to Islam and start migrating westward from Central Asia. |

The Seljuks

| 1071 | Manzikert Battle: Muslim Seljuk Turks defeat the Byzantine army in Eastern Anatolia. |

The Crusades

1087–1099	First Crusade. Christians sack Jerusalem.
1146–1148	Second Crusade. Muslims recover Jerusalem.
1189–1192	Third Crusade.
1202–1204	Fourth Crusade leads to fall of Constantinople and the reestablishment of the Byzantine rule in the area.
1157–1237	Seljuk Turks, defeated by Crusaders, continue to rule over East/Central Anatolia, which is broken into small groups tied to the Islamic caliphate ruling from Baghdad.

The Mongols

| 1237–1335 | Mongol Turks moved south from Central Asian plains and reigned/ruined cities in Iran, Iraq, and Anatolia. Anatolia becomes a tributary province to the Mongol Ilkhans ruling Iran and Iraq. |

The Ottomans

| 1299 | Byzantine forces are defeated by Osman; Ottoman Empire is founded to represent the Caliphate of Islam. |
| 1300–1923 | Anatolia ruled by the Ottoman Empire, one of the longest-lasting empires in history and the most renowned Islamic caliphate. |

Republic of Turkey

1923	Ataturk declares the birth of the Republic of Turkey.
1925	Fez is banned.
1925	Islamic calendar is abandoned; Christian calendar adopted.
1928	Arabic alphabet abandoned; Roman alphabet adopted.
1932	Turkish History Thesis produced.
1934	Family name law adopted.
1952	Turkey joins North American Treaty Organization (NATO).
1960	Military coup
1961	'Second Republic': new Constitution adopted
1971	Military coup (aka coup by memorandum)
1980	Military coup: government seized, constitution suspended, and parliament closed.
1982	'Third Republic': new Constitution adopted.
1997	Military coup: further measures enforced to limit influence of Islam in public life.
1997	European Union rejects Turkey's bid for membership.
1999	European Union readmits Turkey's candidacy.
2001	Turkey struggles with devastating recession
2002	Islamic-oriented AKP (Justice and Development Party) won the elections to be the first non-coalition party to rule the country in decades, and the first Islamic oriented government to survive its course for a number of years.
Current	Bid to join the EU continues to remain elusive. Relationship with the United States and Israel has become progressively strained, as a general result of what has been termed AKP's eastward turn. Public anti-American and anti-Israeli sentiments rose powerfully, specifically in the first decade of the 20th century. *Metal-Storm*[5] and *Mein Kempf* became best sellers in Turkey. Prime Minister (now President, as of August 2014) Erdoğan's political and cultural agenda, dubbed "neo-Ottomanist," continues to attract a great many and deter others. Erdoğan's economic prowess has uplifted Turkey's economy, while his refusal to support the US-led invasion of Iraq in 2003 or to participate in military operations against the Islamic caliphate–seeking group ISIS in 2014 have led to palpable rifts with Western powers.

Whose history?

Writing in 1908, Barton exclaimed that Turkey "differs in almost every respect from all other countries" (p. 11). Anatolia, the land now called Turkey, has an ancient history. Innumerable nations and civilizations have vied for its beautiful fields and mountains. Turkic tribes, currently spread over a wide range of the Asian continent, also have ancient traces in the steppes of Central Asia. The 'Turkish nation,' however, is of a much more recent birth, dating back only about a century or so. The paradox is, however, that within its short life this 'young' nation has developed the collective memory of a great and glorious past. It is hardly a coincidence that many books published in the mid-20th century comment on Turkish history with such phrases as 'a history in the making' (e.g., Mears, 1924; Schick and Tonak, 1987). This process of 'making' transformed as the 19th century gave its place to the 20th and as the Kemalist[6] brand of nationalism rose to prominence. Nationalism was the heart of the ideological content of Mustafa Kemal Ataturk's revolution. In the Kemalist worldview, says Poulton (1997), Turkish nationalism was prescribed as a "monolithic solution" to all questions regarding social, political, economic, and cultural difficulties of Turkey (p. 102).

When Howard (2001) presents the modern Turkish nation as one that "grew up alongside the academic study of antiquity," he is alluding to a unique process of identity engineering. Once the political basics of the new Republic of Turkey were laid in the early 20th century, the need for supportive theories of history became evident. Textbooks written within the Ottoman tradition lacked the ideological content required for the new national identity demanded by the Kemalist enterprise. In 1932 the new 'Turkish History Thesis' was thus presented at the First History Congress in Ankara. In this thesis, which was to become the official discourse of the Kemalist movement, the Ottoman past along with the Islamic heritage were given little, if any, credit. Poulton (1997) explains the disqualification of the Ottoman and Islamic heritage in terms of the stigmatic effects of the defeat of the Ottomans by European forces. In other words, one might understand the Kemalist Turkish History Thesis as a defensive reaction to humiliation. An important message of the Kemalist movement, repeated over and again by Ataturk (see, e.g., the six-day-long radio speech made by Ataturk in October 1927) was that the Ottoman and Islamic heritage is indeed the cause of Turkey's falling behind the caravan of civilization. In order to catch up with the rest of the world, it was imperative, it said, to rid the country of the shackles posed by this heritage in its many forms. In parallel to this disqualification of the nation's actual past was the creation of an imaginary past. Lewis (1975) refers to the product of this construction as a theory that was a mixture of truth, half-truth, and error (p. 359). According to this theory, he explains that

> the Turks were a white, Aryan people, originating in Central Asia, the
> cradle of all human civilization . . . the Turks had migrated in waves to

various parts of Asia and Africa, carrying the arts of civilization with them. Chinese, Indian, and Middle Eastern civilizations had all been founded in this way, the pioneers in the last named being the Sumerians and Hittites, who were both Turkic peoples. Anatolia had thus been a Turkish land since antiquity.

(Lewis, 1975, p. 359)

Even though the official account of the history of Turkey and its people has since been made more in tune with 'reality,' traces of the original thesis have continued to thrive explicitly and implicitly. A recent secondary school history textbook in Turkey read as follows: "we know that the Turks, starting from Central Asia, went all over the world, founded states and civilizations and often changed the course of history. We know all this thanks to historical research done under the guidance of Ataturk" (translated and quoted in Poulton, 1997, p. 102).

A question of perspective

When one speaks of Turks in early history, one is speaking of Turkic peoples of Central Asia. According to the *Encyclopedia Britannica* (2002), "little is known about the origins of the Turkic peoples, and much of their history even up to the time of the Mongol conquests in the 10th–13th centuries is shrouded in obscurity." Furthermore, over the past two centuries, official accounts of history in the Anatolian peninsula have gone through radical changes: First, in early 20th century and due to the Kemalist revolution and its agenda, the official discourse of Turks and their history underwent a rapid yet fundamental conversion; and then, over the century that followed this radical shift, original Kemalist discourses underwent further alterations and modifications, and finally within the first decade or so of the 21st century, a new wave of rewriting the history seems to have started its move. At a more explicit political level, the projects of nation building and "identity engineering" have been the dominant motive in construction of official accounts of the 20th century to such an extent that the scientific accounts endorsed by the government often appear dictated by an agenda bordering on propaganda. It was hardly a coincidence, for example, that the main Turkish historians during the first half of the 20th century were also important political figures. The common denominator especially among the early Republican accounts was the promulgation of cultural, political, and historical superiority of the Turkish "race" (e.g., Lewis, 1975, p. 359). The first History Congress, which took place in Ankara in 1932, had only four subsections: the use of prehistoric sources, Turkish languages, geographical changes in central Asia causing migration of Turkic peoples, and discussions of the contents of 1932 history books. The main perceived need of this congress, according to Poulton (1997), was to provide "an unassailable myth [on which] to build the new nation." (p. 107). The skeleton of this myth was "spelled out" in an article that concluded in these words:

> Many European scholars think their [that is, European] ancestors came from the tribes of Central Asia, which they call Aryans, Indo-Europeans or Indo-Germans, who originated from the Altai-Pamir plateau and brought their high culture to Europe and all of humanity both in prehistoric and historic times . . . The Turkish race had attained a high level of culture in its homeland while the peoples of Europe were still ignorant savages . . . Turkish children will learn that they are part of an Aryan, civilized and creative people descended from a high race who have existed for tens of thousands of years, not from 'a tribe of 400 tents' [a reference to the Ottoman myth of origin].
>
> (Poulton, 1997, p. 108)

It was further reported that the last remarks (rejecting the Ottoman heritage) were especially "greeted by prolonged applause" (Poulton, 1997, p. 108).

Not surprisingly, on the other side of this coin one encounters texts of a very different nature, written by Europeans on Turks. These texts, especially those written during or before the first half of the 20th century, share a comparable degree of propagandist content, albeit of an anti-Turkish nature. They tend to depict Turks as a barbarous nation lacking cultural, civil, or political history, and interestingly, they often insist on the identification of Turks and Mongols. In 1900 European nobleman Sir Charles Norton Edgecumbe Eliot published a book under the pseudonym Odysseus, titled *Turkey in Europe* (note also the allusion to this title in the book mentioned earlier by former Turkish president Türgut Özal). In the chapter titled "The Turks," 'Odysseus' wrote that

> their contributions to the art, literature, science, and religion of the world are practically nil. Their destiny has not been to instruct, to charm, or to improve, hardly even to govern, but simply to conquer. The sterility of their authors has deprived them of the fame which the scale, if not the grandeur, of their exploits deserves. When one tries to piece together these obscure and fragmentary records, what a catalogue of terrible names passes through the memory: 'the scourge of God,' Huns, Avars, and Turks."
>
> (Eliot, 1900, pp. 80–82)

Older European texts generally regard the Ottoman dynasty as a historical phenomenon unrelated to the Seljuks, or at times as a continuation of the Islamic political movements traced back to the Arabian peninsula, perhaps even to the prophet Muhammad himself. This latter tendency had in part to do with the Ottomans' own historiographies, as they considered themselves the continuation of the Caliphate of Islam as established by the prophet

Mohammad. In a book titled *History of Turkey*, de Lamartine (1855) offers a detailed story of Islam from the beginning to the Ottoman era. Of the more than 370 pages of de Lamartine's book, merely 10 discuss briefly the "appearance of Turks in Asia" and then the Seljuks, before the book moves on to the Ottomans as the Islamic caliphate without implying any serious connections or historical continuity in terms of Turkish ethnicity. Another 19th-century book, *History of the Ottoman Turks* by Creasy (1877), simply makes no connection between the earlier Turkish history and the Ottomans as it tells the story of how "Othman" came to initiate the great empire. While this phenomenon reflects more than anything else, the European identification of Turkic people with Islam (a fact again traceable to the Ottoman's own politics and discourses of identity), it also suggests a lack of a dominant discourse, up to the mid-19th century at least, of a Turkish nationalistic nature. Ironically enough, I too have chosen here to put aside a significant portion of Turkish history stretching from the 11th-century arrival of the Seljuks through the Ottomans' rule from the 14th to 20th centuries. In this case, of course, the exclusion is simply due to length restrictions, and in favor of a more detailed examination of the current Republic of Turkey, which starts with the fall of the Ottoman Empire and the coming to power of Mustafa Kemal Ataturk in 1920.

The 'Father Turk' and the birth of the Republic of Turkey

The end of the Ottoman Empire, known internally as the Empire of Islam, came with the end of the First World War and its official surrender to the Allied forces in 1918, culminating in the occupation of Istanbul. According to the astonishingly severe treaty known as the Sèvres treaty signed by the last Ottoman sultan, Mehmed VI, the body of the Empire was to be broken and divided among the Allies. Drawing similarities between the Sèvres treaty and that of Versailles against Germany, McCarthy (1997) writes that

> both were punitive treaties, imposed by victors who adopted a high moral tone to hide self-interest. Both treaties contained economic clauses intended to ensure that the vanquished would never rise again. Both limited the military strength and territory of the loser. However, the Sèvres treaty was harsher.
>
> (p. 374)

The Sèvres treaty was greeted in the Empire with a national day of mourning (Lewis, 1975, p. 247). Eventually an armed resistance against the treaty developed, led by groups that have come to be known under the generic label 'nationalists.' Intriguingly, and with the exception of Greece, the nationalist forces did not meet any military reaction from the Allied armies. As a matter of fact, the Allied forces pursued a different agenda: In 1921 both France and Italy agreed to withdraw from their designated territories in Anatolia, "in return for future economic concessions" (Howard, 2001, p. 89). The Greeks, however, did not share the same interest and sought the Allies' permission for military enforcement of the Sèvres treaty on Turkey. This was the time when Mustafa Kemal (Pasha) was given extraordinary authority over the army by the Nationalist forces to fight against the Greeks. Mustafa Kemal carried out his task of war against the Greeks with victory, thus becoming the prestigious Hero of the Turkish War of Independence (1919–1922).

A radical change took place during the turbulent post-War decade: The sultanate system and the Ottoman Empire were abolished in 1922 by the Grand National Assembly of Turkey (Türkiye Büyük Millet Meclisi), and the Republic of Turkey was formally declared on October 29, 1923. As a symbolic parallel to this transformation, the capital city also moved from Istanbul to Ankara. This was a climax in the course of the numerous changes the forming nation had gone through over the past few centuries and was a radical rupture that only heralded more to come. Mustafa Kemal Pasha was to impose most of those ruptures using a mixture of power, charisma, and intimidation techniques. When he once faced objections in the parliament to his views on radically changing the system, he climbed a desk and threatened, "[H]eads might roll," and the discussion was thus settled (Howard, 2001, p. 93). From there Mustafa Kemal's next move was to amend the law to proclaim Turkey a republic, which was followed by sweeping changes in the Ottoman/Islamic administrative, financial, judicial, and educational systems. He shut down traditional *medreses* where prayer leaders and *ulema* would have studied and dissolved Islamic higher education into the state-run educational system. The religious sector, the *ulema* that had played a strong role in social and political arenas, was thus incapacitated by moves that tore down their social, financial, and educational structures. Mustafa Kemal also placed special emphasis on the change from older Ottoman borders to new Turkish ones and on a lack of expansionist aspirations in the new regime (e.g., in his six-day speech; see Ataturk, 1929). Such a delimitation served two basic objectives: an assurance to Europe that Turkey does not, nor will it ever, seek to regain its traditional role as the Empire of Islam; and a juxtaposition of a national/ethnic frame with the (yet nonexistent) linguistic border.

Throughout the following years, swift tribunals widely executed, jailed or exiled Mustafa Kemal's opposition (and sometimes not-so-oppositional) figures. Eventually, all but two official newspapers were shut down, and the only rival political party, the Progressive Republican Party, was closed, leaving the Republic of Turkey with one party: Mustafa Kemal's Republican Party. In the framework of his one-party state and under the heavy shadow of the army, Mustafa Kemal started a historically unprecedented project of Westernization, secularization, and nation building in Anatolia by introducing extensive changes to the ways of life and structures of power. Given the sweeping scope of these interventions, perhaps a more efficient way of presenting them would be by simply listing them. An approximate chrono-logical list of the changes thus follows:

- The dervish (Sufi) orders were abolished, their gathering houses (*tekke*) were closed, and their traditional outfits were outlawed (1925).
- The Fez, men's traditional headgear, was outlawed (1925).

  - Hats (Western style) became legally required to be worn by all men.

- The veil, women's traditional cover, was strictly denounced, later out-lawed in public buildings, universities, public events, and so on (1925).
- The Christian calendar replaced the Islamic one (1925).
- Islamic legal laws were replaced by European ones (1926).
- The phrase 'the religion of the Turkish state is Islam' was deleted from the constitution (1928).
- Roman script replaced Arabic script (1928).
- Kemalist thesis of history was established/supported (1932–1935), claiming that

  - Anatolian antiquity (Hittites, Sumerians, etc.) were "Turkic" peo-ples who brought with them foundations of Western civilization from Central Asian steppes.
  - craniological studies show that Turks belong to Caucasian/Aryan races.

- Kemalist thesis of linguistics was established/supported (1932–1935), claiming that

  - Turkish was the "primeval human tongue from which all others were derived";
  - Turkish was the national language of Turkey;
  - the Turkish language was to become purified from Persian and Ara-bic impurities;
  - publications in languages other than Turkish were forbidden; and
  - traditional Muslim call to prayer (*azan*) was to be done in Turkish.

- European-style family names became compulsory (1934).

  - Regardless of origin and ethnicity, Turkish last names were to be chosen.
  - Mustafa Kemal was given the last name Atatürk (father of the Turk).

- What was deemed folkloric art (music, dances, stories, and literature) received great emphasis while other traditional (religious or Ottoman) genres were pushed to margins, often forbidden.

To sum, the basic aspects of Mustafa Kemal's Westernization project may be considered as ridding Anatolia of Islamic and Ottoman traditions and as constructing a National Turkish identity within a framework of secularism, science, and Westernization. Looking back from the 21st century, however, it becomes clear that the project was much more complicated than Ataturk had assumed. For one thing, Islam was simply too deeply associated with the very notion of Turkness to be separated and removed surgically. As Lewis (1975) puts it, "among the different peoples who [had] embraced Islam, none went farther in sinking their separate identity in the Islamic community than Turks" (p. 329). It is no coincidence that you can still find *Muslim* among the *Webster* dictionary's definitions for the word *Turk*, nor that the "star and crescent" symbol of the Ottoman Empire (which, significantly enough, still serves as the Turkish flag) has come to be the universal sign for Islam. So it is hardly surprising that Mustafa Kemal's de-Islamicization project was not the success he or the West had originally envisioned and that Islam has remained strong underneath the official layers of erasure and denial. Turkish Nationalism in Anatolia, however, was to become Pandora's box of the Republic of Turkey. During the years of war Mustafa Kemal had made it explicit that he believed in autonomy for minorities, specifically for the large Kurdish minority (more than 20 percent of the population) in Anatolia. As Kemalism and Nationalism took roots and grew in strength, however, these promises lost color (see, e.g., Howard, 2001, p. 95f.). In 1924 the parliament passed a bill forbidding any publications in Kurdish. A first Kurdish revolt thus erupted in 1925, led by the religious leader of the Naqshbandi (Nakşibendi) Sufi order, Sheykh Said, and demanding a return to Islamic values. The rebellion was swiftly and brutally crushed. The so-called Independence Tribunals (İstiklâl Mahkemeleri) were established by Mustafa Kemal's government as a legal shortcut to swift execution of the opponents from the Kurdish rebellion. These tribunals proved too efficient to be abandoned afterward and gave much service to a "cleansing" of the system in the following years (e.g., Lewis, 1975, p. 270). The forced Westernization first introduced by Ataturk became the foundation of a trend that has become a defining feature of the republic, along with the heavy presence of the military shadow. The latter has been an important feature bringing its own paradox into the sense of identity in modern Turkey. The military has functioned as the stronghold of Ataturk's ideology of Westernization throughout the 20th century (see the following discussion). Paradox, however, lies at the core of this issue as well, because a fundamental discourse that establishes power and authority for the army (apart from their guns, of course) is ironically enough the tribal traditions of the great Turkish warriors. Let me be more specific.

A study of Turkey and its identity discourses would be incomplete without mentioning the military and its legacy in that society. I shall take the liberty of a brief indulgence here to exemplify this association, of Turkish identity and military tradition, in the context of a poem. This well-known poem by Turkey's national poet Nazim Hikmet (1902–1963) describes Turkey as the head of a mare. The poem is also a good example of the strength and presence of the signifiers of horse and horsemanship in a context of movement from East to West (the perpetual process of which is still symbolically continuing through Turkey's ongoing bittersweet bid for joining the European Union). The poem's opening lines reads as follows (English translation is mine):

> *Having come galloping from Far Asia*
> *Stretching into the Mediterranean, like the head of a Mare*
> > *This country is ours!*
> *Wrists soaked in blood,*
> *Teeth clenched together and barefooted,*
> *And land that looks like a silk carpet*
> > *This hell, this heaven is ours!*

Significantly, not only does this poem emphasize notions of movement, horses, and war; it combines this with that of the land. The Anatolian Peninsula in this poem is merged with the notion of 'Turkhood' in the signifier of a horse on whose back Turks have moved from Central Asia toward Europe. The figure of horse is indeed still quite alive and present in various Turkish cultural spaces. In Turkmenistan, the birthplace of many Turkic tribes, April 27 is currently a national holiday titled 'The Horse Day,' and the mandala-like state emblem has at its very center the image of a horse, the *Akhaltekin* horse, which holds a fundamental place also in identity narratives of the Turkmen government.[7] It is hardly imaginable for a "land like a precious silk carpet" to give the horse bloody wrists, but together with the clenched teeth, this metaphor brings to mind at least two notions: a sustained state of struggle or war and, hence, an arduous journey. Like horses and horsemanship, the metaphors of journey and war are almost inseparable from the Turkish cultural traditions. The Ottoman image was juxtaposed with that of a ferocious military might on the move, both to the Ottomans themselves and, of course, to others touched by their presence. "The terrifying military machine that besieged Renaissance Europe, led by hundreds of drummers and the howling wail of massed Zurnas, was central to the Turkish identity in Europe" (Pettifer, 1998, p. 61). Ataturk's explicit intentions of eradicating the old, signifying chains that bound Turks and thus Turkey to a warrior identity/tradition, had an ironic turn as well. Not only did Ataturk fail to change the military associations and actual presence; in fact, he himself opted to ride that mare to victory. After the crises of 1909, according to McCarthy (1997), the army had taken "a hand in many areas of government, including tax collection and public order in the provinces" (p. 320), a factor that did not change with the introduction of Ataturk's revolution and the new Republican system.

The Father Turk was himself a true soldier, and his establishment of the new Republic became possible only through phenomenal leadership and victory in the Turkish War of Independence (stiklal Savaşı), specifically in the final phases often referred to as the Greco-Turkish war (1919–1922). In fact, with the exception of the latest four, all Turkish presidents following Ataturk have also been military officers (Howard, 2001, p. 20). One result of this tradition has been that the war metaphor and the supremacy of the army have effectively survived as a living metaphor, one that has rendered the army an entity of special privileges, above the ordinary law, and taboo for political criticism. In addition to the simple fact that Turkey currently has one of the largest infantry forces in the world, the symbolic and real forces of the army are also exceptional. "The army never sleeps, . . . they *are* Turkey in their own eyes . . . Ataturk made the army . . . many people still believe that the army is the only real centre of power in Turkey; the National Security Council can move prime ministers like puppets" (Pettifer,1998; p. 53). But this presence is not a simple one. This unspeakable presence is yet another paradoxical fruit of modern Turkish democracy à la Ataturk. When, in a speech delivered during the seventh congress of the Motherland Party (Anavatan Partisi, ANAP) in 2001, Mesut Yilmaz, former prime minister of Turkey, alluded implicitly to the army's role in political decision making in Turkey, even his mere allusions were quite impressive for the Turkish intelligentsia. In an August 14, 2001, article subtitled "Will Turkey Demolish Her Fundamental Taboo?" for the online edition of *Turkish Daily News* Cuneyt Ulsever wrote,

> Turkey's political system is put under the category of "democracy under the guardianship of the army" by most of the international academic circles, but it was the first time internally a Turkish politician recognized, announced and criticized the situation . . . The role of the army in Turkey is taken as "a sacred responsibility" and it is taboo to talk about it.

Turkey joined NATO in 1952, only three years after NATO was established. During the following half-century, Turkey's 10-year coups became proverbial. Not long after joining the NATO, the first successful military coup in the Turkish Republic took place in 1960. The coup was an intervention by the military in reaction to a series of unrests that followed difficult financial years at the end of the 1950s. A colonel, Alparslan Türkeş, announced the coup on the national radio, in words closely resonating with the section from the constitution quoted earlier. Türkeş announced that the army had taken over the state in order to "prevent fratricide" and to "extricate the parties from the irreconcilable situation into which they had fallen" (quoted in Howard, 2001, p. 126). According to the official account, the coup was met with "wild rejoicing," which goes to justify the fact that its anniversary, May 27, was marked as a Turkish national holiday (Davison, 1988). In fact the 1960 coup was only to be the first of what became a regular tradition of military intervention in the political affairs.

About 10 years later, in 1971, once again in a situation where Turkish social and political arena was wrought by dissatisfaction crystallized around anti-American sentiments (e.g., Howard, 2001, p. 145; Vaner, 1987; Poulton, 1997, p. 175f.), the military took it upon itself to take over the political stage. Once again in this coup the official line was that since major political parties had failed to work together, the military was forced to intervene in order to "prevent fraternal strife and restore democracy" (Timur, 1987, p. 20). By this time the influential power of the Army was so deeply embedded within the political reality that the coup took place through a simple 'memorandum' sent to then president, Suleyman Demirel, in March 1971 – hence known in history books as the 'Coup by Memorandum.'

Once again, about 10 years after the Coup by Memorandum, serious economic turbulence and social unrest afflicted Turkey. The Islamic revolution in neighboring Iran sent out additional ripples and emboldened the Islamists in Turkey who voiced their rejection of Ataturk publicly. A third military coup took place on September 12, 1980. This time, however (and perhaps due to the volatile international situation following the Iranian Islamic Revolution), the army's role was more explicit. Tanks and military machinery occupied city corners, and the heads of the four major political parties, including the prime minister, Suleyman Demirel, were arrested along with about 100 of the parliament members. Martial law was announced throughout the country, and the Constitution was suspended (see, e.g., Howard, 2001, for details). During the first 7 months of this military intervention, 122,609 arrests were made by the military (Schick and Tonak 1987, p. 371). Even though the action was more heavy-handed, the discourse replicated that of previous coups. In a first address after the intervention, General Kenan Evren reported a blacklist of crimes, murders, and losses and then proceeded to make a comparison between the situation and the War of Independence following which Ataturk had established the Republic, concluding that "even this simple comparison reveals that a covert war has been carried out in Turkey that did not assign any value to human emotions" (quoted in Schick and Tonak, 1987, p. 371). Here, as in the previous two coups, "[t]he final objective of the military institution" was "to bring civil society into line, so that an end can be put to the perturbations it causes in the functioning of the state" (Vaner, 1987, p. 257). With the third coup the National Security Council (Milli Güvenlik Kurulu Konseyi) took explicit power (Isikli, 1987, p. 328) – the establishment whose duty was defined as maintaining the military's position as guardian of the principles of Kemalism within the institutions of the state.

The three military coups were all justified by the military as efforts to save Turkey's secular democracy, while they all contributed to the increasing intervention of the military in politics, and to a consequent institutionalization of such interventions, says Timur (1987). In a seemingly paradoxical manner, he writes, "efforts to 'save democracy' through military coups led to its growing restriction, and eventual transformation into a military trusteeship" (Timur, 1987, p. 19).

Not unlike the 1971 Coup by Memorandum, in 1997 the military once again intervened to depose an elected government in Turkey, this time through a process later known as a "bloodless coup." This intervention was to remove from power an elected pro-Islamic government introduced by the Welfare Party (Refah Partisi) under the leadership of Necmettin Erbakan (see, e.g., Howe, 2000, for analyses, esp. p. 134f., for military role; also see more details on Erbakan in the case analysis of Senem in Chapter 4).

The unquestionable powers of the military have been challenged in recent years as a result of the reforms demanded by the European Union membership process, on one hand, and a power struggle between secularist Republicans and the Islamist ruling party, AKP, on the other. "The series of cases known as Ergenekon," reported *The Economist* in a 2013 analysis for instance, "has left Turkey's once omnipotent armed forces weak and divided."[8] The word *Ergenekon*, derived from a Turkic (Mongolian) creation myth, is used to refer to a series of high-profile trials that have taken place in Turkey since 2008, in which hundreds of people, including up to 15 percent of the country's top brass,[9] have been accused of membership in an alleged secularist clandestine organization named Ergenekon and plotting against the AKP government (see also the topic of Asena and the Ergenekon myth discussed in the case of Emel, in Chapter 3, as well as the notion of deep state discussed in the case of Senem, in Chapter 4).

There has been much said and written on the role the Turkish military has played not only in the history and politics but also in the very formation of a Turkish sense of identity. As suggested earlier and hopefully reflected in this short sketch of the second half of the 20th century alone, any account of Turkish identity would be incomplete without recognition of the military's place. Let me return now to the political and social trajectory of the national identity-building project initiated by Mustafa Kemal Ataturk.

The Turkish identity-engineering project

Despite the novelty and severity of the changes implemented by Ataturk, a closer look at the last phases of the Ottoman Empire, specifically through the 18th and 19th centuries, would suggest that 'revolution' as a historical phenomenon in Turkey had been in the making for decades, if not centuries before him. Yet it was the eventual realization that the decline experienced by Turks might be due more to the rapid advances of their Western neighbors than to their own decay, which began a new phase of the path that culminated in Ataturk's revolution. This was a path characterized by a gradual increase in appreciation of the power afforded by Christian Europe, followed by a gradual realization of the inferiority of the Islamic Empire in front of the powerful glory of Europe in the peak of its colonial exploits. In parallel with this process one can also observe a gradual decrease in 'collective self-esteem' within the Turkish society and an eventual 'conviction' that there was something inherently more successful in the European way of being in the world, something that could, and in fact had to be replicated, if the Empire was to ever enjoy power and dignity again. Yet such an undertaking proved disastrous for the Empire.

For one thing, the nature of the changes that had taken place in Europe was alien to the Ottoman social and political reality. Renaissance was the outcome of social and economic conditions that were simply not present in the Ottoman world and its history. As Lewis (1975) puts it,

> the great events and movements of European history had broken against the religious and military barriers that separated Islam from Christendom, leaving Turkey unaffected, even unaware. The struggle of Church and State, the Renaissance, the Reformation and Counter-Reformation, the scientific awakening, humanism, liberalism, rationalism, the Enlightenment – all the great European adventures and conflicts of ideas passed unnoticed and unreflected in a society to which they were profoundly alien and irrelevant. The same is true of the great social, economic, and political changes. The rise and fall of the baronage, the emergence of the communes, the rebirth of trade, the rise of the new middle class, the struggles of money and land, of city-state, nation-state, and Empire – all the swift yet complex evolution of European life and society, have no parallel in the Islamic and Middle Eastern civilization of the Ottomans.
> (p. 482)

Indeed, the top-down importation of technologies and, more important, social ideas, cultural practices, and philosophical notions from Europe created an irregular, internally incongruent cultural mosaic. Traditionally, of course, the Turkish world had shown great aptitude for diversity and plurality, where otherness had not constituted social exclusion (e.g., McCarthy, 1997, pp. 127–132). Reflecting this quality of multiplicity, Mardin (1989) describes the Ottoman society in the late 19th century as "a crazy-quilt pattern of tribes, loose tribal federations, ethnic units and religious groups." (p. 43). The main problem, however, was that the worldview to be imported from Europe was not simply 'different' from that of the Ottoman world; it was in some sense also opposed to the Ottomon character. In European eyes, as I mentioned earlier, Turk and Turkhood stood to signify not simply fear and threat but also barbarity and a lack of 'civilization' as such. The European view of Turks was one of derogation and contempt, and thus, internalizing that view through the adoption of European measures could, theoretically at least, cause strong internal conflicts, which I argue is precisely what happened.

Consider the notion of identity for example. Even at as superficial a level as nomination, the name Turkey has come to stand for internal conflict, due to the process I have just outlined. Tracing the genealogy of the term,

Lewis (1975) explains for example that the name 'Turkey' was in fact coined by the Europeans, with its first occurrence being in a 1190 chronicle of the Crusade of Barbarossa (p. 1). It is true, for example, that the term *Turkey* was never used by the Ottoman state; it was used in official self-reference only after 1923 when Ataturk started his career as the president of Turkey. The importance of this genealogy is twofold. First is the fact that the very name adopted by this country for self-identification is made by the beloved enemy, Europe. A second significance of this appellation lies in the derogatory 'sense' associated with the term *Turk*. A North American colleague of mine with a good history of working with Islamic societies mentioned that every time she writes down the word *Turk* she finds herself hesitating, as if she were using politically incorrect terminology. In my copy of the *Webster's Dictionary* (1989), the third meaning given for the word *Turk* is Muslim, and the seventh meaning is "a cruel, brutal, and domineering man." As a matter of fact, even within the Ottoman Empire the word *Turk* was used in a derogatory sense. In his 19-century text *Impressions of Turkey*, Ramsay reports the significance of the word *Turk* in *Turkey*, as follows:

> At the present day the name "Turk" is rarely used, and I have heard it employed only in two ways, either as a distinguishing term of race (for example, you ask whether a village is "Turk" or "Turkmen"), and as a term of contempt, for example, you mutter "Turk kafa" [Turk head], where in English you would say "Blockhead."
>
> (1897, p. 99)

Paradoxically then, while marking the beginning of an ultranationalistic movement, the appearance of Turkey as a term of identity also signals an internalization of the European other's derogatory regard. In part due to such incorporation, then, the healthy interest for catching up with Europe's power and glory gradually gave its place to an anxious attempt at becoming that which Europe was. "Civilization means European civilization, and it must be imported with both its roses and its thorns," wrote the Young Turk thinker Abdullah Cevdet in 1911 (Heper and Criss, 2009, p. 330), and this was a perspective with which Ataturk was in full agreement (*Lewis, 1975*, p. 267). To Ataturk, the eventual advantage of a republican system was opening the road for the 'Turkish nation' to catch up with Europe, indeed to 'become' European: "the Turkish nation has perceived with great joy that the obstacles which constantly, for centuries, had kept Turkey from joining the civilized nations marching forward on the path of progress, have been removed" (quoted in Lewis, 1975, p. 267). In many respects, that same vein of anxiety can be traced into the heart of Turkey's desire as well as its somewhat hopeless struggles since 1987 to join the European Union.

As much as the 20th-century Turkey can be understood in terms of a sustained identity crisis and a desperate struggle to "slough off" old Islamic/

Ottoman identities in order to give birth to a brave new secular and "modern" nation, the first decades of the 21st century have reflected a significant shift in Turkish political affairs the best descriptor for which might be a return of the repressed. The Justice and Development Party (Adalet ve Kalkınma Partisi, AKP), and more specifically its leader, Recep Tayyip Erdoğan, have been described as following a neo-Ottomanist agenda. Neo-Ottomanism is generally understood in stark contrast to Ataturk's agendas of secularism and Westward regard, as a 'return' to Turkey's traditional affilliation with Islamic traditions internally and with the Islamic world internationally. AKP's 'turn' has clearly significant implications, and within its short life (AKP was founded in 2001 and came to power in a landslide victory in 2002) it has introduced a mostly successful and apparently stable enterprise that promises to become a persistent and impactful element in Turkish social and political arenas. Intriguingly, the time when the interviews with psychotic patients analyzed in this book were done coincides directly with the forceful coming to stage of the AKP in 2002. Even though I do not enter any detailed discussion of AKP and its current or future impacts in this book, however, it is quite fascinating to note how easily one could recognize and anticipate based on these analyses precisely the kind of dynamics that AKP is enacting. The AKP's political and ideological agenda, in other words, provides strong evidence for some of the central conclusions of this book such as the deeply embedded processes of continuity, and the intergenerational transmission of political affect through the intricate and implicit dynamics of political subjectivity.

Notes

1 The Republican People's Party (Cumhuriyet Halk Partisi, CHP) was established by Mustafa Kemal Ataturk in 1923 following his initiation of the new Turkish republic.
2 I find great irony in this statement. The past glories, the program claims, are still living, yet they are living not among the people, not inside the culture, they are living "in the depths of its soil" – a striking image of the living dead that calls to mind Derrida's notion of the paradoxical Zombie.
3 The *Oxford English Dictionary*, for example, describes the fez as a former "national head-dress of the Turks."
4 The fez and other headgear played an important role in the sense of identity during the Ottomans. The dead, for example, were identified by tall rectangular or round stones erected above their graves with a fez or other headgear carved on top. These graveyards can still be seen in Istanbul and in other parts of Turkey.
5 This is a novel describing a world war that starts with the clash between Turkey and the United States and ends with a Turk exploding an atomic device in Washington, D.C.
6 *Kemalism* is a term commonly used to refer to the social and political agenda of Mustafa Kemal Ataturk.
7 See, for example, explanations of the state emblem on Turkmenistan's American embassy website under "Discover Turkmenistan" at http://turkmenistanembassy. org/state-symbols/.

8 *The Economist*, "Turkey and its Army, Erdogan and his Generals," February 2, 2013. Available online: http://www.economist.com/news/europe/21571147-once-all-powerful-turkish-armed-forces-are-cowed-if-not-quite-impotent-erdogan-and-his.

9 See, for instance, the article by *Russia Today* titled "Erdogan vs Army: 15% of Turkish Top Brass on Trial, Hundreds Resign," February 9, 2013. Available online: http://rt.com/news/erdogan-turkish-army-beheaded-799/.

3 Vicissitudes of political subjectivity

The story of Emel[1]

An intriguing challenge in writing a meaning-oriented cultural-psychiatric case analysis is the question of linearity, not the least because the associations often go around in circles – like a spiderweb, as Emel put it aptly. I start by going in small circles around an arbitrary center, like a spider, only to expand gradually into a web as I attempt to remain true to the psychotic state. While it is easy to do such a thing in a clinical encounter, it is a challenge to implement and defend a methodology based on this approach in writing a scientific text. I hope, however, that this first analysis will approach that objective by introducing a nonlinear account that gradually expands the range of involved associations while at the same time it funnels its point toward a focused and meaningful conclusion. Such an approach may produce inevitable moments in which fragments of patterns and partial interpretations, stories, or formulations are hinted at, then deferred to pick up elsewhere in the analysis. There may be occasions where an interpretation appears to the reader as magical or unwarranted or where obvious and ripe interpretations seem to have been skipped or ignored. The reader, in other words, may discover the need for patience and for containing anxiety when reading the following three chapters. I venture to suggest that such anxiety be taken as a sign that the analysis is doing what it should be doing: moving through the disorderly waters of psychosis while promising to put the reader back on solid ground at the end, hopefully with a handful of worthwhile souvenirs. Let us start with the story of Emel.

Emel

Emel is a young woman of 23 according to the hospital records, though she looks slightly younger, perhaps 20 or 19. She is hospitalized in ÇAPA (pronounced *Chapa*), a hospital associated with Istanbul University, and she is being followed by Dr. Azar, a 27-year-old female resident in psychiatry from that university. Emel is the elder of two siblings; her younger brother, 20 years old, graduated from the vocational high school in trade and industry[2] and has been doing his military service for the past 2 months. Emel's parents are both alive and present in her life. Her father is a retired worker.

Dr. Azar tells me the father used to work in a hospital; the father himself says he worked for the Bank of Agriculture. Emel's mother, a homemaker, is 45 years old, 7 years younger than the father, who is 52. Emel has not been married and, as far as the family is concerned, has never had a relationship with the opposite sex. She herself speaks a few times in the course of her interview of a 'fiancé' or a 'boyfriend' who has left her. This 'boyfriend/fiancé' concept turns out to be less clear than it sounds at first.

Emel has recently been diagnosed with schizophrenia. This is her second hospitalization due to a psychotic state; the first time she was hospitalized about 1 year earlier, in the same hospital. After the first hospitalization she was released without medication but was brought back to the hospital after 6 months, which was 2 months before this interview. Her parents say her latest episode started about 2 weeks after her brother left home for his military service, an event that they believe is related to the onset of her current crisis. Her latest symptoms, according to the clinician, include verbosity, agitability and anxiety, sleeplessness, and loss of appetite, along with hallucinations and what the clinician calls delusions of grandiosity, as well as a paranoid sense that men seek to sexually abuse her and a strong belief that she is pregnant. Emel's parents later add their own observations, including her recent inexplicable violence, not listening to them, a continuous sense of withdrawal into her own room and her own world, a loss of her faith in God, as well as seeing and speaking to persons who are not there (namely, her own brother) or jinns who she believes are intent on harming her. The doctors' initial suspicion of manic episode or bipolar I disorder was later revised to the current diagnosis of paranoid schizophrenia. She is on anti-psychotics but, according to Dr. Azar, without benefit for the past month or so despite a recent increase in her medication. Emel's physical health is described as good by her clinician, with no known current or previous problems.[3] According to her parents, there is no known history of mental health problems in the family.

Data collection

I conducted three interviews: a first interview with Emel herself, followed by one with her clinician, and eventually one with Emel's mother and father. All three interviews took place at the psychiatric ward of ÇAPA. The following descriptive analysis reflects the sequential order of the themes discussed in the interview with Emel. One objective of this analysis is to capture, so far as possible, an overall sketch of the major themes in this interview: the way they are associated to Emel's understanding of herself and her situation as a hospitalized psychotic young woman diagnosed with schizophrenia in Turkey and the extent to which they may be understood to be instrumental in forming her experience of psychosis. A second objective is to facilitate a search for culturally common patterns of association and signification salient to the understanding and experience of psychosis in Turkey. Content from interviews with family members or clinicians are frequently used to augment the analysis by providing a wider background, enriching, clarifying, supporting, or lending contrast to the patient's discourse.

Themes

A number of dominant themes surface to varying degrees of salience throughout the three interviews. Although primed in a variety of contexts, they demonstrate a 'thread-like' quality, a continuity of associations that make it possible to recognize them as they resurface in various points and different guises and to notice that they function like camouflaged warps and wefts of an often-ripped fabric that holds Emel's discourse. The interviews with Emel and the people around her (i.e., her parents and her clinician), are structured by main themes such as love, purity, health and intoxication, dichotomy, and identity (personal and/or collective) that establish broad areas for analysis. Secondary themes include a brother-lover and her love relationship with him, the notions of chemical properties of foods and substances, blood and its pollution/purity, and death and rebirth, any of which may be used as vehicles to address the main themes structuring her discourse. Here in Emel's case note that the overarching themes, especially the couplet of love and identity, provide a blueprint around which more specific concepts, themes, and metaphors such as dichotomy or purity are put to work to produce meaning. As in the other cases, Emel actively 'borrows' various signifiers from the semiotic landscape of her cultural environment and skillfully weaves them into an idiosyncratic yet fascinating web of meanings in an effort to express and give sense to her unusual subjective experiences.

Analysis

As I start the interview with Emel, I am quickly struck and impressed by her exuberant presence and her frank will to power. She takes on the task of marking the start of the session by saying, "OK, you may ask your questions now." I respect her desire and put my thoughts into a question. No sooner have I started, "Now. . .," then she overrides my locution: "I am going to speak!" she declares, further clarifying where she would like to stand in our dialogue. Realizing the potential seriousness of this for derailing the interview, I decide to frame my soft approach, so I go on: "Tell me your name." She responds with a quasi-automated bundle of information, ideas, and story fragments:

Patient (P)   My name is Emel . . . I was born, I came to the world 2 months to the first day of the first month. I was 7 months old when I came to this world. . . . I get fits. I get fevers all the time. I had meningitis. They took some liquid from my back. I have hernia in my back. I cannot carry heavy objects. When I do, forgive me, it strains my tummy. And it still continues. It's like, some people, ladies, can use the washroom in one minute. Men take longer. Because they are men, so we are different. You are a gentleman, and I am a lady.

The game has begun, and I cannot deny the mild anxiety that comes with the realization of having taken the first step into a whirlpool of thoughts, affects, and fantasies that is Emel's world: we are no longer in Kansas. As I sit back now to rethink what Emel told me in that long interview, I have the privilege not only of having read and reread the content of our conversation but also of having at my disposal the interviews with both her parents and her clinician. I know, for example, that Emel had a serious illness at a young age. I know that her parents confused the time of that illness in their interview: first, they decided, collaboratively, that it was when she was 8 months old, but then they agreed, again collaboratively, that it was when she was 2.5 or 3 years old. Thanks to those other interviews, I now also have clues to kernels of truth in other themes that appear here and there in her narrative, such as the theme of death and rebirth. The question remains to be asked, of course, of what exactly such fragments of objective reality may mean for an analysis or toward an effort in 'understanding' a psychotic patient's meaning system. I will return briefly to this question later in this chapter; however, a more detailed treatment is postponed to later chapters.

Illness and difference

One feature that became rapidly clear in my interview with Emel was a saturation of her sense of identity with notions of illness and difference. After uttering her name as a primary signifier of identity (a primary signifier, mind you, that itself turns out to be a paradoxically complicated construct, as we will see), the second point of reference/identification for her is having been born outside of the ordinary ("I came to the world 2 months to the first day of the first month, I was 7 months old when I came to this world"), an abnormality that is then immediately tied to illness: fits and fevers, meningitis, and more. Illness naturally leads the association to physical points of reference like weakness and pain, which in turn evoke the next signifier of identification, gender: "You are a gentleman, and I am a lady." Without a pause or any prompts from me, she continues to tell me more about the 'problem' in terms of which she identifies herself:

P   My problem [*sorun*: question, illness, issue, case] is . . . I have a brother . . . in the army. He is supposed to be coming back today. So . . . And I smoke cigarettes.

Interviewer (I) Pardon me . . . you have a brother . . .?

P   My brother was both my mother and my father.

I	How is that?
P	Both mother . . . both *mommy* and *daddy* [italics signify original language]
I	Both mother, and . . . ?
P	I am here because of sorrow. I do *panic attack*. I cannot distinguish fantasy from reality . . .

The 'problem'

Having established and introduced an identity in terms of illness, Emel now moves on, automatically, to describe and explain that illness: "my problem is [that] I have a brother in the army." This seemingly irrelevant remark in fact proves itself to hold an essential reference to a significant recurrent theme in Turkish accounts of madness: love/union and rejection/separation. Even in the absence of an awareness of a possibly cultural model formulating this utterance, however, it should be noted as significant that Emel would immediately associate her illness with having a brother in the army. This significance leads me to solicit more details, in response to which she becomes yet more cryptic: "my brother was both my mother and my father." While it is too early in the interview to make a richer sense of this remark, it is already clear that the association of her brother and his absence with her illness is related to the importance that this brother has had for her, a brother who crosses genders and generations to become all: father *and* mother. Later on in the interview Emel introduces two concepts that will help make more of this remark: a direct association/juxtaposition of this brother with the figure of a lover or fiancé and an invading theme of split that she attributes to various elements of her identity, ranging from her own name to the Turkish state, to Ataturk, to the East and the West, and to her two parents representing opposite poles of a fundamentally dichotomized universe. Having that in mind, I call your attention to the two aspects already associated with the brother: love and loss, on one hand, and dichotomy and unification, on the other.

Love: loss, sorrow, and illness

When I asked Emel's doctor if there were "any significant events, important stories, events, in Emel's life?" the doctor answered my question as follows:

Clinician (C)	She says she had a boyfriend. I am not quite sure when this might have been. Apparently they broke up when he left for military service. Perhaps this was the time when she was first hospitalized here, but I am not sure about the date. In the second episode her brother goes to do military service. This was 2 weeks before [hospitalization]. This is all I know.

As I pointed out before, according to Emel's parents, there is no question in this story of a boyfriend – or a fiancé, as Emel prefers to put it.[4] As for the clinician's response, a few points merit attention. First, these departures/separations (of a boyfriend and of a brother) are the first and the only concepts she can think of in her search for "significant events and important stories" in Emel's entire life. Second, she suggests that Emel's breakdown is associated with a boyfriend who departed for his military service. She holds to this presumably causal association despite the fact that she does not have any idea when, how, or even "if" such an event has actually taken place and despite the fact that the parents deny the existence of any boyfriends. Finally, the clinician suggests that in the second hospitalization, a brother is involved, one who has also left for the military service and whose departure is also strongly associated with Emel's crisis.

The importance of the brother and his departure is confirmed on a number of occasions and in all three interviews. The mother, for example, traced the second hospitalization event in these words:

Mother (M)   They [the doctors] said she was fine, that they were treating her without medication. I asked if she would get ill again. The doctor said anything is possible, and that he would monitor her. Everything was going well, and then her brother went to the army.

A causal role attributed to the departure of the brother is implied in the phrase "everything was going well, and then her brother went to the army." But the references are numerous. On another occasion during the interview with Emel's clinician, I asked about the family and its role in the course of Emel's illness. The doctor mentioned first that the father might have a drinking problem, but she was quick to add that she did not think that problem had anything to do with the illness. So I asked if she thought the family played any role in this illness. She said the following:

C   Well apparently she is very attached to her brother. When he went to do military service she started to become aggressive. She asks her mother specifically to bring his picture, his picture from the army. They haven't told her where he was sent to do his service so that she would not be upset. You know in the Eastern Anatolian region, the borders are kind of dangerous, there's more deaths. They haven't told me either, it must be a place like that. They haven't told her so she wouldn't be upset.

Once again, the brother's departure is the only other important family-related fact that the clinician has to suggest. An interesting aspect of this model of causality is the intricate transformation the brother signifier has to undergo in order to comply with the illness narrative shared by all involved parties. In other words, there is a shared *implicit* agreement between all parties, that the signifiers 'brother' and 'lover' are juxtaposed at some level. Consider the following excerpt from Emel's interview when I inquire about her hospitalization story:

I   Now, Miss Emel, How did you come here?

P   My family brought me here.

I   Your Family?

P   Uh-huh . . . I broke a glass at home

I   What happened? Why did you do that?

P   I put the cigarette out here [points at her arm]. . . .

I   OK.

P   Three months ago.

I   OK.

P   It was about my boyfriend.

I   OK. Which friend?

P   Before he went to the army . . .

I   OK.

P   We were going out.

I   Uh-huh.

P   He went for military service. He put me here, he forced me here. He tricked me.

I   OK.

P   He lied to me.

I   I see.

P   I never forgive lies. I used to lie a lot. I would steal money from my father.

I   Uh-huh.

As I mentioned earlier, so far as the "objective truth" is concerned, there has never been a boyfriend in the picture. The parents, for instance, described the events that led to Emel's second hospitalization this way:

I   How is she now?

F   It's getting better. She was a lot better [after first hospitalization]. About 2 months ago her brother went to do his military service. She was very close to him. She was very sad about that, that's what I think, I don't know. After that she was ill again. I wasn't at home, she broke the glass. They got a car and took her here . . .

Love: a semiotic trick

It is possible to consider a boyfriend about whom the family did not know, or even to imagine a scenario where the brother and the sister were involved in an incestuous relationship. But a third alternative is more viable, both culturally and in terms of all three interviews. This is the interpretation that through a semiotic juxtaposition of the two signifiers 'brother' and 'boyfriend,' the factual 'brother,' the young man who has left home to do his military service, is appropriated to fit in a preexisting cultural formula that has traditionally functioned to explain psychotic illness in the Turkish society. That formula consists of love, separation, and an ensuing sorrow that can lead to madness. In the preceding excerpts and in those that will follow, two implicit logical components can be identified as central: first, the premise that Emel's access to an object of love has been denied and, second, that the denial and lack of access has forced her into the current state of illness through an excessive sadness: "It was about my boyfriend . . . He went for military service. He put me here, he forced me here." Further into her interview, Emel points out again the relationship between a sense of disillusionment with the love from her boyfriend/brother and her "crazy" behavior in these words:

I   Why did you break the window?
P   I thought my boyfriend was cheating on me, and he had actually cheated on me. I know about that.
I   When you think of that . . .
P   I get very sad [*Üzgün*: mournful, melancholic].
I   You get sad.
P   I cry.

The close association of the absent brother with an almost erotic love is also reflected in the parents' accounts. After the brother left for the military, for example, one of the early reactions that signaled to the parents a state of abnormality was that Emel became deeply and unusually occupied with her looks and appearance. The following are her mother's words:

M   Before she came here her brother went to do military service. [*turns to the father*] Right? 10 days before [coming] here, her brother left. It hadn't been a month yet.
I   OK.
M   She became talkative again. She was talking about him a lot and she started to put on lots of makeup. She just couldn't get enough of that makeup.

Emel herself later returns to identify the 'boyfriend' figure who has gone on to the military as her own brother, emphasizing her experience of loss and sadness:

P   [*Sniffs*] . . . I am very upset . . .
     [About 5 sec of silence . . . continues to snivel]

P   I really miss my brother.

I   Your brother, where is he now?

P   He is in Cyprus.

I   What is he doing in Cyprus?

P   He is a lieutenant.

I   A what?

P   Lieutenant.

I   What does that mean?

P   It's a high-ranking position.

I   OK.

P   Like a doctor.

I   I see.

P   That means he is someone important.

The juxtaposition of the brother and boyfriend/lover/fiancé signifiers becomes still more explicit on a later occasion. The following excerpt is taken from an interaction in which Emel was speaking of her illness in a state of confusion and self-alienation:

P   [I want to have m]y mother, *mommy*, my father, and how do you say brother in English?

I   In English?

P   *Boyfriend*!

I   *Boyfriend*?

P   *Mommy*, father, *boyfriend*, and "*I am.*"

Given the basic familiarity of Emel with English, as demonstrated in her occasional use of terms and concepts in English, it is not easy to assume that she is simply making an error, when amusingly suggesting the word *boyfriend* for *brother*. Besides, the repetition of this juxtaposition through the interview gives reason to assume a more intricate play of references is involved in her translation game. The following excerpt shows a clear example of that juxtaposition, the places of *brother* and *boyfriend* are interchanged, and this time the game is played in Turkish:

P   There might be people who don't like me. It's not like everyone has to like me.

I   I see.

P   For example, to give you an example, I like my boyfriend better than my family.

I   Hmm . . .

P   He just got back from the army . . . It has been a month since he got back, but they are hiding it from me, they lie to me.

I   Is that so?

P   My mother is a little self-oriented. You know what I mean?

I   Selfish?

P   She thinks about herself.

I   Your mother thinks about herself.

P   My father about me.

I   Your father thinks of you.

P   Mothers are more fond of their sons here [in Turkey].

I   OK.

P   Of the Boyfriend.

I   Hmm.

P   The father side prefers me.

I   OK.

Love: loss and sorrow

Emel's reaction to the separation from her brother is associated strongly, so far as all these accounts indicate, with a sense of loss and sadness. The parents put it this way:

M   We showed her a picture [of her brother], and she cried.

Father (F)   She started to cry.

I   Is that a good thing or a bad thing?

M   She said he had lost weight. I told her he was already thin. She said no, he has lost weight . . .

F   She got so emotional because she misses him.

M   She was always asking about him . . .

F   She misses him.

You recall Emel's own account of her sadness/madness as a result of the separation. On another occasion she described her lonesome sadness in these terms:

P   I listen to the silence when I go to sleep at night. I would rather talk to myself than to others. It's better just by myself.

I   What do you tell yourself?

P   I talk about my family, you know, how my brother is gone, is in the army.
.. . He is going to send me a picture today, I will show you the picture.
OK?

As suggested earlier, the model used by Emel, as well as her family *and*
the doctor, to associate the departure of her brother/lover with her psychotic
illness is culturally appropriate. Emel's assertion "I am here because of sorrow" should be heard within a cultural chain-events model of love and an
original union, followed by separation, loss, and an ensuing sorrow.

Sorrow is a richly loaded term in the local system of signification. The
Sufi poet Rumi, whose points of view inform the collective self-image of
today's Turkish culture,[5] starts his famous *Mathnavi* with a poem 'on behalf
of' the *ney*[6]: "Listen to the *ney* as it tells you stories. .. ." Literally, the word
ney or *nåy* (which rhymes with *high*) signifies a reed, a plant with a special
place among Sufi and Middle Eastern cultural metaphors. It also signifies
the breath or the larynx: it stands for *voice* in a metonymic relation. The *ney*
additionally is the integral (often the exclusive) instrument of Turkish Sufi
music. Its sound represents the wailings of the soul and is used as a metaphor
of the human being, specifically when its fate of separation from its origins
and its share of sorrow is involved: "Listen to the *ney* as it tells you stories/as
it sings the sorrows of separations." In Rumi's opening poem, the *ney* in fact
takes on the first-person voice, and the poem is "spoken" by the *ney*, who
tells the reader or listener of its sorrow, the sorrow that is an inseparable
part of having become the *ney*, just as it is an inevitable aspect of becoming
human. The sorrow, we learn, results from the fact that the *ney*, in order
to become a *ney*, in order to find a voice and become able to "speak," has
to be cut away from the reed-bed and "[e]ver since the time I was cut away
from the reed-bed/I became the breath of sorrow for men and for women/
Anybody who is torn away from their Origin/cannot help but long for the
times of Unity." In other words, through the painful process of being torn
away from the "Origin" the *ney* becomes able to sing and humans become
able to "speak."

This is a longing that the Sufi is called to heed, because this longing is
all that is worth "speaking" about: "we regret," says the poet Saa'di, "any
words we ever uttered other than the story of our longing for the Beloved."
One can hardly avoid noticing the resemblance of Rumi/Sufi theories of
the human capacity to process symbols (or to become a subject of language
and "speak"), to Lacan's idea of the painful transition of the subject from
the original union with the Real to the eventual initiation into the Symbolic
(as manifested in the capacity to use words and communicate via symbols),
or Kristeva's conception of "speaking" as a means of simultaneously representing and fending-against the horror of that separation. Later I discuss
the close relationship between this set of signifiers and the notion of love,
love that can easily lead to madness. Rumi's second story in *Mathnavi*,

for example, is the story of a maiden who is suffering from an apparently incurable illness and who fails to be diagnosed until a wise physician (the legendary Avicenne) demonstrates that the woman's illness has to do with love, that it is caused by separation from the man she loves, and that a unification with her beloved is the only cure.

'Problem' revisited

It is easier now to make sense of Emel's formulation of her psychosis when she says, "My problem is [that] I have a brother in the army . . . [he] was both my mother and my father . . . [and] I am here because of sorrow. I do *panic attack*. I cannot distinguish fantasy from reality." Emel's "problem," we are being told, the cause of her illness, is that she has a brother who is gone, a brother who represented a unification of diverging elements, and she is now hospitalized due to the sorrow because of that loss, a sorrow that leads to two things in turn: panic attacks and hallucinations. And these two are medical terms of reference for her "illness" that she has learned in the hospital: in fact, for panic attack, she even uses the actual English terminology. Another significant fact about this formulation of love and madness is that it is a model shared by all three parties: it is endorsed and used as an explanatory model for Emel's illness in the discourses of Emel, her parents, and the clinician alike.

Identity

When I moved on to collecting other primary facts and asked Emel her age, she replied as follows:

P   I will be turning 23 tonight. If you would allow me, I would like to celebrate my birthday here.

I   Is that so?

P   So what is my astrological sign? Since I was born on the New Year's. For instance, December 24th is 5 days, one week before January 1st. My dad had me recorded a week earlier . . . not my dad, but the administrator working at the population records office.

I   Oh . . . I see.

P   OK . . . I am talking . . . then . . . my grandmother was a teacher. She passed away. My parents passed away when I was young. My mother's name is Sükriye. My grandfather's name is Veli. My grandmother was married twice. My uncle is actually my father. I have asked for blood test, my . . .

I   What did you ask for?

P   DNA test. To find out who my parents are.

She tells me that she is 23 years old, connecting this to the central theme of who she is and what she may be about. "If you permit me, I would like to celebrate my birthday here," she says, connecting her birth to the hospital ("here"), where she is kept with a diagnosis of schizophrenia. The birth/rebirth motif is taken up more prominently later with a detailed discussion of the significance of this theme. Take note here that she associates that issue with two more facets of identity: fate – "so what is my astrological sign?" – and blood/lineage – "my uncle is actually my father, I have asked for blood test . . . DNA test to find out who my parents are." Fate represents an important aspect of local reactions to trauma and illness in general. In Emel's interview, however, fate did not develop as a recurring theme, and I do not dedicate much space to its analysis here.[7]

Blood and lineage

Fundamentally important in the process of locating one's self as a social subject is the family, to which Emel moves immediately: grandmother, grandfather, mother, father, uncle. The question of family and blood appears regularly throughout the interview as Emel struggles to locate herself. Consider the concept of blood more closely, starting with a brief excerpt:

P   So [Ataturk] is my grandfather. We are from the same earth [*toprak*: earth, soil, land].

I   You are from the same earth . . .

P   Yes we are from the same earth . . .

I   OK.

P   No one has my blood type. Only my father and I have it. A-S, it's A-S type.

I   A-Z [A and Z are pronounced very similarly in Turkish].

P   A-S.

I   Oh . . . A-S.

P   Positive . . .

I   OK. No one else has that type blood?

P   No.

I   What kind of blood is that?

P   Turkish blood.

The notions of blood and lineage surfaced directly or implicitly through-out Emel's discourse, slowly making it possible to discern a network of associated concepts. The idea of a pure 'Turkish blood' is associated strongly with the legacy of Ataturk, whose phrase "damarlarimizdaki asil kan" (the pure blood in our veins) continues to be used and reproduced widely in

Turkish social and political jargon. Following a devastating earthquake in 1999, the Turkish government was alleged to have refused blood donated by the Greek and Armenian governments on the argument that it would spoil or dilute the country's pure Turkish blood. The alleged refusal was reported in *The Observer* (Smith and Freely, 1999) and was later reported separately by US congressman Representative Joe Knollenberg in a speech of December 15, 2000.[8]

On Wednesday, November 19, 2003, the British Broadcasting Corporation (BBC) published a news item concerning the twin bombings of two synagogues in Istanbul on the 15th of that month. The headline read "Turkish Investigators Have Identified the Bodies of Two Men Suspected of Carrying Out Saturday's Twin Suicide Attacks on Istanbul Synagogues" (BBC, 2003), and the opening sentence was as followed: "Istanbul Governor Muammer Guler said DNA tests had shown that both men were Turks." Neither Governor Guler, however, nor the reporter provided any explanation as to how exactly a DNA test could establish the Turk-ness of a dead man. I had already encountered this notion of a Turkish blood in another more personal occasion. One day I traveled about 2 hours into the European side of Istanbul to a local TV station, where a friend's friend had promised me copies of some old movies as well as a TV commercial for the new local drink 'Cola Turka.' Shortly after leaving the TV station, and while taking photographs of the old wall of a graveyard, I was struck by a city bus that had lost control due its high speed. In addition to the privilege of being a foreigner, I was also lucky enough to have the phone number of a physician friend in Istanbul found in my pocket by passersby, two facts that together translated into my being promptly located by an ambulance and transported to a hospital less than two hours after the accident and my receiving thorough medical attention at that hospital.[9] One memory that has stayed with me besides the encounter with death in that frightening accident is when a physician told me that a test had also been done to verify my blood type, and concluded, "Well, now we know for sure that you are not a Turk." Overwhelmed by pain and fear, I did not have the presence of mind to ask what that meant or how a blood test could verify someone's Turk-ness,' but this was a notion that I encountered often afterward.

A frequently quoted phrase from Ataturk says, "Bu ulusu ben değil içimizdeki ruh, damarımızdaki asil kan kurtarmıştır" (It is not I, but the spirit inside of us, the pure blood in our veins that has saved this nation). In a great analysis of the notion of blood and nationalism in Turkish Cyprus, and confirming earlier analyses by Killoran (e.g., 1998), Bryant (2002) demonstrates that for Turks in Cyprus the notion of blood entails a specific significance, essentially different from the Greek Cypriot or North American metaphoric usage of the term. *Blood* is used by the Turkish community, she says, as an intermediary "substance" that connects the person not just to the kin but to the land itself, "along with the accompanying attributes of spiritual purity"

(Bryant, 2000, p. 511), a notion well reflected in the following patriotic lyrics taught to Turkish children:

> *If I squeeze this soil, Turkish blood comes out,*
> *If I excavate this land, Turkish bones come out.*
> *Oh, what these Turks have endured!*

(Nesim, 1987, p. 325)

It is not difficult now to see the way Emel's earlier assertions fit in this associative pattern, when she related, "[W]e [Ataturk and I] are from the same earth . . . no one else has my blood type."

The personal and the collective

One observes in Emel's narrative a strong association between her illness and notions of identity, blood, and purity, ideas associated just as closely within the larger Turkish nationalist discourse. The following excerpt further solidifies these associations. Further into the interview, Emel offered a striking metaphor for her illness and the consequent hospitalization: "It's a spiderweb," she said. When I inquired what she meant by that, she offered me yet another cryptic response. She said, "Spider, spiderweb, that means the opposites. Like East and West, like I told you." Unable to hide my confusion, I asked for more explanation:

I   Like East and West? I don't really understand this East and West thing. Could you explain that for me?

P   It means siblings.

I   East, West . . . siblings . . .

P   It means peace.

I   It means peace.

P   Peace. Peace at home. Peace in the world. I was reading Ataturk's writing, Ataturk's address to Turkish Youth.[10] Do you like Ataturk?

I   I don't know much about Ataturk.

P   If I gave you a book would you read it? A gift.

I   Thank you. Why don't you tell me the name of the book?

P   *Bütün Dünya* [The Whole World].

I   The Whole World. What does it say inside?

P   It talks about Ataturk. When he died, when he was born. How he won the battle of Sakarya.[11] How Sultan Mehmet the Conqueror conquered Istanbul.[12]

I   OK. History of Turkey, History of Istanbul. So why don't you tell me about what Ataturk did.

P   He was born in 1981.

I   1981, OK.

P   He died in 1983. His mother's name is Zübeyde, Father's name is Ali Rıza. He went to *ta mektebi* [stone school], then he worked as a *kimyager* with a hoja.

I   OK.

P   After that he slowly, slowly went farther and took the name Ataturk.

I   OK.

P   So he's my grandfather. We are from the same earth.

I   You are from the same earth.

P   Yes we are from the same earth . . .

I   Aha.

P   No one has my blood type. Only my father and I have it. A-S, it's A-S type.

I   A-Z.

P   A-S.

I   Oh . . . A-S.

P   Positive.

I   I see. No one else has that type blood?

P   No.

I   What kind of blood is that?

P   Turkish blood.

I   Turkish blood.

P   Turkish blood.

I   So your blood is Turkish blood.

P   Yes.

I   Your mother, is her blood the same?

P   It doesn't match.

I   Doesn't match?

P   I had blood tests done. It doesn't match.

I   Hmm.

P   She is not my mother. She is my sister.

I   I see. What about your father?

P   My father is my real father.

I   Ah, OK. So your father has Turkish blood?

P   Turkish blood . . .

I have included the opening East/West remarks in this segment as context but postpone a detailed discussion of that theme for now. Suffice it here to point out the theme of conflict and a binary opposition built into this East/West metaphor, one Emel ties here to the idea of siblings, recalling remarks about her brother/lover as the entity bringing father and mother together. Notice that Emel applies the East/West dualism to her father and her mother, with her mother standing for the Western/non-Turkish side and her father for the Turkish/Islamic side. Her next association, "it means peace," is congruent with the earlier mention of a sibling/love object who produces peace/unity by bringing together opposing sides of a schism, that is, the father and the mother, and all the binary oppositions they represent. Of interest at this point is that in this excerpt the personal account of identity blends seamlessly with the collective discourse. The idea of an intermediary catalyst that brings two conflicting worlds together and restores a stable self-identity coincides with the figure of Ataturk, whose famous adage "peace at home, peace in the world" she repeats. Ataturk is now the pivotal point of reference for Emel through which she finds, without much effort, a way of deferring her frustrating struggle for self-identity to a larger and more promising domain, the collectively organized system of meaning and power.

A famous statement by Ataturk sheds further light on the process suggested here: that an individual quest for self-identification may be deferred seamlessly to the collective domain of Turkness and Turkish nationalism via a signifier known as Mustafa Kemal Ataturk. He said,

> There are two Mustafa Kemals: one is I, the flesh and bone Mustafa Kemal. . .the second Mustafa Kemal I cannot describe with the word 'I'. That Mustafa Kemal is not I, it is 'We'. That Mustafa Kemal is the enlightened and warrior collectivity that is striving for the new thought, the new life and the Great Ideal on every corner of this country. I am a manifestation of their dream . . . You are that Mustafa Kemal, all of You . . .[13]

The specific speech by Ataturk that Emel selects to mention is also quite revealing; it describes the very point where political collective identity and subjective personal identity intersect. The speech she says she has been reading, known as "Address to The Youth" (Gençliğe Hitabesi), is a brief but powerful address in which Ataturk alerts Turkish youth that the Republic of Turkey is "the foundation of your existence." He warns that one day malevolent forces from both "within" and "outside" may conspire together to take the Republic toward disintegration to the point where "circumstances may turn out to be extremely unfavorable" when "by violence and ruse, all the fortresses of your beloved country may be captured", "all its armies dispersed and every part of the country invaded . . . [it] may be impoverished, ruined and exhausted." But, in such circumstances, he asserts, you can restore its integrity, by falling back on "the pure blood in your veins." A poem quoted from the Turkish government's Ministry of Culture and Tourism can put this in further context. Alluding to the "second" Ataturk as a universal "spirit" that runs through the Turkish individuals, it says,

> Know that there are two Mustafa Kemals./I am the second, in the infinite/ Invisible like a spirit . . . On the road to brotherhood and plenty/In the light of the creativity of knowledge/I am in the finest thoughts/In new, universal discoveries/I have done away with backwardness, it will not come back . . . If you have woes, remember me/Feel me in your worst moments/ . . . /The Conquerors, the Magnificents never die./Believe me, Mustafa Kemal will never end.
>
> (Yağcioğlu, 2005)

It is not difficult to see how Emel's psychotic experience of the land as the personal body the blood of whose veins is "Turkish blood" and whose spirit is Ataturk, is not altogether incongruent with a larger culturally endorsed model of national and collective identity.

A semiotic trope: yurt

It is worth consideration as we speak of land here that whether Emel talks of home in a phrase like "peace at home, peace in the world" or Ataturk speaks of the country with an enemy inside or abroad, or the country whose integrity needs to be defended, the original Turkish term for both home and country is a single one, *yurt*. The term itself is a signifier of identity as a meeting place of the private and the social and using the same signifier across two or more discourses is evidence for a semiotic continuity across those discourses. *Yurt* is a word with a flexible range of significations, all of which share two senses: a demarcation of interiority/exteriority associated with land, with selfhood, and with sociality and an indication of peace and rest, associated with resting, sleeping, and settlement. The oldest sense known for this Turkic word is the round markers made on land by nomads in Central Asia within which they would then set up their tents or other sleeping facilities for the family, a sense in which the word is still used by nomadic tribes in various parts of Asia (see, e.g., Stronach, 2004). One important feature of the yurt is the fact that in its original sense it is simultaneously dynamic/mobile and constant, because while the nomad sets up the yurt in various locations at various times, the interior space remains basically unchanged, including the same items organized in the same general pattern. A contemporary Turkish dictionary would list such meanings for yurt as dormitory, home, country, motherland, fatherland, hostel, or hotel, among others.

It is easy to see how *yurt* has made a wonderful metonymic candidate for the self as a dynamic space marked to signify the interiority where one can rest sheltered both literally and by social convention. It is thanks in part to such dynamic signifiers that Turkish 'common sense' juxtaposes Ataturk's prescription of falling back on pure Turkish blood in "extremely unfavorable" political circumstances and the poet's recommendation of falling back on the spirit of Ataturk in an individual's 'worst moments.' This is an instance of a culturally available semiotic trope that a subject in need of an 'anchor' can use to simultaneously express its unique experience of the world and approach a culturally legitimized state of meaning, continuity, and 'organization.'

East and West, modernity and tradition

The book Emel offered to give to me was titled *Bütün Dunya*, or *The Whole World*. My search for a book with that title was fruitless, though it is not implausible to assume Emel is actually referring to some publication. There is, for example, a journal published by Başkent University bearing the title *Bütün Dunya*, which defines its agenda as introducing modern thought to the Turkish society. In either case, the notion of wholeness is germane to my analysis here, as is the fact that the content Emel attributes to that book (i.e., the conquest of Istanbul by Ottoman Turks and the reinstatement of the country by Ataturk) continues the theme of national identity and Turkish integrity. Significantly, the two historic events that Emel mentions are major markers in the history of Turkey, both defined in terms of an ongoing East versus West struggle. The first, the 15th-century conquest of Istanbul, is generally considered the high point of the Ottoman Turks' claim to statehood and power in confrontation with Christian Europe, and it was through the second, the Battle of Sakarya, that Ataturk gave a second birth to Turkey by defeating the European/Christian Greek army.

Emel then continues to suggest a direct self-identification with Ataturk by telling me that he was born in 1981: the same year she had earlier suggested for her own birth. Curiously, she then gave the date of Ataturk's death as 1983, that is, only two years after his birth. There is a subtle resonation in her calculation of Ataturk's birth and death with her parent's discussion of her own birth and a time when they assumed her dead, when she was 2 years old, which I consider later.[14]

Hojas and professors

Immediately after attributing to Ataturk those self-referent birth and death years, Emel introduces the notion of magic/*kimya*: Ataturk, after having finished the "stone school," has gone on to study *Kimya* with a *hoca*, or as transliterated in English "hoja." A *hoca* is traditionally a person knowledgeable in religious sciences, and, often, specifically in folk traditions, someone knowledgeable in more esoteric practices such as contacting supernatural beings including the jinn or spirits of the dead, an area that constitutes a branch of *oloom-e khafi-ye*, the 'concealed sciences.' The word *hoca* has double significance, resonating somewhat with the word *master* in English (specifically in its Arabic origin, *khajah*, where the senses of 'lordship' and 'mastery' are more salient) and used in reference to either local healers or academic teachers. However, the term is typically distinguished from the modern concept of 'doctor.'[15] At different points in the interview Emel made it clear that she has a very specific use for each terms as when she spoke to me of her (superficial) resignation to the Western medical discourse:

P   I trust doctors more than hojas, you know?

I   No, why is that?

P   There are no hojas here . . . There are doctors.

I   Yes . . . In the hospital.

P   I accept myself as an ill person. Yes . . . imagination . . . This could be a product of the power of imagination, it could be real too. I want to accept this reality, will you help me?

A closer look at her comment reveals an irony just below the surface. This interaction took place just after she asked me if I were affiliated with "the field of psychiatry." My positive answer located me on the 'modern' side of the modern/traditional dichotomy in Emel's (and in the Turkish) world. It was in strategic response to that positioning and in an effort to appeal to my assumed belief system that she shared with me, without being solicited, her agreement with the modernist discourse. Like so many others in Turkey, however, Emel's compliance with the modernist discourse is more a political strategy than a deeply rooted subjective stance.

One may consider Emel's explanation that "she trusts doctors more than hojas because she is in a hospital" genuine, given the truth that in a hospital doctors rule, not hojas. Just as genuinely, her follow-up remarks express the difficult predicament in which she finds herself stranded, between two discourses, two worlds seriously at odds with each other. Even if she begins with the confident assertion that "I accept myself as an ill person," it takes her only a few words to confess her inability to adhere fully to one or the other, "I want to accept this reality, will you help me?" Emel's predicament resonates with the political context she lives in, both in the pragmatic terms of the strategies of survival a Turk has to employ as a social subject, and in terms of the fundamental discrepancy between the surface and the beneath, the outer and the inner; features that play central roles in configuring what may be called a Turkish 'style of selfhood.' Her strikingly inaccurate response to a question I raised about the use of doctor versus hoja was another excellent example of the 'predicament' I have just mentioned: "People in Turkey," she said, "don't really go to see local healers, and when they say hoja, they are actually talking about doctors and professors."

Purity and pollution: *kimya*

Emel interlaces in her fragile yet fearsome spiderweb of psychosis the notions of East and West, peace and war, the conquest of Istanbul, and Ataturk and his projects, leading to the fascinating twist of having Ataturk study chemistry/alchemy with a professor/hoja. A distinct quality of double significance in the Turkish semiotic space is beautifully demonstrated here. It was only after becoming a *kimyager* and mastering the magic of purity, that Ataturk was worthy of the title 'Father Turk':[16]

P   . . . then he worked as a *kimyager* with a *hoca*.

I   OK.

P   After that he slowly, slowly went farther and took the name Ataturk.

I   OK.

P   So he's my grandfather. We are from the same earth.

But what makes *kimya* meaningful in this trajectory? Emel referred to the idea quite regularly, and her references were often associated with the notions of blood, purity, and (national) identity. Shortly into the interview, for example, Emel demanded to go over our consent form again. Acting true to the quality I described earlier as a 'will to power,' she wanted to put her signature in the blank section meant for the researcher's name. When I pointed out that the space was meant for my [researcher's] signature, she said the following:

P   Researcher . . . is researcher a *kimyaci* [*kim-ya-jee*]?

I   That [part] is for my name!

P   *Kimyaci.* . . . You have selected the field of *Kimya*!

I   I am a *kimyaci*? What is a *kimyaci*?

P   *Kimiyci* . . . is a person who analyzes the blood.

Later on she also said,

P   My name is Emel; I was born on the 24th day of December. I was born in 1981. I wish to become a researcher and a *kimyaci*.

Or elsewhere again,

P   *Kimyager!* Someone who analyses the blood.

I   They call them *kimyager*?

P   Yes, you know, there's this two pieces of glass . . . you look with a microscope. You look like this to see if there are any germs in the blood, you know?

In modern post-Ataturk Turkey, the term *kimya* is used to refer to chemistry. Even a brief glance beyond the modern Turkish dictionary, however, reveals the term to have a more intricate significance, a significance partially kept in the apparently irrelevant sense in which the term is used to mean 'something extremely important.' I call this sense 'apparently irrelevant,' because for all means and purposes there is no relationship between chemistry and this sense of value – yet people still maintain the polysemy. The reason for this invisible association is of a diachronic nature; that is, the connection lies in pre-Republican times. Along with such disciplines as *simya*, *himya*, and *rimya*, *kimya* is (or 'was,' so far as Turkey is concerned) a branch of knowledge known in the Islamic Middle East as *oloom-e khafi-yeh*, or the "concealed sciences." *Kimya* is the equivalent of alchemy, the branch whose objective is to find the Elixir, the substance of purity also translated in English as the philosopher's stone. Put in other words, *kimya* is the branch of knowledge concerned with finding a way of transforming inferior 'impure' substances to the pure one, gold. The association of chemistry and alchemy in (Ottoman) Turkish, Persian, or Arabic should not appear novel to French or English speakers (or to the speakers of most other European languages), because chemistry or chimie also have its roots in alchemy, etymologically and genealogically.

In the Middle Eastern/Islamic scientific and philosophical traditions, *kimya* is not only the branch of science that searched for purification of metals into gold; it also had strong medical implications. Jaber bin-Yayyan (traditionally known to Europeans as Geber) was of the opinion that the pure substance, gold, could be applied toward physical healing, not only in humans but even in animals or plants (e.g., Stanton, 2003, p. 80f.). This sense is still traceable in his legacy of the notion of *al-iksir* (elixir, aka the philosopher's stone), which signifies, simultaneously, a substance that would "change metals into gold" and a substance with the effect of "indefinitely prolonging life," as well as "a sovereign remedy for a disease" (*Oxford English Dictionary*, 2005).

Not surprisingly, the terms *kimya* and *iksir* are used quite frequently in Sufi discourse as metaphors for healing and for purification. Imam Ghazzali's 11th-century seminal treatise on the human 'Self,' titled *Kimya-ye Saadat* (*The Alchemy of Happiness*), and the more recent book on Ibn Arabi titled *Quest for the Red Sulphur* (Addas, 1993), are living evidence of that long lasting association. In that same tradition, another word closely associated with *kimya* is *love*, a sign specially associated with both madness and purity, understood to bring purity through intoxication or *bikhodi* (the state of having no self) wherein the 'superficial' layer of personhood (the self, the *nefs*) is cleared and inner purity is unleashed. The *nefs*, which should ideally be overcome, tamed, or trained, is the part of a person responsible for pursuing gains and avoiding losses and is generally associated with reason and logical thinking. Inner purity, by contrast, is commonly associated with and conveyed in terms of *kalp* (Arab. *Qalb*: the heart), which is associated with intuitions and direct relation to the hidden truth of existence, is responsible for 'love' and is scandalously unreasonable or 'crazy.' Rumi says that "[t]he light which shines in the eye/is really the light of the heart/The light which fills the heart/is the light of God, which is pure/and separate from the light of intellect and sense" (*Mathnavi*, Book 1; trans. Helminski, 1998, p. 107). Love, says Rumi elsewhere, is "the sea of not-being, and there the intellect drowns" (Helminski, 1998, p. 49). The connections between love and intoxication/madness will be further developed in the case of Ahmet (see Chapter 5).

Purity and pollution: chemical properties

Of interest here is the recurrent pattern of associations produced by Emel around the notion of purity: purity of blood and purity of the spirit function as a point of convergence for individual selfhood and collective identity, and along with 'wholeness' or 'unity,' purity is strongly associated in Emel's system of references with health and recovery, while she associates her illness with pollution or 'poison.' The following passage, reviewed earlier, ends in an enigmatic declaration:

P I accept myself as an ill person. Imagination! Yes, this [illness] is a product of the power of imagination . . . I want to accept this reality. Will you help me? I want to be clean like this pen!

This idea of 'cleansing' herself in order to heal from her illness repeats elsewhere in association with a *kimya*–magic model of explanation for her illness. Smoking cigarettes, for example, is associated with the purity-versus-pollution motif, a theme that Emel tries to introduce early in the interview but that I fail to notice until later. Recall that when introducing herself she said the following:

P My problem is . . . I have one brother . . . in the army. He is supposed to be coming back today. So . . . And I smoke cigarettes.
I Pardon me . . . you said you had a brother . . .?

The association of smoking and illness in this passage is by no means accidental; it is part of a larger explanatory model of illness as a state of impurity entailing the presence of a pollutant, physically and/or spiritually. She brings back the notion of smoking shortly after that original introduction, once again as she tries to decide the nature of her illness and what it might be about:

I . . . Why did you come here, Miss Emel?
P I am psychologically unstable. They immediately told me it was schizophrenia. But that's not my problem, my problem has to do with ear nose

and throat. There is an inflammation in my ear. . . . I mean, I may have the mumps or jaundice . . . I smoke three packs of cigarettes a day.

I   Hmm.

P   I smoke three packs a day. The doctors are giving them one by one now. I am testing myself to see if I can quit smoking or not.

I   I see.

P   I could have quit actually.

I   Do you want to quit?

P   I do, but not just now. I can't just quit. People can't stop smoking just like that. Do you smoke?

I   No I don't.

P   How nice. Congratulations.

I   Thank you.

P   Congratulations!!

I   Thank you!

And later on she comes back to the question of smoking, this time in the context of 'what kind of person' she is, which she first associates with religion and being a Muslim and then with the question of smoking cigarettes. It should be mentioned here that both her parents and her clinician emphasized that a significant shift in her attitude due to this 'illness' was that when she became ill she was prevented (by the illness/jinns and despite herself) from acting like a good believer. Emel had explained that the jinn did not allow her to be a believer and do her prayers.

P   So . . . according to you what kind of a person am I? Can you describe me?

I   I don't know you.

P   We just met. My name is Emel.

I   Yes.

P   Your name?

I   Sadeq.

P   Mr. Sadeq.

I   Yes.

P   Have you become a Muslim?

I   Yes.

P   Oh how nice.

I   Yes.

P   Would it be all right if I smoked five cigarettes a day?

I   Five cigarettes?

P   Would that be too much? Smoking . . . American cigarettes

I   I don't understand. . . . What do you mean?

P   Cigarettes . . . cigarettes . . . That wouldn't be harmful, right? Also I can't sleep at night without drinking milk.

I   You can't sleep at night without drinking milk.

P   I love milk and yogurt.

I   Milk and yogurt.

P   I was actually poisoned.

I   How? What happened?

P   I had yogurt . . . After that I had a banana . . . that's it. 500 milligrams of yogurt all by myself. Then they gave me some medicine. I slept for four days; I couldn't get out of bed. Do you think that's fair or unfair? I don't understand.

It is possible to discern in the preceding excerpt, as in the earlier passages concerning vitamin and poisoning, an underlying logic that connects her illness to an almost magical notion of different substances and the way they may act together to poison a person, as in having bananas and yogurt together. The notion of foods that do or do not 'match' is a common idea in the Middle East as in many other traditions and should not be considered a psychotic thought as such; this is a logical pattern she is borrowing from the local meaning system. What I would like to point out here, however, is the implied idea that pollution or poisoning may be mobilizing her illness and that this poisoning is associated with chemical properties of foods and substances. The following passage captures that sense when, in another part of the interview, she explains her illness with reference to the chemical properties of foods and substances:

P   I have a vitamin D deficiency.

I   How?

P   I have iron deficiency.

I   Why?

P   Because I don't eat enough spinach.

I   I see . . . so iron . . .

P   Lemons have vitamin C. Oranges too . . . Do tomatoes have vitamin D? C or D, I can't decide. . .

I   Now . . . these vitamins . . .

P   Should I repeat?

I   No. What happens when you don't have enough of these?

P   I take vitamins. Now I use cigarettes as an antidote [*panzehir*].[17]

I   Antidote?

P   You can't have yogurt and cigarettes together. It becomes an antidote because there is nicotine in this. It's addictive. It's like that.

Purity and pollution: the *nefs*

The polluting property of cigarettes that Emel has already linked to her illness is later on connected directly to the Sufi concept of *nefs* [self] and its purification. In yet another instance of her search for giving a sense to her condition, Emel says the following:

P   What do you think my illness is? Does it have to do with the nerves? Is it about personality? I have lost my confidence in myself.

I   Why have you lost your confidence?

P   I want to regain my confidence.

I   How can you do that?

P   I will tame my *nefs*. . . . Look I asked for cigarette and they wouldn't give me. . . . I will give myself more value from now on. Cigarette is poisoning me. It has a very bad smell too, doesn't it . . . May I see your watch?

Nefs [Arab. *nafs*] is a specialized Sufi term not commonly used in daily conversations. The closest English translation for *nefs* would be 'self' or 'ego.' In Sufi teachings the *nefs* is pictured as a dangerously wild and powerful yet clever entity, at times a dragon, at times a cunning fox, and at times a magician. "Nafs," says Bakharzi, "is like a flame, both in its display and beauty and in its hidden potential for destruction" (Fediman, 1997 p. 66). It is the Sufi's objective in life to 'overcome' the *nefs*, to free oneself from its ruling and to master it with the ultimate objective of bringing it to pure servitude of God. Both God and the Devil can play with the *nefs*: the latter by tempting it and the first by testing it. Emel conveys the relation between the *nefs* and cigarettes in two respects: first, cigarettes are poisonous and act as pollutants and she should therefore move to a process of purification and taming of the *nefs* by quitting cigarettes. Second, her *nefs* urges her to smoke cigarettes and further taint her clarity. In other words, the implication here is that if she managed to 'control' her *nefs*, she would quit smoking and stop the pollution and respect her 'true self' and thus be able to avoid asking the nurses for cigarettes (i.e., gain power). The motif of pollution and purification then becomes an important theme in her illness narrative, as reflected in the ensuing interactions:

P   Do you know Balık Aydın [literally, "Fish Enlightened"]? . . . There was a whale they found there once.

I   A whale?

P   I saw it myself.

I   You did?

P   By myself.

I   By yourself!

P   Yes.

I   How was it?

P   500 tons.

I   Oh . . .

P   I pulled it along and buried it. I felt sorry for it . . . the poor thing . . . It was polluting [*zehirlemek*: to poison, to pollute, to taint] the water.

I   Polluting the water?

P   It was polluting . . . because it was dead.

I   Yes, OK.

P   But it's back now. It comes back every year. . . . It's running away from the hunters.

I   Running away from hunters?

P   I really like fish. What about you?

Purity and pollution: death and rebirth

The theme of cleansing and purity in the preceding excerpt is associated with another significant concept in Emel's account: that of death and rebirth. The death/rebirth notion is repeated in different occasions by both Emel and her parents. The parents put it in these words:

M   . . . [Emel] was 2, 2-and-a-half years old. . .

F   She was 2 to 3.

M   She just seemed dead like this [gestures] . . .

F   It was as if she had died, she died and passed away . . .

M   She was dead like a piece of wood. She died, had nothing, no life no blood.

F   There was a clinic nearby we took her there.

M   Then she woke up and started to cry . . .

I   How long did that last?

M   A little.

F   About 5 minutes I think.

M   Only about 5 minutes. . .

F   I think it was about 10 minutes.

I   5 to 10 minutes?

M   She turned white like a piece of board . . .

F   She was colorless.

M   No blood, no life, she had no color. She stayed like this, like a dead body. Then, after we took her to the clinic, she woke up and she started to cry.

And Emel herself said the following at one point:

P   I was born early.

I   You were?

P   Hang on. I didn't learn this from my mother. I learnt it from my aunt. After my mother gave birth to me . . . I had a fit. I was 740 grams when I was born. Then I died and then I came back to life. There is a name for that. . . what was it?

And then in another occasion, also concerning her birth, she says the following:

P   My mother did not want to stay in the hospital [for my birth].

I   OK?

P   She went home. She was a housewife. She did housework and she had a miscarriage, and then they buried me as dead. Then God gave me life and strength and so I came back to live again.

After bringing in the theme of death and rebirth in the earlier excerpt, Emel made a new connection between that and a process of cleansing that resonates closely with tenets of the Sufi doctrine. Associated there with the death of the whale and the ensuing act of purification through the burial and revival by her is the symbolism of fish, specifically in the context of the story to which she links that signifier. One of the most immediate associations in Islam with fish, especially with larger "fish" such as whales (the Quran does not make that distinction, it simply says 'fish'), is the story of Jonah (Yunos, or Yunus). The Quran says the following of Yunos:

> Then the fish swallowed him, while he was tainted by acts worthy of blame. Had it not been that he repented and glorified Allah, he would certainly have remained inside the fish till the day of resurrection. But We cast him forth on the naked shore in a state of sickness, And We caused to grow over his head a spreading plant of the gourd kind. And We sent him [as our messenger] to a hundred thousand [people] or more.
>
> (Surah 37, Ayahs 142–147)

Yunus, tainted as he was, says Allah, is sent to the nether world, the world of the dead, buried in the belly of the large fish, where he finds an opportunity to purify his soul by repenting, and is then brought back to life and thrown onto the dry land, not only to recover from his 'state of sickness' but indeed to become Allah's chosen one, a prophet, as well. The process of purification is an important concept in Sufism, where the individual gradually 'tames' his or her *nefs* and attains purity of the spirit and growth toward unity with Allah. Jonah himself, for instance, is used as a metaphor of that process by Sufis, quoting the fact that he needed the period of loss/death/burial in the belly of the fish to purify his *nefs* from the blight of anger that poisoned his spirit: "when the nefs says meow, like a cat, put it in a bag, like a cat" (Rumi). It is in this sense that Emel insists, "I want to tame my *nefs*."

Fish are also associated with purity in Turkish and Islamic religious and folk traditions. One of the oldest surviving traditions of the Anatolian peninsula concerns the 'fishponds of Abraham' in the city of Urfa [aka Şanlıurfa], to which in fact Emel makes direct reference:

P   I really like fish. What about you?

I   I like them as well.

P   Have you ever been to Şanlıurfa?

I   No I haven't.

P   It's really nice there.

I   Have you been there?

P   No I haven't been.

I   What is there in Şanlıurfa?

P   There are fishes . . . There is a pond with fish, like a pool . . .

I   Really?

P   Have you heard of Ibrahim Tatlıses?

The fish pond in Şanlıurfa to which Emel is referring has in fact been called "a last living link with the city's heterodox past" (e.g., Dalrymple, 1997, p. 73). Urfa, locally referred to as Şanlıurfa[18] and known in earlier centuries as Edessa, is a museum city with a history dating back more than 9,000 years, according to some sources. According to local Muslims, Urfa is in fact the ancient city of Ur, known as the birthplace of the prophet Abraham, the common father of Judaism, Christianity, and Islam. According to local folk belief, it is also the city where the Prophet Job lived, and a city blessed by Jesus. Urfa is one of the most sacred cities in Turkey. The fishpond of Abraham, locally known as Balıklı Göl (Fish Lake), is the focal point of the city. According to legends echoed directly in the Quran's story of the prophet Abraham,[19] the regional king known locally as 'Nimrut[20] the Hunter'[21] had the prophet Abraham thrown into a big fire after Abraham vandalized the city's holy shrines and temples, but God made water emerge from the fire and saved Abraham from the flames' harm. That water then remained to form the current lake and pieces of burning wood from the fire became the fish in the lake.

The story of Abraham who did not burn in fire is often used in the Islamic metaphoric system to speak of purity: it was Abraham's purity that made the fire ineffective on him. Rumi, for example, relates a conversation that took place between Abraham and the archangel Gabriel when Abraham was cast into fire, where the angel offers him help, and he rejects that offer, claiming that he does not need any help because the fire will only demonstrate his purity, since he is already one with God through love (*Mathnavi*, Book IV, story 17). Propounding that same logic, Rumi also tells elsewhere in his *Mathnavi* the story of a layman's quarrel with a philosopher over truth and purity, which ends in this way:

> [The layman] said, "When genuine gold and base coins argue,
> Both saying 'you are fake, I am genuine,'
> The ultimate test is fire, when the two are cast into the furnace."
> So then the two men leapt into the burning flames;
> The philosopher was burnt to ashes, but the God-fearing man
> Came out cleaner than before.
> (Mathnavi, Book IV, Story 6, orig. trans. Whinfield, 1898)

Purification and unity: Ataturk and Turkish nationalism

Both Emel's story of the whale purified through death and rebirth and Abraham's symbolic purification in fire recall the chemistry of madness/pollution and healing/wholeness and the resonance of that pattern of associations with the search for purity in *kimya*, which Emel describes as a science of testing blood's purity, implying the same pure Turkish blood that she shares with her "grandfather," Ataturk, through the land. The signifier of fire that Emel uses to convey purity and healing is almost identical with the two other notions: love and alchemy. The metaphoric use of 'fire' to refer to love is a standard practice in Sufi literature. On the purifying power of fire (love), Rumi recounts the following conversation between two coins:

> The base coin says [to the pure coin] with pride,
> O pure gold, how am I inferior to you?
> The gold replies, the touchstone is at hand; be ready to meet it!
> Death of the body is a benefaction to the spirit;
> What damage has pure gold to dread from the shears?
> If the base coin were of itself far-sighted,
> It would reveal at first the blackness it shows at last.
> If it had showed its blackness at first on its face,
> It would have found the alchemy of love in due time;
> If it became broken-hearted through its own ills,
> It would look onward to Him who heals the broken;

And be made whole at once by the Healer of the broken.
Divine grace places base copper in the alembic,
Adulterated gold is excluded from that favor.
             (*Mathnavi*, Book. IV, Story 3; orig. trans. Whinfield, 1898)

As I suggested earlier, the implicit logic that emerges in Emel's system of associations concerning purity and illness is strikingly similar to that of the Sufi doctrine, according to which the human soul "has to be purified, dissolved and crystallized anew to achieve its 'golden nature'; which is immutable purity and luminosity" via a long and painful process of "alchemy" (Burckhardt 1970, p. 24). Referring to that same "painful process" of alchemy, Moris (1997) writes that

> [h]uman perfection can only be attained after long periods of time when the soul patiently undergoes a painful process of painful alchemy or transformation. The soul, like the base metal, lead, has to be transmuted zto become gold; that is, only a self which has purged itself of vices and base qualities arising from the dominance of the nafs [*nefs*] . . . [for attaining which,] man has to "die unto himself."

Recall that at the end of the last excerpt from Emel's interview, after having brought into play the ponds of Abraham, she asked whether I knew İbrahim Tatlıses. İbrahim Tatlıses is a popular singer in Turkey, whose obvious relation to the story of the fish is the fact that his name is the same as the unmentioned protagonist of the fish lakes, Abraham (Turk. İbrahim). But by this twist what Emel manages to do turns out to be more intricate than an association of names. Here is how the interview continues:

P   There are fishes . . . There is a pond with fish, like a pool . . .
I   Really?
P   Have you heard of İbrahim Tatlıses?
I   Yes.
P   I am his girl [*kız*: daughter, girl], Asena.
I   You are his girl?
P   Uh-huh . . . Asena.
I   Asena . . .
P   I have two names: Asena, Emel.
I   I know the one that is Emel, what's the other one?
P   My father's side call me Emel, my mother's side call me Asena
I   Asena?
P   According to Islam . . . excuse me but . . . Christianity they say this side.

I   Christianity?

P   Islam they say [claps her hands on one side of her body] this side . . . Christianity [claps hands again, on the other side]. In reality they're all one [*bir*] . . . Siblings, brother . . .

I   OK. So your mother's side . . . ?

P   Foreigner.

I   Foreigner?

P   Uhuh

I   How do you mean foreigner? What is that?

P   Someone who hasn't changed their religion.

I   I see. That means remained Christian?

P   Remained Christian.

I   But your father . . .

P   Muslim.

As muddled and pointless as this genuinely psychotic excerpt first appears, close investigation reveals implicit connecting threads within it. Singer İbrahim Tatlıses did have a famous 'love of his life' by the name of Asena at the time our interview took place. Below this commonsense surface, however, Asena assumes new significance in two respects: its fit within local mythology and its fit within local politics and discourses of binary oppositions. The word *Asena* is almost homophonic with the name of Emel's mother, but only 'almost,' because though sounding similar, the mother's name is an Arabic/Islamic name while Asena is from Central Asian mythology. I discuss further specifics of Emel's troubled identification with her mother and its strong links with her binary division of the world later, but first let us consider the mythological connotations of the name Asena.

Asena is a name associated with mythologies of both Central Asia and Asia Minor. For Turks, Asena is the mythological she-wolf who saved Turkish blood when she led the Oghuz Turks away and westward from the barren and drought-ridden steppes of Central Asia (e.g., Kinzer, 2001, p. 107; Pope, 1997, p. 8). Some researchers also identify Asena with a Sumerian goddess of fertility who mated with a certain Nimrut to give birth to the great hunter twins: Hunor and Magor, conveniently enough identifiable as the ancestors of the Huns and the Magiars (e.g., Bobula, 1982; Hamori, 2004).[22]

What is evident about the name Emel selects to give herself is a significant association with Turkish identity and nationalism. Ataturk himself carried the title Bozkurt (Gray Wolf) in reference to this myth of origins and in recognition of his significance as someone who, like Asena, brought back to life the almost dead Turkish Nation (see, e.g., Armstrong, 1932). The following text written by a Turkish man is an indication of the scope of this signifier for the average Turkish person:

The gray wolf is the ancient and noble animal representing the nation of Turks stretching from the Northern Pacific Ocean, west through Siberia, to Eastern Europe and the Mediterranean Sea. The gray wolf is intertwined in countless stories, legends, and mythologies of the Turks. One mythology relates that in a great battle the Turkish nation was destroyed except for a baby prince, who was left to die in the battlefield. A lone she-wolf named Asena happened upon the babe and took him away to the legendary Ergenekon mountain range in Northern Siberia. Within this mountain, the boy was reared by the wolf to maturity whereupon Asena and the prince gave birth to the new Turks. . .

(Turk, 2004)

Ironically enough, Ataturk, the he-wolf, and Emel/Asena, the she-wolf, share not only their strong identificatory associations but also a quality of internal discrepancy, ambiguity, and *extimity* in regard to their Turkish identification.[23] They are simultaneously insider and outsider, the very reason for existence of a Turkish blood, yet themselves are 'tainted' by an unspoken sense of the 'non-Turk' (see the following discussion regarding dichotomy and wholeness and Selanikli).

Identity and the play of oppositions

In the preceding interview passage inspired by mention of Ibrahim Tatlıses, the 'loaded' name, Asena, gains significance as Emel uses the concept of 'names' to anchor her elusive sense of identity within a binary opposition that mobilizes an array of immediately accessible binary metaphors such as East/West, Left/Right Christian/Muslim, Turk/non-Turk, and, once again, father/mother. She later makes the binary opposition implicit in her double name choice more explicit, saying the following:

I   OK. What was your other name?

P   Asena.

I   Asena, what does that mean?

P   It's the opposite of Hazine.

I   Huh?

P   The English of Hazine.

I   That's English?

P   My mother's name is Hazine.

I   Hazine?

P   Hazine

I   I see.

P   I am changing my identity for Hazine . . . It's the opposite. English is the opposite of Turkish. And the opposite of Turkish is English, in my opinion.

I   I see, OK.

Here again Emel is quick to identify the way out of this binary opposition, through/toward a wholeness associated directly with brother/love: "they are all one, siblings, brother," she asserts (see the earlier excerpt). Note that the term *brother* is used in singular form rather than plural, to wit, the intended meaning is the concept 'brother,' rather than the notion of brotherhood. You may also recall an earlier passage where the same association was expressed in this way:

P   Spider, spiderweb, that means the opposite. Like East and West, like I told you.

I   Like East and West? I don't really understand this East and West thing. Could you explain that for me?

P   It means siblings.

I   East, West . . . siblings . . .

P   It means peace.

I   It means peace.

P   Peace. Peace at home. Peace in the world I was reading Ataturk's writing, Ataturk's address to Turkish Youth. Do you like Ataturk?

Purity of wholeness and pollution of duality

On yet another occasion Emel brings back the East/West opposition when she is talking about recovery. She is complaining about the duration of her hospitalization, claiming that she has not been able to leave the hospital for 8 months and that she needs to leave the hospital and go "outside." She then asks me how they say *outside* in English, and I pronounce the word *outside*. She plays with the word for a moment, and then once again rapidly sets it in an unusual association:

I   [It is] [o]*utside.*

P   *Outside . . . outside.*

I   '*Outside.*'

P   '*Otside?*' or '*Outside*'?

I   '*Out-side*'

P   '*Outside*' . . . like the opposite of . . . East and West synthesis, *now*, in this moment.

I   East, West. What is the difference between East and West?

P   None, for me there is no difference . . .

I   So you mean . . .

P   They were separated. For inheritance.

I   For inheritance.

P   Yes.

I   Who was separated?

P   My aunt separated from her husband.

I   I see.

P   My mother separated from my father. I am left alone in the middle . . . I am a ball, like a soccer ball.

I   That's difficult.

P   They throw it here. They throw me here. They shoved me here and they are *outside* enjoying themselves. And Emel can take her punishment . . . isn't that?

I   Hmm.

P   This is really unfair. I am left like this because of inheritance . . .

I   Whose inheritance?

P   My grandfather . . . He used to live in Salonika.

Once again in what struck me as a whirlwind of imagery and metaphors, Emel has delivered a bundle of concatenated ideas that at first appear fully disjointed yet yield intriguing associations on closer investigation. The general theme centers on duality and opposition versus oneness and unity, a sense of duality that permeates various aspects of 'life' and one which, if it were to be set right, should turn into 'oneness,' or in her words, a "synthesis." Her predicament, she emphasizes here again, is due to a dual opposition of forces, outside and inside, father versus mother, aunt versus uncle, and, of course, West versus East, the binary opposition that leaves her like a soccer ball in a field: deprived of stability and a definable locatedness. And that, she says, is all due to a war over her ancestral heritage, what has remained from her 'grandfather.'

Identity and the politics of purity: the Selanikli

Emel earlier claimed Ataturk, the father of Turks, as her grandfather, identified with her, of the same blood and of the same earth, and she identified herself with Asena, the mother of Turks. Remember also that in an earlier passage Emel suggested that while her father is of pure Turkish blood, her mother is not so, or elsewhere that her mother is in fact a Christian. In order to search for relevant cultural and historical plots I investigate the term *Selanikli* (*Salonikan*), and with that I introduce another important and paradoxical phenomenon of the recent Turkish history, known as the *Dönmeler* (converts) associated with the mysterious cabalist messiah Sabbatai Sevi (aka Sabbatai Zevi or Shabetthai Zebi, 1626–1676). The Selanikli phenomenon is an issue that raises questions of identity and 'purity' for Ataturk himself, as a Turk and as a Muslim.

Let's us consider a few instances that illustrate the significance of that story to Emel's narrative. I begin with some 'nonpsychotic' content from the interview with Emel's clinician. At the time of this interview (as well as those with Emel or her parents) I was unaware of the *Dönme* notion and its obvious significance in this story, which is why I failed to address the hints present in the clinician's account[24]:

I   Now, do you know the religious situation in the family? I mean their beliefs, etc.?

C   Well the mother covers her hair . . . and they are . . . hmmm . . . her mother's family has migrated from western Thrace, I don't know her religious orientation. I didn't specifically ask about that but she does have Islamic appearance, her head is covered but I don't know the denomination.

I   So you don't know.

C   No, I haven't specifically asked about that.

I   You said they have migrated?

C   Yes

I   How? Where are they from?

C   Well . . . They have migrated from Greece. Her mother's side.

I   Oh, Her mother's side.

C   Yes. I don't know about the father.

I   I see.

C   The mother's side has migrated from Greece.

I   OK, is this an important factor for the hospital?

C   I don't think it is significant for her condition, but the patient's mother's side of the family is from Sarköy. Near Sarköy . . . do you know Sarköy?

I   No.

C   Well there is a district near Istanbul. Tekirdag.

I   Right.

C   It's a town there, the mother's side of the family is from there, generally there is a high migrant ratio in that region. Either from Bulgaria or Greece. This family has migrated from Greece.

I   Ok. So the mother and father . . .

C   They are not related as far as I know.

I   I see.

C   They are not related. But where is the father's side of the family from?

I   You don't know.

C   I didn't speak to the father. I didn't feel it necessary to ask her mother either.

Even without knowing the significance of these regions, it should be possible to detect an implied relationship between the mother's place of birth and Emel's story. When I simply ask about religion in the family, the doctor tells me about mother's migration from Salonika, and in a manner imbued with vagueness and uncertainty: "Well . . . the mother covers her hair . . . and they are . . . hmmm . . . her mother's family has migrated from western Thrace, I don't know her religious orientation." Their geographic origin, in other words, causes the clinician to not be able to simply call the mother Muslim, despite the fact that for all means and purposes she *is* a Muslim, calls herself one, and acts like one. The average Turkish person would have rapidly made the connection between the clinician's remarks and the *Dönme* status implications. But I did not. Even without that insider knowledge, however, I did perceive from that interview that Emel's mother's family coming from that part of the country was of significance. Having naively sensed tension around the issue, I pointed directly at it by asking whether the mother's family background "is an important factor for the hospital." The clinician gives a promptly double-edged "no . . . but" response. Intrigued, and still naïve to the reason, I experienced a similar tension surrounding the question of the mother's background in the interview with Emel's parents. The unease associated with the mother's family background and an apparent wish to disown and dissociate from that background can be seen in the following sample from the parents' interview:

I   [addressing the mother] What does [your name] mean?

M   Well I don't know, my parents . . .

F   Her parents, the elders named her. She doesn't know what it means. I don't know what it means myself either.

M   My grandparents.

F   Your grandparents.

M   That's what they named me.

I   Where is your family from?

M   Salonika.

I   Salonika, I see. I was going to . . .

M   But he, he is from [turns to the father] . . .

F   I am from here [note that "here" does not signify Istanbul; it actually means Turkey, as opposed to an imagined "there," outside of pure Turkishness, as signified by being a Selanikli].

M   He is from the Black Sea region.

F   I am from the Black Sea region.

I   So you are from the Black Sea. Sinop in the Black sea region. Black Sea is supposed to be a nice place. Do you go there sometimes?

F   Yes I do. My father has land over there.

I   So you still have ties . . .

F   Of course. My uncle's children tend the land there.

I   [to the mother] Do you go as well?

M   No. [assumes that I have asked about visits to her own village]

I   You don't go.

M   We don't have anyone left.

I   In . . .

M   No!

I   Do you go to Sinop?

M   To Sinop, yes I go to Sinop

I   You go to Sinop but you don't go to . . .

F   Their grandparents came here from Salonika.

I   Your grandparents?

M   My parents.

F   The parents.

I   Your father came to Istanbul?

F   He migrated. They were Turks; they came back here from there.

I   Oh really?

F   Migrant.

I   So you have no more family left?

F   No! We have no more ties.

But what does it mean to be from Salonika, to be a Selanikli, and why would Emel's mother be so intent on disowning that heritage to the extent of denying ties to her own Turkish birth place? To be Selanikli, or *Dönme*, has a specific yet vague meaning in Turkey. While literally it means being from Salonika (or a convert, in the case of *Dönme*), in practice none of these needs to be present in a person to be suspected of being Selanikli, or *Dönme*. That is, a person may be born in Turkey (as Emel's mother was), and born directly into a Muslim tradition (as Emel's mother was), yet be considered Selanikli or *Dönme*. Originally, the terms go back to the 17th-century Jewish messiah Sabbatai Zevi, who claimed his messianic mission in the city of Izmir (then Smyrna), and developed a noticeable following. When Sabbatai eventually claimed to have converted to Islam (arguably due to Ottoman pressure) followers of Sabbatai (who came to be known in Turkish as *Dönme* or Selanikli) developed a strategy of adjustment: to be a Muslim in public and to adhere to Jewish traditions in private. In fact Sabbatai himself, who was given a place within the Ottoman government after his conversion, was eventually sent to exile by the Ottoman state because he was caught singing the psalms in a tent with a group of Jews (Kohler and Malter, 2005).

"The fate of Sabbateanism in Republican Turkey," writes Neyzi (2002), "points up to the Janus-faced Turkish national identity" (p. 138). When Ataturk's strong Turkish nationalism replaced the Ottoman discourse, it implanted a number of paradoxical dilemmas within the Turkish conduct of identity. He zealously promoted a secular brand of modernity and nationalism defined in direct opposition to the Ottomans' multiethnic and religious-traditionalist collective identity. In practice, however, Ataturk employed an operational definition of Turkness wherein a true Turk was defined exclusively as a Sunni Muslim who spoke Turkish. In addition to adding a deeply paradoxical dimension to the question of Turkish Identity, this introduced new problems for the so-called Selanikli, who had already employed a strategy of double identity to cope with their predicament. The Selanikli had identified themselves with a pro-European discourse of modernity in tune with Ataturk's official discourse, but Ataturk's pro-modernism fell short of offering an opportunity to assimilate more comfortably within the Turkish society. In fact in the new context a more pernicious trend of stigmatization became their lot. The stigmatization entrapped the Selanikli while broadening the term referring to them. Now any immigrants from European parts of the former empire who chose to migrate to the new country would be Selanikli by default: a Turk, but not a real one, tainted by 'something' not quite clear, something associated primarily with Judaism, but in the folk view, also with Christianity and more broadly, with the West in general. This impurity was formally and legally substantiated by the Turkish Republic in 1942 when a Capital Levy was imposed as a measure of economic maintenance in war time: along with Armenians and Jews, those deemed Selanikli were to pay higher taxes despite the fact that they were officially Muslim (e.g., Aktar, 2000). The second irony in the relationship between Ataturk's Nationalism and the Selanikli had to do with Ataturk himself. Not only was Ataturk born in Salonika (and thus literally a Selanikli) and had blue eyes and light-colored hair, but he is well known to have been trained as a child in a Selanikli school and under a Selanikli teacher (e.g., Neyzi, 2002).

Identity: from dichotomy to wholeness

By now Emel's construction of her mother and her mother's family in opposition to her father and a pure Turkish blood should be clear, specifically as she deals with a sense of self-identity as unhinged as a soccer ball. I examine here a few excerpts in which Emel is drawing on this culturally provided model for locating her mother, and herself in relation to that mother. At one point in the interview she associated her mother and her own identity in the following words:

P   My mother was a good mother to me. She is also my sister. Not completely my mother. She is going to adopt me. Now I am waiting for my identity [*Kimlik*: 'who-ness']. My name is Emel, my last name is ***. I am still celibate [*bekar*: etym. virgin; single, bachelor]. I am not married. I want to enter a beauty pageant but I have trouble distinguishing between dreams [*hayal*: imaginatin, fantasy] and reality. . . .

Recall that after she spoke of the different identities she inherited from the father's versus the mother's side and clapped her hands on the opposite sides of her body to demonstrate the binary opposition of East and West, Emel described her contradictory inner world in terms of a Christian mother and a Muslim father. These terms resonate closely with the culturally provided notion of the *Dönme*:

I   OK. So your mother's side . . .?

P   Foreigner.

I   Foreigner?

P   Uh-uh.

I   How do you mean foreigner? What is that?

P   Someone who hasn't changed their religion.

I   I see. That means remained Christian?

P   Remained Christian.

I   But your father . . .

P   Muslim.

She had also spoken, earlier, of her own uncertainty about whether she could count as a 'pure' Turk. In that instance she had produced that sense of impurity in close association to the question of being a Muslim or not, and eventually to her Salonikan background, which she likens to the foreignness of a tourist:

P   Do you know the church in Balat? The Orthodox Church?

I   Yes?

P   I live near there. In Balat. So I . . . Do you believe in the Bible?

I   Do I what?

P   Do you believe in the Quran?

I   Yes.

P   May I see your hand?

I   My hand? Here . . .

P   It is written Allah Muhammad in your hand.

I   Is that written?

P   Mm-hmm . . .

I   You see that?

P   This is the letter E . . . My . . .

I   OK ?

P   Letter *E* . . . E-mel, there is also an O[25]. . . You get it?

I   I get it.

P   Is there anything you want to ask?

I   Yes there is . . .

P   Just so there are no misunderstandings, my Turkish is also not so good. We are immigrants from Greece. . . During Ataturk's time.

I   Really?

P   Uh-huh . . . from Salonika.

I   How's that?

P   From Salonika, Athens, Bulgaria.

I   I see . . . so your grandparents come from there?

P   Uh-huh. . . During my grandfather's time, when Ataturk started the War of Independence women helped out . . . carrying food on their backs . . . Ataturk moved them to Istanbul. For instance, you know how tourists come here over the summer for 3 months?

Recall also the excerpt quoted earlier in which Emel speaks of identity in terms of blood and purity, declaring her own blood type as A-S and emphasizing the difference between her father's 'pure' Turkishness and the status of her mother. As this excerpt ends she declares the following:

P   She is not my mother. She is my sister.

I   I see. What about your father?

P   My father is my real father . .

I   Ah, OK. So your father has Turkish blood?

P   Turkish blood . . .

Earlier, when discussing how Emel gave herself the second name, Asena, I had pointed out that Asena, in addition to having strong identity-related implications via mythology, was also closely homophonic with her mother's name. It is easier to make more sense of that fact in the context of the excerpts that depict Emel's ambivalent relationship to her mother, specifically when it comes to the question of identity. The ambivalence is reflected in two main features of her discourse: at the collective level by repeatedly contrasting a stable and 'pure' paternal identity with an uncertain, ambiguous, and polluted identity associated with the maternal heritage, and at the personal level through a highly problematic identification-by-contrast with the mother. Consider the following excerpt, for example:

P   My name is Emel.

I   Yes I know. Emel. Do you know what Emel means?

P   It's a want, desire.

I   Desire.

P   Desire.

I   OK. What was your other name?

P   Asena.

I   Asena, what does that mean?

P   It's the opposite of Hazine.

I   Huh?

P   The English of Hazine.

I   That's English?

P   My mother's name is Hazine.

I   Hazine?

P   Hazine.

I   I see.

P   I am changing my identity for Hazine . . . It's the opposite. English is the opposite of Turkish. And the opposite of Turkish is English, in my opinion.

I   I see, OK.

It is out of the scope of this analysis to address the question of whether Emel is struggling to overcome or escape a dichotomized world or whether she is actively involved in a process of dichotomization as a means of locating herself. Neither scenario, however, alters the fact that her discourse of self and identity is saturated with the theme of dichotomization or that this theme fits more or less seamlessly within the larger collective questions of Turkish nationalism and identity. Both these discourses are unmistakably built around and into a fundamentally dichotomized universe:

P   You know the underground passage when you leave here?

I   Yes.

P   You turn left after that . . . It's left for me, it might be right for you. Because my heart is on the left side. What about yours?

I   Mine is also on the left.

P   Then we are in the same country!

Love: wholeness and recovery

Love, the loss of which had pushed Emel into sorrow and madness, comes back later, this time associated with union and recovery. Far from being discrepant, however, this association is yet another instance of the foundation of Emel's meaning system resonating with that of her cultural context, where health and a recovery from her predicament of madness and bifurcation are associated with love and reunion. Love in this configuration represents union and wholeness, and in it, opposites come together within the same order of meaning. This is a notion she had hinted at in her earliest utterances, when she spoke of the brother in whom converge the father and the mother, "my brother was both my mother and my father," the same 'mother and father' who were in turn identified with West and East, respectively, and the series of other oppositions from left and right to teams competing on the opposite sides of a soccer game.

Emel's discourse portrays a case of psychosis embedded in local history and politics and drawing on culture-specific constellations of signifiers, metaphoric references, and logical associations. Like many other victims of psychotic illnesses, Emel appears to be engaged in a distressing quest for rest, for an anchor, and for the lost magic that used to keep parts and pieces of her existence together in a functional 'wholeness.' Perhaps the primary thing that distinguishes her quest from that of another person living in another cultural context is the locally endorsed system of meaning and power within which and in reaction to which she develops her desires and experiences as a social subject, including both her experience of illness and the imagined recovery she strives for. In a poignant moment she spoke to me of her search for rest, peace, and wholeness in these words:

P   Can I ask you a question?

I   You can.

P   If you fall in a derelict [*ıs-sız*: foundation-less, lacking structure, forlorn, left alone, uninhabited] and silent [*ses-siz*: soundless] island, you fall in the sea and there is nobody beside you, whose presence [*olmak*: being, existence] would you want beside you?

I   Who would you want?

P   Me? My fiancé, my mother, my father, and myself as a fourth person.

I   Who is the fourth? Come a little closer [to the desk/tape recorder. Patient is pacing in the room], tell me again who you would choose?

P   My mother, *mommy*, my father, and how do you say brother in English? [remember, *italics* indicate words in original language]

I   In English?

P   *Boyfriend*

I   *Boyfriend?!*

P   *Mommy*, father, *boyfriend*, and *I am.*

I   And who?

P   *I.*

I   "*I*"?

P   Me!

I   Ah, I see. . . . You would want to take yourself to the island.

P   Uh-huh . . .that's who I want.

If you fell into disorder and voiceless loneliness, and you wished for order to be restored, for the loneliness to go away, what would you wish for? Emel wished for all the bits and pieces to come together; for her brother, the lost love, to come back; for mommy and daddy to coexist on the same island once again; and for herself, her self, for the long lost sense of "I am", or at least just the "I" of it, to come back and join in, she longs to be an I anchored in the Other.

It is not a meaningless coincidence that she demonstrates her brother–lover juxtaposition in this moment. Love is quite related to wholeness and a recovery from the world of oppositions, according to the Sufi philosophy. It is through love that unity with the beloved becomes possible, and it is through that unity that the sick self gains health. The 'sick self' is often described in terms of a person with a vision deficiency who therefore sees two where there is only one object, and a recovery from that deficiency would enable them to perceive the true unity of the universe. "O man of double vision!" says Rumi, "listen attentively: seek a cure for your defective sight . . .," and he explains that "once the illusion of seeing double is cured", then one will be capable to see the unity of "One" (*Mathnavi*, Book II, story 1, my translation; see also Schimmel, 1992, p. 146). And it is in this tradition that I understand Emel's island. What she is explaining is that it is only in the presence of the boyfriend/brother, in the union of love, that mother and father will come together; the brother that, she had suggested earlier, is both father and mother to her, the union the loss of which has driven her to madness to begin with. The magic of 'I am,' in other words, can hold once again in the island of union.

Conclusion

The relationship between Emel's utterances and the cultural and political environment in which Emel lives is undeniable. It is tempting in fact to assume there exists a method to her madness, an invisible or implicit network that maps her utterances and formulates her metaphors. It is important, however, to realize that from my theoretic stance that would be an erroneous deduction. While it is obvious that fragments and pieces of what can be approached as a 'story,' or loosely formulated thematic conglomerates do surface in Emel's discourse, I remain content with just that, resisting, in other words, the all too usual urge to 'understand' her 'world.' Even if as a nonpsychotic interpreter, securely anchored within a functional meaning system and well versed in the local cultural logic and associative constellations, I am able join the broken pieces of Emel's narrative together to demonstrate how they 'belong' in a larger network, to assume that Emel is also enjoying the privileges of that systemic navigation requires an unwarranted step.

For Emel the so-called network has given its place to a frightening labyrinth whose disjointed alleys she experiences as uncannily familiar, yet the overall structure of which decidedly eludes her. On my mission to 'interpret' her utterances and to 'unearth' a presumed interior logic, and after puzzling again and again over the bits and pieces of an imaginary lost structure for which Emel (and the many other psychotic patients that I interviewed) seemed to be desperately longing, it gradually became clear that such a structure does not exist. Instead of a final structure, however, the best the patients are able to do is to roam endlessly among nightmare-like compounds of half-familiar alleys and streets that resemble isolated pieces and bits of a map torn into pieces, a map that, as far as those patients are concerned, may or may not have ever represented a real city. Instead of searching for lost cities then, I was soon convinced that I should remain content with attributing to the patients only what I could empirically observe, that is, a process of mobilizing partial networks of ideas, of signs, and of belief structures, without synthesizing them into a more comprehensive system of anchored subjectivity.

Solace for that disillusionment came to me only later as I realized that the number of composite structures of signs and associations that emerged again and again in various interviews was not as chaotic and boundless as one could imagine. A number of significant patterns repeat themselves, not only around a single case but also across various cases and stories, as the following case studies demonstrate. More significantly, those same partial structures that give psychotic patients transient and fleeting islands of 'meaning' and relief, seemed also to contribute to the narratives of truth and identity in nonpsychotic individuals, a fact reflected in the close ties between Emel's private associations and those of Turkish cultural and political realities.

Notes

1 Emel is a pseudonym.
2 *Endüstri Meslek Lisesi.*

3　With the exception of a onetime serious incident around the age of 2 or 3. See the later discussion for details.

4　It is easy to understand her preference for this term [*nişanlı*: lit. 'marked,' fiancé], specifically because there is a large number of Turkish folktales and songs built around the agony of two lovers 'marked' for each other and eventually forced into separation

5　It is virtually impossible to find a document discussing Turkey and its culture without reference to Rumi and his points of view. Rumi's poem, "Come!" has become the hallmark of most official documents published by the Turkish government, second perhaps only to Ataturk's remark on peace ("peace at home, peace in the world"). Here is a translation of Rumi's "Come": Come!/Come whoever you are./An unbeliever, a worshipper, a lover of leaving/If you have fallen a thousand times/Come!/Come whoever you are, for this is not the door of despair/Come,/Just as you are.

6　Rhymes with *hay*: a reed or the musical flute made of that plant.

7　As in many other areas of the world, the relationship between fate and identity is a strong one in the Turkish/Middle Eastern Muslim worldview. A proverb says that "if the kilim of one's fate is woven in black, it cannot be whitened with water from Paradise." Intriguingly, one's fate is not decided simply by the supernatural powers, but there seems to be a psychological element involved, as this folk lyric puts it: "my fate was set wrong since the beginning, because my mother fed me on milk of sorrow [i.e., my mother was sad as she fed me]." Paradoxically, fate does not imply a sense of imprisonment to the Muslim mind, in fact it is a wonderful thing if you are lost, uncertain, or simply unable to discern your own good. Fate is when Allah becomes involved in such popular phrases as '*in-sha-Allah* [if God wishes so]' or '*ma-sha-Allah* [what God may wish].' It means that in a final analysis even your bewilderment has an actual path, a map that exists regardless of the experience of being lost. Signifying your fate, the signs of the zodiac not only decide what you are and who you are; they may also, indeed, be able to tell 'where' you are. One may see in the preceding excerpt from Emel, however, that she finds herself deprived even of a basic point of reference such as her date of birth or her zodiac sign.

8　The inclusion of this information does not indicate my confirmation of the blood refusal allegations. In the spirit of fairness, I am well aware that these allegations might be politically motivated propaganda rather than historical facts, despite the apparent credibility of the sources I have provided. Factuality or lack thereof, however, would not affect my argument here, because the very existence and survival of these allegations (they appear in many documents, official and otherwise) is possible only due to the context I am suggesting here, that is, the special status of the concept of 'pure Turkish blood' in Turkish nationalist discourse.

9　My gratitude goes to my dear friend and colleague, Dr. Kemal Sayar, and his family for their supportive presence and their caring help during that difficult time.

10　This is an important and central speech by Ataturk, in which he calls the Turkish youth to respect the 'pure Turkish blood' in their veins and to make sure they transform Turkey into a civilized and modern nation.

11　The Battle of Sakarya is the famous and much celebrated battle fought by Ataturk against the Greeks. The defeat of the Ottoman Empire against the Allies in World War I had led to a treaty known as the Sèvres treaty, which virtually disintegrated the Ottoman land altogether. After winning the battle at the Sakarya River, however, Ataturk's Nationalist Army gained the strength to refuse the Sèvres treaty and to demand new arrangements, which eventually led to the formation of a new country called Turkey. The Battle of Sakarya is celebrated as the birth event of modern Turkey.

12 Here she is referring to the 15th-century conquest of Istanbul by Muslim Turks.
13 See original quotation, for example, on the website of the Turkish Ministry of National Education: http://www.meb.gov.tr/belirligunler/10kasim/yazilar/vecizeler.htm.
14 Ataturk was born in 1881 and died in 1938.
15 The expression *hoca* is sometimes used, however, by patients to address their doctors, as a term of respect and a confirmation of the doctor's scientific merits and social status.
16 *Ata-türk* literally means Father-Turk.
17 *Panzehir*: anti-poison. This is a paradoxical statement, because on a few other occasions, including the very next sentence, she speaks of cigarettes as having poisonous effect on her health. It is impossible to draw a final conclusion, but it is quite plausible to assume she understands *panzehir* to mean 'poison' or 'poisonous' because it contains the term poison (*zehir*) in it. The original etymology of *anti-poison* is from old Persian (*pad-zahr*) and is most certainly unknown to her.
18 'Glorious Urfa,' so termed after the role played by this city during Ataturk's War of Independence.
19 See, for example, the Quran, Surah 21, Ayahs 51ff.
20 Also known as Nimrud and Nimrod.
21 Note also that Emel moves on to the fish directly after mentioning the hunters who chase that whale.
22 See Nimrut 'the Hunter' discussed earlier. Nimrut or Nimrod also appears as a hunter in the Old Testament, see, for example, Genesis, 10: "like Nimrod, a mighty hunter before the Lord . . ." Additionally, the Ponds of Abraham are also believed by historians to go back to a Sumerian goddess of love and fertility; see, for example, Dalrymple (1997, p. 75).
23 *Extimity*, or *Extimité* in its original French form, is a term coined by Jacques Lacan, converging the notions of exteriority and intimacy to indicate the presence of "the other" within the very structural core of the self. See, for instance, Rahimi (2007) for further discussion of the term and its application.
24 I am grateful to my friend and assistant Emre Unlucayakli for introducing me to the Selanikli history, among other interesting ideas.
25 O: in addition to being a letter of the alphabet, O is also the third-person singular pronoun in Turkish, representing both genders, as well as objects/animals (i.e., equal to English pronouns *he*, *she*, and *it*).

4 Power, faith, and the politics of identity
The story of Senem

In this chapter I present the story of Senem, a 37-year-old housewife and mother of five children. Senem was staying in Turkey's largest psychiatric hospital known as Bakırköy Hastanesı, where she had been brought by force with the help of the police after she had shown violent behavior, including attacking her husband, locking him out of their home, and starting a fire on their balcony. Violence, however, was not present during the interviews that I had with Senem. When I met Senem she had been in the hospital for about 1 month, during which time, like most other patients she had received a succession of eight or nine electroconvulsive therapy (ECT) treatments, starting on the second or third day after her arrival. The interview with Senem produced fascinating data, most of which can be organized under a number of recurrent themes, themes that originally appeared diverse and unrelated but that analysis brings to light a certain 'relevance,' a relevance that can be seen most clearly once the case material is viewed against current and past cultural and political patterns in Turkey.

To start with basics, the issue of power, which I refer to by the metaphor of 'voice' here, is an organizing force in Senem's discourse. The centrality of the question of power in this story is a telling sign of the struggle involved for 'subjective survival' within a meaning system. Such a struggle can be understood as 'private' insofar as it reflects various drives desiring subjects might experience and attempt to articulate or negotiate, but simultaneously it needs to be understood as collectively constructed, representing the dynamics specific to a certain symbolic order as a system of power/meaning. It is in a struggle for subjective survival against the very system of meaning in/of which the subject is made that he or she experiences a sense of being as an intentional subject. Problems arise in a case such as Senem's, however, when due to specific circumstances of the subject's trajectory or his or her environment, that subjective struggle grows to unusual proportions.

When the trauma or violence experienced by a subject passes a certain threshold, the extent of destabilization may become so overwhelming as to force the subject to assume extraordinary modes of subjectivity in order to survive the trauma; modes of subjectivity so unique as to be deemed 'outside' of the commonly accepted realms of 'sense,' that is, psychotic. Conceptually, however, the fact remains that even in producing such novel configurations, the subject has to rely on raw material available in their semiotic landscape. Here in this chapter, for example, I examine the story of a woman whose sense of selfhood has been severely traumatized by violent events in her life, and whose environment, the social, political, and religious context in which she has lived, has been configured in such a way that a culturally legitimate 'power' has been inaccessible to her as a subject in her specific 'position.' Note that when I speak of power here I am speaking of discursive power, power that comes in the form of legitimacy of a discourse in a symbolic order. A 'victim' position, for example, is often an instance of such a culturally legitimized position of power. So I am suggesting here that Senem had been deprived of *any* culturally endorsed claim to power or a *voice* in which to live her resistance, including that of a victim.

The themes of which I have spoken are discussed throughout the following case analysis, but before starting, I would like to briefly explain the organization of the analytic work in this chapter. Senem's discourse is built strongly around the issues of a birth event that remains 'enigmatic.' Following her explicit demand, we started the interview (during which her mother was also present) discussing that birth and progressed gradually into other significant themes. My analyses here follow that progression. In a second interview with Senem, however, when she was by herself, she gave me further information about that birth that she had not revealed in the presence of her family. The new information was powerful enough to add a new and significant dimension to my understanding of her story. In presenting this case I have decided to follow the interview content as it unfolded in time, remaining as genuine as possible to my own experience, then turn around and look back and 'update' my analyses when the new information comes in. I hope the reader finds this more effective in terms of both the overall interpretation of the case material and the development of ideas.

As in the story of Ahmet (see Chapter 5), I find the hospital and what it stands for come to the foreground and gain significance in Senem's story, as the historical and social aspects of the place itself weave into the patient's experience of her illness. I therefore start with a brief overview of Bakırköy Hastanesı.

Bakırköy Ruh ve sinir Hastanesı

I met Senem in a female-only 'block' of the large psychiatric hospital, Bakırköy. Bakırköy is the best-known psychiatric hospital in Turkey, and people from far and near often travel to Istanbul to bring their loved ones for treatment in this hospital. It is a "Teaching and Research Hospital for Health of the Spirit [*Ruh*] and Illnesses of the Nerves [*sinir*]," says the sign over the gate, adding that it has been in service for more than 80 years. As if to give an eerie hint at Foucault's historiography of mental care, the Bakırköy establishment was already an icon of isolation and medical policing as an asylum where those afflicted by leprosy were kept away from the public, before it was dedicated to madness. The current Istanbul Leprosy Hospital at Bakırköy is a descendent of that original establishment, even though now most of the leprosy patients in Turkey tend to be in eastern and southeastern Anatolia (Saylan et al., 2000).

The history of the Bakırköy psychiatric hospital dates back to 1927, at the peak of Ataturk's reform days, when a group of patients suffering from severe mental illnesses who had been kept in another center (Üsküdar Toptaşı Bimarhanesi) were dispatched to Bakırköy Mental Health center. Bakırköy thus started, constructed to represent a modern, medical, and liberated perspective on mental illnesses (see, e.g., Bayülkem, 2002, p. 47f). Over the 80 years of its new life, Bakırköy has come to stand for the notion of mental illness across Turkey. I have seen movies in which a character's mental ruin after a love disaster or a fallout with his or her family is symbolized and summarized in a simple shot of Rodin's *Thinking Man*. This is not just any *Thinking Man*, of course, but a shot of the Bakırköy *Thinking Man*: a large, solidly built white man of concrete, staring deeply into a small pond of water surrounded by serious-looking male heads (busts) planted on human-high pillars, staring at each other in fraternity and deep thought. This petrified gathering of thinking men struck me at once as the center of gravity in the Bakırköy hospital, but, as if to highlight its importance, the hospital's logo, a thinking man cutout, is devotedly stamped on signs, boards, and objects throughout the vast sanatorium. The book I referred to earlier, Bayülkem's volume on the history of psychiatry in Turkey, has the white thinking man against a red background as its cover design.

Senem has come here, she says, to escape the patriarchal dictatorship of her husband and to take asylum from the repressive lifestyle of a young mother in her position. "When you're sane, you have to worry for everybody," she says, "so I went crazy so the world would worry for me." I spoke to Senem at the Bakırköy hospital, the first time along with her mother and her 16-year-old daughter, and then two days later by herself. A few days after the second interview I got to see Senem once more, this time along with her doctor who had just given me an interview and was now there to give Senem and her mother her release papers: Senem was going home after having spent about 1 month in the hospital.

This has been Senem's first hospitalization, in fact her first psychiatric contact ever, despite my impression from her own and her family's accounts that at least some of her far-fetched reasoning and belief fragments had been present for years (this was also confirmed later by her doctor: "Our patient has approximately 7–8 years of history and she has never had any psychiatric treatment until now"). Despite all her 'strange' ideas and behavior, the family did not consider her 'problematic' and in need of help or treatment, until she became violent and actively challenged her husband's authority, locked him out, burned objects on their balcony, and threatened that if he forced his way into the house she would attack him with a cleaver.

On the last day, as she was about to leave the hospital she told me that she was indeed feeling better. "I can look at my husband now . . . We are like husband and wife." Something, in other words, is now 'restored' due to the whole process, starting with her psychotic beliefs, culminating in burning a fire on their balcony, and concluding with her stay in Bakırköy. It may seem obvious to some that what is restored is Senem's sanity due to ECT or the antipsychotics. But I am not so certain that is true. For one thing, on the last day of her stay at the hospital after all the treatment, she still believed in the same 'delusional' discourse that she had articulated in recent years. I tend to believe what Senem meant to express was that now she had a voice, even if only as a madwoman. Bakırköy, in other words, worked as a catalyst in her quest for power, giving her a legitimate, if marginalized, social status as a madwoman. It is, you may agree, better to be mad and have some power than to be mute and have no power at all.

Senem

Senem is 37 years old, and she has been married now for 19 years. She was born in a small village in the north near the Black Sea and moved to Istanbul "when I was 28 days old, anyway, before 40 days." She has one older sister, and no brothers. Her (actual) name, which means 'joy' or 'pleasure,' was given to her 'for' her mother's brother – it was the name of a woman that he was madly in love with but failed to marry:

Interviewer (I)	Who picked her name?
Mother (M)	Her name . . . my brother, my brother in the village had this love.
I	Uh-huh.
M	He could not get her.
I	OK.
M	He could not marry her, my late father did not let him. . .
Patient (P)	[interrupts the mother] He was very sad about it, always talks about it . . .
M	He did not let him marry her [brief pause] and well, because of that, my brother's heart ached a lot, it burnt him . . .
I	I see.
M	I mean because he couldn't get to his love . . .
P	Would you like some [cigarettes]?
I	I don't smoke, thanks.
M	As he could not be with his beloved, my brother said to me, "Sister, if you had a baby, could you name her Senem." And I said OK.

I   I see.

M   It's for that. I named her Senem for that reason.

Of Senem's immediate family of origin, her mother is alive, and so is her older sister, but she has lost her father. Senem's husband is alive and in fact plays a central role in her illness story, but I did not get a chance to see or speak to him because he did not have a habit of making hospital visits. Senem has given birth to six children, but one of them died shortly after birth. Or so they say. As far as Senem is concerned, that child never died; he was taken to be 'twinned' and used in a project of proliferating the Turkish nation. Here is how she explains that:

P   I mean, perhaps they take the extra children of a family [*bir aileye fazla gelen cocuklarını*] . . . place them in dormitories [*yurt*] . . . or you raise them in the dormitories yourselves . . . all so that Turkhood [*Türklük*], its lineage won't dry up. Don't do, like, well, what is it, for instance? For instance, I didn't give birth to a child . . . [5-sec. pause. Mother talks in the background, but incomprehensible]. And let us say, at that moment, I have the wherewithal to raise a kid, but not two . . . they can certainly take the second child . . . as an adopted child. I mean, this was done, these things were done. [raises her voice slightly] I proved . . . these but why . . . are they afraid ? A fear, something is in everybody . . . I am just asking for a blood test, that's all really.

Of the five living children, the second one is a 16-year-old female who also participated in the first interview, and the rest are boys ranging in age from 18 to 2, none of whom I met.

Senem has a primary school education. From her way of telling the story I get the impression that Senem was forced to stop after primary school against her will and was sent to work. She then insists at one point that she would have liked to continue with her school. She says the following:

P   I have primary education. After that, I attended knitting and modeling-stylist schools. I have a diploma too.

I   OK.

P   I mean . . . I didn't attend secondary school, but at home . . . I've read all the secondary school books so I could help my children. I am continuously developing my knowledge.

I   Hmm.

P   I mean, although I did not get to attend the, the school, I did not want to sit, sit at home do, do . . . doing nothing.

Her doctor, however, implies there is a deficiency behind Senem's quitting school. She tells me of Senem's delusions, specifically of "the delusion that her husband cheats on her. She thought her husband was with other women, she had disloyalty ideations. This is what we found. She was bad-tempered and nervous." The doctor then moves to connect these to Senem's education:

Clinician (C)   So her thoughts are like that. I mean, she says, for example, that she couldn't study after elementary school. She says she couldn't continue because she was afraid. But her family says that she wasn't a successful student in reality, her teacher was never kidnapped or killed, she didn't want to study herself. . .

And later she adds further:

C   . . . [S]he graduated from elementary school, she worked in a clothes manufacturing workshop for 7 years, she was courteous and hardworking in her workplace, in 1987, when she was 19, she got married, but this wasn't an arranged marriage, she got married with love, willingly. She gave birth to six children, five of them have lived, four of them are boys, one is a girl. One of her children died 2 days after the birth.

I would like to call your attention to the fact that the image implicitly sketched by the clinician here has something of a 'positive' quality to it. Senem graduates from elementary school; she is not very interested or intellectually capable, so she decides to stop school and starts working as a courteous and hardworking girl until she falls in love and gets married to the love of her life, has children and . . . one could almost expect to hear the 'happily ever after' phrase, if this weren't the story of a patient with psychotic illness at a mental hospital. I am pointing out this quality, because as it turns out, at least from Senem's own point of view, her life events have not been pleasant. The contrast, I suggest, is not accidental or meaningless but a reflection of the central theme of Senem's illness: the quest for power and for a voice with which to speak as a subaltern subject. Senem's illness has already been named, 'paranoid schizophrenia,' though she has been seen for 1 month only, and this is her first psychiatric encounter. Ironically, when I asked the clinician, "In your opinion, what is the main issue for this patient?" she responded by telling me first about schizophrenia and what it means, and eventually she suggested that in fact life events might have triggered Senem's psychotic illness. She said the following:

C   Now, when we say the main issue, the cause of schizophrenia hasn't been found yet, it is understood that schizophrenia is caused by an organic deficiency in the brain. But there isn't any evidence that completely proves that. But, there can be a genetic disposition. In Ms. Senem's family there isn't a history of psychiatric disorders, because in schizophrenia genetic disposition is very important, but there isn't any. It can be caused by the events she had lived through, and if the reason can be established in the future, maybe in reality it may be caused by different illnesses or by a malfunctioning or a pathology form birth.

There is an obvious, if reluctant, hint in the clinician's narrative here that life events might have in one way or another influenced Senem's illness, partly because no obvious evidence has been found for biological and genetic factors in her case. This idea of psychotic illness triggered by life events stands, of course, in contrast to the clinician's own presentation of the case, which sought to portray an average, trauma-free life story. But an average, trauma-free life story was not the picture that emerged out of my interviews with Senem and her family either.

Interviews

When I first met Senem, she struck me as a beautiful, curious, animated, and strong woman. I had not had a chance to speak in detail to her doctor before the meeting, partly because she was in a female ward. I had been stationed by the hospital in a male ward, and for visiting with female patients, I needed to go to their wards and then come back to my base in the assigned 'block.' So I knew very little of her history and circumstances before the actual interview, which is to say that I was quite naïve to what her story might be about, and for that same reason, my interview was not guided by any specific preconceptions. In fact I did not get a chance to speak to her doctor until after my second interview with Senem. But in reality that did not pose any difficulties, given the impressive eloquence of Senem, on one hand, and the eager participation of her mother (and her daughter), on the other. Senem was interested in learning about me, who I was and why I was interested in doing an interview with her. She asked me a number of questions as soon as I was introduced by the nurse, and finally she settled by turning to her mother and telling her, "He is a researcher, as far as I can tell, a psychologist-researcher." I was quite comfortable with that understanding, this was certainly more agreeable an introduction than some other occasions where I was introduced to a patient by his or her doctor: "This is Dr. Rahimi; he is working with us. Now you make sure you tell him everything, OK?" In a number of occasions I had had to make it clear for the patients, over and above the usual informed consent process, that I was *not* working with 'them' and that he or she did not have to tell me everything either. But here in this interview Senem had already located me well enough, and I could now go on with my business.

'The birth'

Before I had a chance to ask any questions, Senem asked whether we were going to start by talking about 'birth' [*doğum*]. From her tone of asking that question I had the impression that 'birth' might bear a specific significance in her story, so I decided to start on that note.

I   OK, so you said we are going to start by talking about the birth. Is that right?

P   Yes. Today we discussed the situation with the doctor and with Ms. Seda [perhaps a nurse] as well. Well, if there is any delay or something in one's birth, I mean if the birth delays in a mother's womb, or there is the placenta [*eş*: placenta, partner, one of a pair, double] thing, you know . . .

The issue of birth turned out to be indeed a central theme in Senem's discourse in a number of ways, and it was emphasized in her doctor's interview. According to the doctor, when Senem's firstborn (a boy) died shortly after birth, the hospital and the parents did not show her the dead body, nor did they show her the place where the child was buried. And that failure, the doctor believes, then became a nucleus for her paranoid delusions that the child is actually alive but has been taken away from her for mysterious reasons.

C   Ms. Senem sees her child alive after she gives birth. They told her that the baby has to stay in the incubator, but after going home, after two days, her mother-in-law said, "There is no child, forget your child, your child is dead." They didn't show her the corpse of her child, they didn't even show her, her baby's grave. Therefore, this may be the source of her delusions that her children were kidnapped or had twins.

Duplicity: twins

I have selected to use the term *duplicity* to address a fundamental theme in Senem's story. The dual signification of the term is in fact quite a welcome feature, given the true sense of duplicity that so permeates the sad story of Senem, be it in terms of an environment that in the name of love and honor is capable of submitting its own members to the cruelest of fates, or in terms of a world of objects and subjects that almost always have two fundamentally different, if not opposite, senses at once. I should also point out in passing that I have consciously bypassed a traditional psychoanalytic interpretation of the theme of the double here. The 'bypassing' is not so much in rejection of the psychoanalytic reading as it is in search of a broader treatment of the theme. It is possible and indeed fruitful to approach the question from a fundamentally cultural and collective point of view.

Even if the death of the child functioned as a nucleus for her illness, Senem's delusions have extended well beyond the dead child by now. There is a fundamental depersonalization applied to people around her, and doubling is a central feature of this depersonalization: almost everybody is duplicated in one way or another, and the people around her are almost always copies of some absent, lost, or stolen originals. The original versions are basically inaccessible, be that her so-called stillborn child who was taken away and twinned to save the Turkish blood; her living children whose twins she sees as characters on TV or as patients at the hospital; her husband whose double comes home to sleep with her; her own twin who appears alternatively as a teacher, a political figure, a soldier of freedom, and a martyr; or her real parents from whom her parents took her away when she was just born. The only character who seems to be the 'original' in all this is Senem herself, whose wandering twin, a male figure by the name of Celal Bey (Mr. Celal; pronounced *Jelal*), appears in various scenes and contexts.

In fact, the "placenta thing" that Senem speaks of at the very opening of the interview is already reflecting that theme in a powerful way. Unlike the English *placenta*, which finds its etymology in the notion of 'flatness' and can be understood as a more or less descriptive term, the Turkish *eş* (pronounced *esh*) has more intriguing semiotic resonances. *Eş* means 'one of a pair,' as is commonly used to refer to one of a pair of shoes, for example, or to refer to one's wife or husband. *Eş* is also used to mean equal, symmetric, twin, and in a number of other cases in which the sense of equalness and pairedness is intended. In her own interview Senem used the word *eş* not only to refer to her placenta but also in different contexts to refer to her husband (*eşim*: my spouse) or even to attribute to herself a sense of uniqueness (*eşsiz*: peerless). Senem continued her placenta story in these words:

P   If the placenta thing stays inside for a certain long period of time, I mean it affects the newborn child negatively. If the parents have not received any psychological therapy, if it is brought up with tense nerves, this is definitely reflected [*yansıyor*] on the child; 90 percent of the time it will be reflected.

So the *eş*, she tells me, is quite an important thing; it is not just a flat piece of organic cake (placenta); it is a very specific interaction with the baby after the baby is already born. I return shortly to this connection once I have introduced more instances of the way the *eş* functions within Senem's discourse. Note here the mysterious relationship between the child and its *eş*, its double, as well as the explicit indication that this is a psychological relationship. Let me point out here, that the term *eş* also becomes central to the story of Senem's psychosis in another, ironic way, via its 'husband' sense.

She made the relationship between the child and its *eş* explicit when she spoke of a second birth at noon of the day following her own birth, that is, 12 hours later than her birth – which had itself been at midnight. This second birth took place, she said, because the placenta, the *eş*, remained in her mother and was born later in the form of a certain 'Celal Bey,' who is therefore her brother. She said the following:

P   Yes, I went to [my kid's] school. Eh, yes, Mr. Celal showed great attention to us. Like a brother . . . I mean, I am scared, I see him as a brother and he sees me as an elder sister. I am scared, he is paying attention to my children, I am scared that they might spread false words about us.

I told my kids, "Look now, this chap may be your uncle because when my mother gave birth to me, it was apparently 12 at night and after 12 hours, she apparently gave birth one more time because of the *eş*, the *eş* came later, you know . . .

I should point out, of course, that the mother flatly denied any truth to this *eş* story. According to her, Senem's birth had been a fully normal birth with no unusual events. When Senem gave this last description, for example, her mother interjected, with a tone simultaneously of great caring, patience, and concern: "Now where did *this* idea come from?!" she said, and when Senem insisted, "It came from you," the mother insisted, "No, absolutely not. You were born in the morning. In the morning! You were born in the morning, my loved one!" Of interest to my point here is that the 'placenta thing' is part of an exclusively private reality for Senem.

Duplicity: the number 12

There is another interesting aspect to Senem's description of her birth and the placenta event that deserves closer attention. Along with the placenta, number 12 plays a repetitive role in Senem's account. The number 12 in fact appears in various occasions and for varying reasons throughout the interviews. It took Senem's parents, she prefers to think, 12 years of not being able to conceive, until her mother finally became pregnant with her:

P   Because for about 12 years they are said to have a great longing for having children. They were not able to have kids.

M   13 years.

P   Was it 13 years?

M   Yes.

On the other hand, her own child, the one who died, was also born at 12 o'clock, she tells me: "[I]t was a *Kandil* day, the birth day of our Prophet. We went to the hospital and the child was born exactly at 12 noon . . ." When during the crisis that led to her hospitalization Senem left home without telling anybody where she was, she wandered around until exactly midnight, at which time she showed up at her mother's place:

M   . . .We were of course all worried, her husband too, if someone leaves home and disappears until 12, someone from your family for example, what would you do?

Similarly, the day Senem locked herself in she refused to let anybody into the apartment, except for her mother, whom she eventually let in, but that happened only at noon the next day. The following are her mother's words:

M   [Her husband said i]f she is sick, I will go and get the doctor that she
needs, you can't do it, he said, I'll do whatever I can. The man cried and
cried . . . but still she did not let him in, we sat for a while, we sent him
home, it was 4 in the morning, she had not let me in yet either . . . she
didn't let me in until noon that day, until 12 noon of the following day.
Anyway, she opened the door at noon and let me in, and of course, what
can I say to my own child? She is doing this because she is sick . . .

Later on, when Senem tells the story of a 'flag' incident in which she saves
the school from a 'flag trouble,' once again we see number 12:

P   . . . I dried them [Turkish flags] by ironing them out, and then I took them
there [to school] and we put the big one outside, then, I had 12 flags, and
we put them in the classrooms, we passed that day like that . . .

Again, while telling me about her 'search' for meaning of certain events
(this is a search, incidentally, that her family believes has led to her madness),
she talks of a series of 12 books that she completed:

P   I studied *hadis* [Arab. *hadith*: field of studying traditions of the prophet
through vignettes and quotations attributed to him] books, Islamic Law
books, I read 12 volumes . . .

We are too early into the content here to be able to make much sense of
this repetition, but I would like to point out a simple sense in which the *eş*
and this number 12 might be seen as related. They are similar, because they
both are in-between entities; they are both signifiers that serve to simultaneously separate and enjoin two realms. As the placenta functions to both
attach and separate the fetus from the mother's womb, so does 12 o'clock
serve to enjoin and divide the 24-hour whole into distinct halves, and the
12th month in local calendar serves to signal the end of the old year and
the beginning of the new. "Twelve," says the *Penguin Dictionary of Symbols*, "is the number by which space and time are divided" (Chevalier &
Gheerbrant, 1994, p. 1043). Twelve is not only a universally held means
of dividing the heavens into zodiac signs and the year into months, it has
a specifically rich history of significance in all Middle Eastern religions,
from the Sumerian and Assyrian ones to Judaism, Christianity, and Islam.
The Quran, for example, mentions the number 12 on a few occasions,
and almost every time the number is used to indicate a term of division.
In Ayah 60 of Surah 2 (The Cow), for example, Allah remembers "when
Moses asked for water for his people, We said: smite with your staff the
rock. And there gushed out twelve springs, so that each tribe knew their
drinking-place." This division into 12 tribes is repeated in a few separate
occasions in the Quran (e.g., Surah 5, Ayah 12, or Surah 7, Ayah 160). In

another instance, Allah speaks of how he has divided time by twelve, and in fact that specific division is used not only to refer to the division in time, but also to produce a marker of 'identity,' as a means of distinction from the pagan 'other' that creates cohesion within the pious 'own,' and thus to distinguish between right and wrong. He says,

> [t]he number of months in the sight of Allah is twelve; so ordained by Him the day He created the heavens and the earth, [and] of the twelve four are sacred, and that is the right calculation. So do not make mistakes about that, and fight the Pagans all together as they fight you all together.
>
> (Surah 9, Ayah 36)

Similar to the 12 Jewish chiefs or the 12 Christian apostles, Shiite Muslims also have 12 imams.[1] Of their 12 imams the 12th is a significantly special one, who could be understood as the Muslim messiah (see the later discussion for more on the recurrent significance of the Muslim messiah theme). The 12th imam disappeared at an early age but has not died; he is present and alive, though not in our usual reality; he exists in an in-between state between this and the next world, and on Allah's command he will reappear to save the world. Intriguingly enough, this 12th imam is typically referred to using one of his two common epithets: 'the Absent imam' (*imam-e ghaeb*), or 'the Present imam' (*imam-e haazer*). These specific associations (the Muslim messiah and the liminal status of being Muslim yet Christ(ian), dead yet alive, absent yet present, etc.) should be kept in mind, as they will become relevant as Senem's ideas of her 'absent' son continue to emerge. The associations of number 12 are too lengthy to be detailed further here. Suffice it to note that what remains unchanged across cultures and traditions is the two senses of division and joining of this number, such that by its commonly circular attributes, the number 12 simultaneously represents a closure and an opening, an end and a beginning, a leave and a return, a death and a (re)birth. To bring this all to the simpler and more present fashion introduced by Senem herself, these children and their twins are all born at 12 o'clock, and in intervals of 12 hours from each other: they are each born at the very 'turning point' of the clock, and they complement each other in the grand 24-hour cycle, by being born exactly 12 hours of each other.

Duplicity: *eş*

As mentioned earlier, Senem uses the term *eş* in three separate senses in her interview: to mean 'partner,' when she speaks of her husband, for example; to mean 'placenta,' when she speaks of the birth stories; and to mean 'double' or 'same,' for example, when she wishes her husband would consider her unique and peerless. Whereas Senem's mother habitually referred to Senem's husband by using the term *beyi* [her *bey*], Senem herself used the term *eşim* [my *eş*] to speak of him. Even though none of these usages constitutes a departure from conventional norms, the nuances deserve closer attention, especially because the two women use these terms systematically. The term *bey*, which Senem's mother prefers, has inherent in it the sense of superiority. The *Turkish–English Dictionary* (Yildiz, 2014) gives these meanings for *bey*: "gentleman; sir; mister; ruler; master." It is not uncommon to use this term as the mother does, specifically among less educated or more traditional people. Senem, however, selects to refer to her husband as *eş*, whose closest English translation in this sense would be 'partner,' and whose connotative nuances I noted earlier. I propose that in both these patterns (i.e., in her refusal to call her husband her master, and in her reference to him with the same term she uses to speak of her birth/placenta event) we are witnessing the use of an interesting semiotic trope. The relationship between her husband and the questions both of birth and of her psychotic illness became evident to me only later in the second interview and will become clear here once I examine the place of the husband in her story. For now I consider the other sense in which the term is employed in this account.

The placenta (*eş*) is a powerful signifier in many cultures, including the Middle Eastern and Central Asian ones. Altai and Mongol Turks considered the placenta sacred, a container for spirits. The placenta was associated with the goddess Umai, who helped women with infertility problems and in whose name the placenta would be buried in a special spot within the *yurt* (nomadic home, see the discussion in case of Emel in Chapter 3). A specific talisman would be created at the time of that burial to guard the newborn from the spirits' harm (e.g., Bezertinov, 2000, p. 81). In many traditions all the way from China and Central Asia to Africa and the Middle East the placenta has a history of being regarded as a virtual 'twin' of the newborn and thus of being treated with special care, including ritualistic burial (e.g., Adams Leeming & Adams Leeming, 1994, p. 71f.; Gow, 2001, p. 107f.; M. Rice, 2003, p. 108f.; Rhode, 1994, p. 82f.).

Throughout the interviews it became very clear that for Senem the placenta played the role of that 'leftover' of the person that becomes the double, the alter ego. It is a fact that the placenta takes on new practical significance where actual twin conceptions are involved (e.g., Piontelli, 2002, p. 13f., etc.), but as with the number 12, in the delusional context of Senem's twin births the placenta is also an in-between sign, one that simultaneously joins and separates the baby from the womb; one that *is* the baby, yet not quite; and one that *is* the mother, but not quite: it is a leftover entity from the process whereby the infant is separated from the mother. In Senem's discourse, the placenta is employed to signify that leftover of the self that then forms the double, a sign that enjoins and separates Senem with/from two figures: her imaginary double/twin and her lost baby.

Duplicity: Celal Bey

To recap, the 'placenta thing' with which Senem starts the interview led rapidly to the heart of her delusions, both in direct semantic reference and via more implicit semiotic associations. Given this, one can justifiably expect to find other relevant signs anchored in this network. The figure of her twin, Celal Bey, is one such sign, as is her lost baby. You may recall Senem's early remarks about Celal Bey:

P   Yes, I went to [my kid's] school. Eh, yes, Mr. Celal [*Celal Bey*] showed great attention to us. Like a brother . . . I mean, I am scared, I see him as a brother and he sees me as an elder sister. I am scared, he is paying attention to my children, I am scared that they might spread false words about us. I told my kids, "Look now, this chap can be your uncle because when my mother gave birth to me, it was apparently 12 at night and after 12 hours, she apparently gave birth one more time because of the *eş* things, the *eş* came later, you know . . ."

The name Celal, a common Arabic name and one of the names of Allah, literally means 'glory.' This name reappears in Senem's discourse with some frequency. He is the twin of Senem born of her leftover placenta. In the scene Senem reports, Celal Bey is a teacher who shows great attention to her and her children, so much so that she becomes anxious that people might suspect a secret romantic relationship between the two. She seems to present a brother and a twin almost juxtaposed with a lover. At some point in the interview, I asked Senem about some visions that she had hinted at in passing:

I   You said something about some images. What sort of images were you seeing?

P   Images, I see myself being a teacher. I was seeing myself being tied to a tree and burned. I have a brother, his name is Celal. Celal. . . They tie me, both of us, to a tree and burn us in a village square. Well, that . . . and that . . . we are living in some old wartime period, I mean, he brings some kind of victory, glory to somewhere, to a village in the name of Turkhood [*Türkluk*], he puts up a flag and stuff, and I am the teacher at that village. They start saying stuff like "Hey this woman has a stain [*leke*], this woman is smart, with her intelligence she is opening the eyes of the people, let us kill these siblings . . ." They tie us to a tree back to back. They burn the tree, they pour gasoline, and we burn to death. I see these images.

Here is Celal Bey again, this time not a teacher, but, living up to his name, he is now a hero warrior who has won glory in the name of Turkhood, the erecter of the Turkish flag, and the twin of intelligent Senem, who has taken the 'teacher' role herself. Similar to the earlier episode in which Senem is a mother and Celal Bey is a schoolteacher, the twins are being unjustly persecuted by ignorant people. It is not clear why they are being burned despite all the glory and enlightenment they have brought the village, but the narrative reveals that she is accused of having a 'stain.' The connotative network of the Turkish word *leke* is quite similar to that of its English equivalent, 'stain.' *Leke* stands for a discolored spot, usually indicating a clean surface dirtied, tainted by something of a different color. The notion of color is quite significant in Senem's story in fact, as we will see later. Keep in mind this idea of Senem as tainted and set on fire because of that 'spot' of uncleanness. Let us also take note of the sense of irony that pervades this scene. It is not just the burning of Celal Bey, the hero of Turkhood and the raiser of the Turkish flag, in the central square of a Turkish village that is ironic, Senem's own fate also appears paradoxical, in the sense that in the Republican discourse the notions of intelligence and knowledge have been always associated tightly with honor, light, and clarity, rather than taint and darkness. In what seems to amount to a serious reversal of the value system, the ignorant villagers are convinced that her knowledge and intelligence is tainted by a stain so serious that she can be cleansed with fire alone.[2]

Before going further into the genealogy and significance of Celal Bey, I should point out that in 'reality' Celal Bey is not a person known by Senem's mother or her daughter (to whom he is a teacher, according Senem). Consider the following conversation:

P   Later, earlier, more . . . I see myself living a few centuries back. There's again Celal Bey . . . in my dream. Again I see him being my brother, the same person. Now there is a Celal Bey in our lives, what I mean by our lives is, child, he was my child's teacher, then he became the deputy principal. He is showing close attention to my children, at the school they are attending. I told my husband [*eşim*] that Celal Bey could be my brother. And then apparently he went and searched about it and he was telling me the other day, "How can Celal Bey be your brother? The man is apparently 52 years old." And I said, "They must have shown you the wrong man . . . must have shown you a 52-year-old man! How can he be my brother, when I am still 37 years old?" [sounds amused] I told him, "They showed you the wrong person, this means that there are people out there who do not want our good . . ."

I   Hmm.

P   They are planning and organizing these things like this.

M   [unclear] come now . . .

I   [to the mother] Do you know Celal Bey?

M	No, I don't. I suppose he is a teacher at their [points at Senem's daughter] school. I don't know him.
I	[to the daughter] So you know him?
Daughter (D)	Well, she said, my mother, she said . . .
I	Is he your teacher?
D	No, he was the teacher of my . . . my younger sibling.
I	I see.
M	She [the daughter] said when her mother [Senem] saw Celal Bey, she [Senem] told us [children] those things about him, and that's when I [the daughter] suspected that my mother was ill, she [daughter] said.
I	Hmmm.
M	She [daughter] said that she [Senem] said when she saw him, "He is my brother and your uncle."

Duplicity: the private and the collective

Let me examine the character of Celal Bey now, and reconsider the significance he might have in understanding Senem's story. One important feature of Senem's village square vision is that it constitutes a projection of her subjective experiences in a collective arena. Senem's sense of persecution is depicted in the form of peasant masses burning the elite twins of glory and knowledge, Senem the educator and her twin the hero. The collective nature of this vision is not limited to the fact that a group of people has gathered in a village square, but it is expressed in terms of Turkish nationalism and allusions to a republican discourse of collectivity, through such signifiers as Turkhood, knowledge, and the Turkish flag. We have here yet another instance of a personal subjective experience expressed in a semiotic formulation adopted directly from the local collective experiences of political and social events, and this sense becomes only more evident as she tells me more about Celal Bey and her world at large. The village square vision, in other words, is a personal experience of psychosis expressed in terms of a collectivity divided into/by the two discourses of knowledge, nationalism, and heroic glory, on one hand, and tradition, violence, and backwardness, on the other.

The collective and the private: the flag

In that first interview, when the three female generations were present (their presence was by chance rather than arranged), I noticed that Senem's daughter was wearing a Turkish flag T-shirt: all red, with writings about loving Turkey on its back and front. At one point in the second interview after Senem spoke of her children, I brought up that T-shirt. I quote here this excerpt in a lengthier form not only because it contains a number of interesting and important references but also because the progression of associations deserves closer attention:

I   Your daughter, the one that was here last time, she seems to like Turkey a lot.

P   Yes, they're all like that my kids. They tie a flag on their backs and walk around.

I   Is that so?

P   Yes, they tie it like this [demonstrates] on their shoulders.

I   Hmm.

P   We call it Superman [*Biz superman diyorlar bize*].

I   I see.

P   Now, when they walk, like this, you know how the wind blows into the flag, we call it Superman. They do that a lot at our home.

I   Where does that come from?

P   You mean the love of Turkey?

I   Hmm.

P   I won't let go of Turkey that easily, you know how . . .

I   So it comes from you . . .

P   Wait, I'm telling you about those wars. I'm telling you the story of Ataturk's times. I am telling the story of the presidents after him that were killed. For example, there is a Celal Bayar, there were others . . . they were hanged in the islands, these were all taken to the rope [*ipe gerildiler*].

I   Why, who did that?

P   Over the freedom of thought.

I   I apologize, I don't know the Turkish history very well.

P   That could be. Now they all tried to bring some things to the middle [brought up some issues] about the freedom of thought [*düşünce özgürlüğünden dolayı bir şeyleri ortaya çıkarmaya çalıştılar*].

I   OK, I see.

P   And now you see, in Turkey we have this kind of thing, as soon as somebody does something smart, something really intelligent, right away they get their head chopped down, that means they kill him or her.[3] This is well known about Turkey.

I   Why?

P   So that s/he wouldn't speak! If s/he speaks, that won't be good for the other bad side.

I   I see . . . So has it been always like this, or is this something new?

P   Eh, no, it's ever since the Republic history has been established [*cumhuriyet tarihi kurulduğundan beri*], it's been like that. They've hanged a number of presidents . . .

This segment was evoked by my question about her daughter's wearing a red Turkish-flag T-shirt, which was in turn triggered by her description of the upbringing of her children and their social behavior. In response to my suggestion that her daughter liked Turkey (in fact her daughter had said in the earlier meeting, "I am crazy with love for Turkey") Senem tells me of how her kids wear the flag quite frequently at home, and associates this directly with power (Superman). Another significant detail in the story concerns the color red. Senem had been showing an extreme allergic reaction to red during her stay in the hospital, so much that the staff had noticed she would find an excuse and pick a fight with anybody wearing any red pieces of clothing. This is a significant detail, of course, and I give it more attention shortly. But for now, let's just consider the ironic 'twist' that it puts into the segment we just read, about the family's love for the Turkish flag and the children's wearing the flag and becoming 'supermen,' and more specifically about the fact that her own daughter would wear that red T-shirt to visit her at the hospital. The ironic internal discrepancy that runs through this segment is in fact not dissimilar to the hallucinatory vision, in which she and her twin Celal Bey are burned in a twisted response to their glorious deeds and enlightening services, she spoke of earlier. It is this very paradox, apparently produced out of a fundamental destabilization and a confusion of the places of love and hate, glory and shame, or good and evil, that links her 'love of the flag' to the story of Celal Bayar. Let me be more specific. Like Senem's twin Celal Bey, Celal Bayar was a hero of Turkish nationalism who suffered an ironic reversal of fate. Unlike Celal Bey, of course, Celal Bayar is a 'real' character. He was a friend and colleague of Ataturk's who fought with him for the independence, then served him as prime minister, and later became the president of Turkey himself. Celal Bayar started as a hero of the republican ideal along with Ataturk, and was one of the main engineers of the Republican economic system (e.g., Hale, 1994, p. 89). The cover design of a recently reprinted book by Celal Bayar (1998) titled *How To Think Like Ataturk*, shows Ataturk and then a second, 'double' of Ataturk, and the book is introduced in these words: "It is not possible to become Ataturk, but it is possible to think like Ataturk." Despite a great reputation, and an economically successful 10-year presidency, Celal Bayar's term was abruptly ended by a military coup in 1960. He was ousted, imprisoned, and sentenced to death following the coup (though not executed eventually; see, e.g., Hale, 1994, p. 87f., for details). The fate of Celal Bayar fits quite well then in this theme of ironic reversal, or internal confounding of value systems, in which Senem loves the Turkish flag but develops an allergy against the color red and attacks almost anybody wearing red, the same Senem who brings knowledge and enlightenment to her fellow Turks but is burnt by them accused of some kind of stain. It is also within the invisible pathways of that same associative network that she moves, immediately and for no apparent reason, to speak to me of wars and people who have fought to bring glories to her country and to raise the red flag but who were eventually ousted and punished. The hidden association eventually coagulates in her explicit claim that "in Turkey we have this kind of thing: as soon as somebody does something smart, something really intelligent, right away they get their head chopped off." The claim she makes is not necessarily a psychotically produced one. In fact here again we have a brilliant instance of subjective experience of psychosis expressed in terms borrowed from the collective arena of local political history. It is a common understanding in Turkey that a basically invisible power mafia (known locally as *derin devlet*, the 'deep state'; see, e.g., O'Neil, 2013; Robins and Aksoy, 2000; Unver, 2009; or Yilmaz, 2005) is the true decider of the country's affairs, rather than the visible government. Fethullah Gülen, a figure quite significant to Senem's discourse (see below), speaks of the deep state in an article titled 'Gülen's Warning' in the daily *Zaman*:

> In Turkey there are special units formed outside the state. . .maybe there are 50,000 of them, maybe 100,000, maybe even more than 100,000. . . even if it is spearheaded by the 'deep state' within the state, what is happening should be opposed. . .the public should be warned so that they are not deceived . . .[4]

As I write these lines, Turkey's government continues an unprecedented and protracted struggle against the so-called deep state. In August 2014, for instance, 31 police officers were suspended from duty, suspected of connections with the "deep state"[5] In an earlier article titled "Bombing Throws Spotlight on Turkey's Deep State" the Reuters news agency described Turkey's "deep state" in these words:

> The 'deep state' is made up of elements in the military, security and judicial establishment wedded to a fiercely nationalist, statist ideology who if need be are ready to block or even oust a government which does not share their vision . . . "There are two states (in Turkey)," former President Suleyman Demirel told NTV television . . . "There is the state and there is the deep state . . . When a small difficulty occurs, the civilian state steps back and the deep state becomes the generator (of decisions)."[6]

Due partly to this fact, the common belief goes, very often intelligent people and those who truly care for the nation are abused, removed from power, or destroyed, because such progress would mean an end to the deep state's monopoly and to a traditional system of power. An instance would be the prosecution of Turkey's Nobel laureate author and intellectual Orhan Pamuk, an event widely understood to have been arranged by the 'deep state.' In an article titled 'In Turkey, the Novelist as Lightning Rod,' Kinzer, in the *New York Times*, speaks of the Turkish 'deep state' as a power resisting 'modernization': "Turkish society is now racing towards European-style democracy, and the new openness here alarms diehard defenders of the old order, known collectively here as 'Deep State.'"[7] And later, in February 2008, the British Broadcasting Corporation, BBC, reports that indeed Orhan Pamuk had been on the deep state's assassination list.[8]

So in this scenario intelligent people and those who truly care for the progress of the country become endangered because of the power mafia that feeds on people's ignorance and is invested in keeping the status quo. Note also that this scenario is quite similar to the dynamics of Senem's vision, which is to say once again another layer of public experience, or a publicly shared semiotic configuration, is being adopted to express an idiosyncratic internal experience. As usual, the network that is mobilized to fuse these two is not a simply two-dimensional one; it is intricate, mostly implicit, and multidimensional. For example, consider the notion of intelligence used as a central signifier in this formulation and the way it functions to link these two domains of experience to each other.

The collective and the private: intelligence

Smart is an adjective with which Senem identified herself as a social subject, and intelligence was also pointed out as a cause of her madness, by her and by her mother. Consider the following excerpts:

I   Now, tell me a bit about yourself, what kind of a person are you?

P   I am a very mixed person [*karmaşık*: mixed, complex, composed of many elements] . . . Not everybody can solve me [*Beni her insan çözemez yani. Çözmek*: disentangle, solve, decipher]

I   How is that?

P   I was just telling you, an hour earlier reading history books, an hour later I could be reading the holy Quran.

I   Yes.

P   And when I get bored of that I could pick up the guitar and play it . . . I teach the kids how to play the chess, I teach them, ironing, teach them how to cook . . . I mean I give them all the knowledge of life.

You may remember also that in describing her vision in which she was being burned she had said the following:

P   . . . [People] start saying stuff like "Hey this woman has a stain, this woman is smart, with her intelligence she is opening the eyes of the people, let us kill these siblings . . ."

At another point Senem told me about her neighbors in the apartment block where she lived, and she drew a distinct line between them and herself and between her level of intelligence and education and theirs. She said the following:

P   [What the neighbors and I read] are not the same. They are not. I read the books written by academicians, university graduates. They, however, they read books from here and there, books about tea and hazelnuts . . . What I mean is that someone had written a rough, unsophisticated book and they were reading it with gullibility and lack of reflection. I am showing them the Truth, but they do not want to heed that. And if they do not . . .

M   Look, from now on you will not obsess yourself with reading books, OK?

P   If they do not want a . . . I won't care either.

M   But your neighbors think that you are very smart.

P   My neighbors should appreciate me, that's true.

M   They appreciated her a lot. Very smart, they say . . .

P   [They say] you are a person to listen to, you are very knowledgeable.

The neighbors, ignorant and uneducated, do not want to see the Truth and knowledge that Senem has to offer them. Their ignorance has subscribed to her madness creating the context for her being struck by evil spells of an evil hoja (see the next section). The contrast between her sophisticated self and the ignorant neighbors later becomes more explicitly associated with larger issues of modernity and tradition and specifically the different readings of Islam, which I address shortly. But here in this excerpt it already becomes clear that Senem sees herself in her social environment in terms similar to those so vividly displayed in her visions, a martyr of enlightenment, knowledge, and "the freedom of thought."

Religion and Nationalism

Not long into the interview, Senem's mother told her how it was important for her to 'come back to normalcy' because of her responsibilities, namely, her children and her husband. This in turn triggered Senem to speak of her life and her chores and responsibilities at home, which she then associated with times before the illness. Senem spoke with an air of nostalgia of the days before, and even the early days after she married and became a mother.

She spoke of the social interactions she had and how the freedom entailed in these guarded her from internal turmoil ('stress' is often to be taken to lie at the root of all mental ills) that she associated with her current lifestyle and her current neighborhoods. Let me quote that segment:

P   So, that's how it is . . . my life. When I first got married, we used to have a clothing factory. I would go down and work there. I would see new people. I mean that's how I used to get rid of my stress, by working at the clothing factory and keeping myself busy there, I was getting rid of my stress from home [*bu şekilde stres atıyordum, evdeki stresi konfeksiyonda çalışarak veya kendimi meşgul ederek orda . . .*] and relaxing by working there and talking to people. And now I am totally enclosed inside the house. And we also changed our house. From our old neighborhood we moved to a new place. I didn't know the people there. They are strange, weird people, not for, not like us.

I   How do you mean?

P   I mean . . .

M   They are very nice. You were quite content with your neighbors, and they've been very nice to you.

P   My neighbors could be nice but there's . . .

M   [unclear] . . . called you by phone . . .

P   I don't . . . [3-sec pause] I don't trust my neighbors . . . because each and every one of them has a husband with beards like that . . . they do not do their daily prayers right. I told them, something like, we are such and such with a certain [political] party . . . they wear baggy trousers and gowns [*şalvar giyiyorlar, cüppe takıyorlar*] but . . . I was seeing who was coming in and out of their houses, I mean not . . . they are blaming everybody. Everybody . . . me for instance . . . that's to say, we have weekly Quran gatherings, we go and all, then they read, I don't, so then they don't like you . . . whatever I do is wrong according to them. As long as what I do is right according to me, let it be wrong according to you, what do I care!

I   Like what, for example?

P   I mean, I . . . how should I put it . . . I read . . . read the Turkish translation of the Quran. So naturally, uh, my books are very different from theirs.

The thematic progression in this segment is not complex: it starts from her responsibilities at home evoking memories of the old times when there was freedom instead of homebound restriction, which in turn animates her feelings around the new apartment where she has been living and her unhappiness with the neighbors who are religious-traditionalist (with their beards and their traditional outfit) but who are in fact suffering from ignorance so much that they cannot even do their daily prayers right. The 'certain political party' with which she speaks cryptically of being 'such-and-such,' is actually an important reference for her that I will discuss later. But for now I would like to focus more specifically on the last part of this excerpt, when she explains the reason her neighbors find her wrong: "I read the Turkish translation of the Quran, so naturally my books are very different from theirs."

The Quran and Turkish nationalism

The question of translating the Quran is a significant and passionately disputed issue, not only in Turkey but also across the non-Arab Islamic world. In Turkey, however, the question becomes even more pronounced because it simultaneously coincides with two fundamentally troublesome issues: linguistic nationalism and modernity. "According to a doctrine introduced to Turkey from Persia at the end of the 14th century," says Bernard Lewis (1975), "the image of God is the face of man, the mark of man is language, and language is expressed in the 28 letters of the Arabic script, which thus contain all the mysteries of man, God, and eternity" (p. 425). The tradition pointed out by Lewis, in which the actual (Arabic) words enjoy significance as concrete and direct representations of the divine is neither new nor obsolete. The tradition goes back at least to the Quran itself, a number of whose chapters start in code-like words that have no meanings in Arabic, they stand totally 'outside' the meaning system except in terms of that very 'lack of known meaning.' In fact these 'words' are so sacred and so pronouncedly defiant of any meaning systems that in reciting the Quran one must 'word them out.' For example, the third surah, known as Aal-i Imran (the family of Imran), starts with a 'word' that would be read by a noninitiate as *alm*. But, as any good Muslim should know, *alm* is not really a 'word': it does not have a meaning (one known to humankind, anyway), and it should be spelled out: *alif, laam, meem* (*ey, el, em*) rather than *alm*. There are extensive texts by Muslim scholars dedicated to these terms found in 29 of the Quran's 114 surahs. According to the *Tafseer Al-mizan*,[9] "the letter symbols do have an explanation, however, their final interpretation is known to Allah and His purified servants."[10] Of interest here is the tradition itself, in which the actual physical appearance of text symbols bear great significance. Senem later on told me that she has actually learned to read the Quran in Arabic as well as Turkish, and she told me that her favorite surah is Yaa-Seen, a surah actually named after its cryptic code word: YS (*Yaa-Seen*). She then offered a stronger association with these cryptograms when I asked if there are any specific surahs she likes better:

P   My favorite surah? Yes, there is 'Yaa-Seen,' for example, there is 'Faatiha,' there are other surahs, there are secrets, codes . . .

I   There's what?

P   Codes, there is 'Ayet-el Kürsü,' then there was another one, I can't remember, there's 'Yusuf' . . .

The fact is that apart from Faatiha, which means 'opening' and is literally the 'opening' surah of the Quran, all the other surahs she has indicated here contain meaningless 'codes,' and of course, she herself immediately produces the unambiguous association with 'codes': "there are secrets, codes . . ." Once again, in addition to the apparent 'secret' and mystery associated with these code words, there is the question of physical appearance of the Quran and its importance.

In an article titled "Why Koran Is Such a Hot Button," dedicated to the US soldiers' infamous desecration of the Quran in Guantanamo Bay camps in 2005 and the Muslim world's reaction to that, the *Christian Science Monitor* explains the fact that unlike the Bible, the Quran cannot be translated because it was "transmitted to Muhammad from Allah by the angel Gabriel nearly 1,400 years ago and written down precisely as Allah intended."[11] Similarly, the Muslims' daily prayers are specifically supposed to be said in original Arabic. This 'literal' tradition persisted throughout the Ottoman Empire. By the beginning of the 20th century, however, the tradition had grown into a serious conflict with the burgeoning ideals of Westernization and modernization. The conflict had developed due to the perceived opposition between tradition and modernity, the first associated with ignorance and darkness and the latter with knowledge and enlightenment. Islam, tightly associated with tradition, was gradually singled out as the cause of backwardness along with Turkey's cultural attachment to Islamic traditions and specifically Arabic culture (see, e.g., Lewis, 1975, p. 401f.), and something was therefore to be done about that. The idea of removing Islam from the society was not just impossible; it was unimaginable. The thinkable alternative then was that it was not Islam that caused the problem, but the 'traditions' attached to it that bogged it down. Islam needed to be 'treated' to take away those aspects of it that hindered social progress and modernity. It was at about this point in history that Ataturk entered the stage. The conversion of Islamic texts into Turkish (one of Ataturk's reform items) thus assumes a double significance: first in terms of Ataturk's Nationalist project, in which a Turkish translation of Arabic texts goes without saying and, second, in terms of his Westernization and modernization project, wherein Islam needed to be 'translated and improved' and written in the letters of enlightenment, in Roman alphabet, to befit a progressive country (see, e.g., Lewis, 1975, 'Script and Language,' p. 425f.).

It is in this context then, that one can recognize the sense of Senem's suggestion that she is more intelligent and more progressive than her neighbors, because she "knows what she reads," because she reads her Quran and does her prayers in Turkish rather than in Arabic. Of course, even this simple assertion is not quite what it seems in the profoundly tricky world of Senem's meanings and significative associations. Consider the fact that she also decided to learn to read the original Arabic Quran, or the fact that the day of her home crisis, when she burned a number of charmed timbers on her balcony, she also burned a Quran "written in red ink." Senem's mother denied the existence of any red-ink Quran, and so far as I know, it is highly improbable for a Quran to be printed in red ink. We know, however, that Senem had a Turkish-translation Quran at home, one that she had asked her older sister to wrap in a Turkish flag and give her as a wedding gift. We also know that color red is a primary signifier of Turkish nationalism in Turkey (see the next section for more detailed discussion of the signifier 'red' in this story). Given all this then, the red-ink Quran that Senem burned along with other red items that day on her balcony comes to stand for a Turkified Quran, the Quran that was wrapped in the flag, the modern Quran she has just bragged of reading in Turkish, as opposed to the Arabic ones that her backward neighbors read. So here once again a series of statements fit with mainstream discourses of progress and modernity, but only superficially so, because a closer examination quickly reveals discrepancies that unravel the surface logic of the statements into a paradoxical system of references. We will come back to this.

Impurity and cleansing: the color red

Along with the running theme of ironic discrepancy, another major theme strongly connects Senem's village square and balcony stories: the theme of impurity and cleansing. Both events are constructed around a burning fire that was meant on both occasions to act as a cleansing agent: in one event it was to cleanse a certain stain off Senem as a social subject; in the other it was to burn everything 'red' and erase a charm off Senem the private subject. A question that I cannot help entertaining is, 'Could the stain for which Senem was to be cleaned be understood as a "red" stain?' When Senem's psychiatrist told me of the day Senem had made a fire on her balcony, she said, "[Senem] collected bushes and tinder in the balcony and lit a fire, and then she threw everything red she found into it, including a red door knob and bloody hygiene pads." Elsewhere in that same interview, the psychiatrist also told me of a fight that Senem had raised at one point with her husband, because while he had been traveling abroad Senem noticed bloodstained sheets in their apartment and thus believed that the husband had had a secret relationship with another woman. Her husband, of course, was traveling in Romania at the time, according to the doctor. We do not have enough data to decide whether those 'tainted sheets' were 'real' or of a hallucinatory nature, but in either case the association here with that event and the pursuant 'red-burning' event and the village square vision is hard to miss. The color red is a semiotic 'hub' in Senem's story that serves to link the personal to the collective. Consider the fact, for example, that elsewhere in the interview (see the following discussion) when Senem told me of her ideas about the red Turkish flag she said, "Red symbolizes the bloods that have been shed for our flag. I mean all that blood that has been shed for the Republic, for our freedom . . . so that's a bloody thing, it's a bloody rag, excuse me for saying that." The association between 'bloody rag [*kanlı bez*]' and stained hygiene pads is immediate in the Turkish semiotic system, especially in the discourse of a female subject. The association between the 'stain' and color red is simply too pervasive through the discourses of the patient and the clinician to ignore. When the clinician spoke, for example, of the fact that Senem would pick fights with anybody in the ward who had any red pieces of clothing, she made it clear that Senem herself never made such a connection (between her picking fights and the red item) but, instead, that she would often accuse the other woman of having been "dirty" – establishing once again the association between color red and a sense of being stained. But how are we to understand the significance of such an association, between color red, female blood, the Turkish flag, and an almost transcendental quality of being stained? I will come back to this question shortly with new information.

Reversible signifiers

Even after our initial unpacking of layers of associations and meanings in Senem's psychotic actions and fantasies, a curious feature remains unexplained, that is, the ironic and confusing quality that may best be described as a reversibility of some key signifiers in Senem's representational system. Consider the idea of Nationalism and the flag, for example: it stands to signify love, glory, and pride, on one hand, and anger, violence and shame, on another. Senem made numerous references to the flag, generally in an explicit language of love, respect, and patriotic nationalism. Remember the patriotic twin, Celal Bey, who had won glory for the country and who had raised a Turkish flag in the name of progress and freedom of thought. I quote more fully here an excerpt where I discuss the flag and its significance with the family:

I   [to the daughter] That T-shirt of yours, let's see . . . it says "I love Turkey," eh?

D   Yes.

P   Yes.

I   So it is not for a soccer team or something?

D   I am sick for Turkey ["Türkiye hastasıyım ben" can also be translated "I am crazy for Turkey"].

I   [So it's] only a thing about Turkey then?

D   Yes.

I   Sick for Turkey [*Türkiye hastası*] . . .

D   My everything is Turkey.

I   Oh, is that so?

M   Is it written "Turkey" on the back?

D   Yes.

I   What is written?

D   It says "Turkey."

I   It says Turkey. . . sick [*hasta*: sick, crazy] for Turkey, is that what you said?

D   Yes.

I   [to the daughter] Where does that come from?

P   My children hold a deep respect for the Turkish nation . . . They love Turkey to a strange extent [*acayip* from Arab. *ajeeb*: strange, bizarre].

I   And yourself?

P   Me too.

I   So, you, too . . . have the Turkey sickness [*Türkiye hastasisiniz*: are sick/crazy for Turkey]?

D   But her [Senem's] love for Turkey is much more than ours!

I   [to the patient] So you're the most . . .

P   If anywhere I see . . .

D   Even here [at the hospital] we are doing Turkey stuff all the time. . .

I   I see. Why do you love Turkey so much?

D   [All talk at the same time; few words unintelligible.]

P   At school, she [the daughter] had a thing . . . there was some sort of a celebration, the flags would be pulled up, anthems would be sung.

I   Uh-huh.

P   So the school employees . . . they've burned the edge of the flag when they ironed it.

I   Oh.

P   So I said, my house is very close to the school, I mean you can see the inside of the classrooms from the balcony, you can see inside, we are that close.

I   Uh-huh.

P   Everything was done, but then they saw that the inspectors were going to come to the classrooms, so there needed to be flags put up . . . And no one has any flags. So I said I go and get some from home in 5 minutes, I have twelve flags, I will fetch them.

D   She has the biggest flag ever!

P   I have one particularly big flag, my sister gave it to me as a present for my wedding . . . she was going to get some gift, she was thinking about what to get, and I said, "You'll get a big Turkish flag, and you put the holy Quran inside of it, you'll wrap that up, and will give that to me as a gift."

I Uh-huh . . .

P I still kept that flag and the Quran . . . That flag finally ended up in that school, when I arrived home . . . my son had taken it out to some soccer games [so it was dirty], I washed it in a fast program [of the washing machine]. I took them out right away, and I had already turned the iron on before opening the machine . . . I dried them by ironing them out, and then I took them there and we put the big one outside, then – I had about 12 flags in total, and we put them in the classrooms, we passed that day like that.

I Uh-huh . . .

P Thank God.

I Now, where does this love come from? How come you all love Turkey so much?

D [wondering tone] I really don't know . . .

I You don't know.

M Probably from loving one's land [*toprak*: earth, land].

D It is maybe because we were born in Turkey . . .

M Sure.

I But in Turkey . . .

P Every Turk loves Turkey [laughs].

I There are 60 million people here [in Turkey], but not everybody wears flags.

D I don't know why, everything I have is all red and white. And I like the colors red and white a lot.

I OK.

D And I like Turkey very much.

I Very nice.

D I mean, maybe that's why . . .

I OK, I see.

You may recall also an excerpt quoted earlier, which was taken from the second interview I had with Senem without her family. In that excerpt I brought the conversation back to the daughter's flag T-shirt, from which point Senem then departed to speak of the strong love for the flag at home, the superman metaphor, and eventually the ironic fate of Celal Bayar, the lover of Turkey and the raiser of the flag who was eventually ostracized, persecuted, and exiled to an island. A review of the content in what was just quoted will allow a closer discussion of that internal discrepancy to which I have been referring as an implicit paradox, reflected in the fates of Celal Bayar and of Senem and her own twin, Celal Bey. The primary theme in the preceding excerpt is the love of Turkey and thus its red flag. The daughter's red T-shirt appeared overly conspicuous even for Turkey, where the flag is certainly revered as a sign of national identity.[12] The fashion in which she describes herself as "sick for Turkey" is similarly strong. Senem's daughter is using super-loaded signifiers to express a sense of loyalty and respect for the Turkish culture. I do not have sufficient information on this daughter to analyze what this means to her. We do know, however, that Senem has been showing an 'allergy' to color red during her illness. We also know that her allergy has not been subtle or indirect: she has burned all red objects at home and picked fights with people wearing red items. It is highly improbable that the daughter is unaware of this feature in her mother's illness. So the question returns: What is wrong with this picture? The girl pronounces herself 'sick' for Turkey. The term she uses for this expression is *hasta*, which is quite similar to its English equivalent, *sick*, in the sense that it could be used to indicate either physical/functional inadequacy[13] or, in a more derogatory sense, a social/psychological inappropriateness.[14] But in Turkish, the term also means 'in love with,' a sense that forms yet another connective thread in the association of love with madness. Even though we need to presume it is in this last sense of 'in love' that Senem's daughter calls herself sick for Turkey, it still becomes tantalizingly close to making a literal connection when she then describes her mother in the same way and emphasizes in fact that Senem's love for Turkey is much greater than that of the rest of the family. Love is once again called up, it would seem, to speak of mental illness. But also preserved in this semiotic maneuver is the sense of paradox already found to permeate this story. Here it takes the form of an ironic double significance crystallized in the word *hasta* and its simultaneous connotations of the positive excitement of love on the one hand and the negative grief of illness on the other. It is no wonder that Senem should describe her own and her children's love for Turkey with the word *acayip* (bizarre, odd, or extreme). And when I ask the family the naïve question of why they are so sick for Turkey, the closest they come to an answer is "because we were born here"? Senem and her daughter insist in fact that even in the hospital they have continued to serve Turkish interests. According to the clinician, however, apart from the fact that she has taken on herself to help a number of younger patients whom she considers to be her children (their doubles, to be more accurate), the only significant activity she has done that we can interpret as 'Turkey related' would be attacking people who wear red. Irony appears in the form of descriptions that seem to refuse to lend themselves to a final anchoring and persist in an in-between semiotic space. This trick is not the same as an empty 'floating' signifier that can assume different meanings in different times. Here we are dealing with signifiers that refuse to give in and fail to submit to a final 'meaning' by virtue of a capacity to 'hang' between fundamentally opposite referents such as love and hate, good and evil, glorious and tainted. The story is once again unfolding in an in-between zone as was the case with the number 12 and the *eş*, the zone where signifiers keep for themselves the right to signify 'both–and,' rather than 'either–or.'

Paradox and internal discrepancy

I return now to the question of internal discrepancy reflected in the ironic fates of privately fantasized and publicly recognized characters Celal Bey and Celal Bayar. This was captured in a collectively shared view of Turkish politics (chopping off rather than holding up intelligent heads), which I also referred to in terms of an apparent reversibility of certain signifiers (love/ hate, etc.). Senem not only made a number of references to the red Turkish flag, generally wrapped in the explicit language of love, respect, and patriotic nationalism but also mentioned the flag through alternative modes in her discourse. Consider now the following excerpt, in which she presents another description and relationship to the notions of nationalism, in general, and the flag, specifically. At one point in the interview I asked Senem about her conception of her illness and the way she believes it has affected her life. I asked her if she finds the recent events have changed her life in any way. "Yes," she responded, and she went on:

P   I sit here and talk [to you] now! Before I couldn't be pleasant to a person for a long time, I would definitely get into a fight. The person in front of me wouldn't accept my thoughts, and I wouldn't accept his or hers. I mean after talking for one or two minutes the form of our conversation would change, it would turn into an argument. You see, there's something called freedom of thought, everybody is forced to use that [*mecbur*: forced, compelled]. I mean me too I talk using that, and . . . I don't know . . . I wonder if I'm going to get out and go to prison too . . .

I   But why would you go to prison?

P   Well, you know, because of the flag. The kids wanted a flag from me, and I didn't have a red pen at home.

I   OK?

P   So I drew like this, on a white paper, I drew the crescent and star.

I   OK.

P   The crescent and star. And the rest I colored with blue, with a pen, like this.

I   Blue?

P   I drew it, and the kids they took it and hung it off the balcony like this . . .

I   Yes . . .

P   And anybody who'd see that will complain.

I   Hmm. Why would they complain?

P   You know, they'd say she has changed the color of our flag.

I   I see. But why did you do it in blue?

P   Because there weren't red pens, blue stands for intelligence, you know? Blue color!

I   No, I don't know.

P   Yes.

I   How is that?

P   The color blue symbolizes intelligence.

I   Intelligence.

P   Yes, it symbolizes water.

I   Hmm, I see.

P   And water symbolizes life.

I   I see, OK.

P   [excited] Watch, the skies are blue, blue symbolizes the heavens, symbolizes intelligence, I mean that is the purpose of color blue.

I   And what is the meaning of color red?

P   [voice drops] Red symbolizes our blood.

I   Blood, I see.

P   I mean, red symbolizes the bloods that have been shed for our flag. I mean all that blood that has been shed for the Republic, for our freedom . . . so that's a bloody thing, it's a bloody rag [*kanlı bez, affedersiniz*],[15] excuse me for saying that . . .

I   No, that's OK.

In response to my inquiry of the role and place of her illness events she starts by defining both illness and recovery in terms of power and opposition. For her the recovery is indicated by the fact that she can now speak to someone without entering a power struggle over his or her respective points of view, by the fact that a conversation can remain a play within the language game rather than in a war of differing systems: "I sit here and talk now!" She explains this quality of letting other people speak in terms of "freedom of thought," suggesting that while her illness appeared in the form of her not allowing other people to speak, she now is a subscriber to the idea of "freedom of thought," she now sits and talks and lets others talk, without getting into a fight. Quickly after, however, as if to make the spirit of her remarks more explicitly 'political,' she moves to associate all this with real politics, prison, and the notion of 'freedom of thought' in the actual political arena.

What Senem is doing here is making an association between her conception of her illness as a state of opposition and an aggressive absence of tolerance, and social/political persecution due to actually employing "freedom of thought." In other words, here the freedom of thought, which is first introduced as a space of peace and acceptance that coincides with recovery from illness, is quickly subverted and associated with a state of terror for her: "Everybody is forced to use [freedom of thought] . . . me too, I talk using that . . . I wonder if I'm going to get out [of here] and go to prison." The paradox is subtle but powerful nonetheless: to begin with, the idea that people are 'forced' to use freedom of thought is already a paradoxical concept. Furthermore, the 'freedom of thought' that she has used may actually take her to prison. And all this is constructed around the flag story. Remember her love of the Turkish flag and her hatred of color red? The paradox is repeated here, in a more specific way that may provide a closer understanding of its terms. She made a flag for her children using the color blue. Needless to say, the excuse of 'not having a red pen at home' is, first, highly unlikely in a house of five children most of them students and all lovers of the color red and, second, insufficient to explain either her drawing a blue flag (rather than, e.g., waiting to get a red pen or using a normal black pen or pencil) or the public displaying of that blue flag over the balcony, specifically given the strong explicit pro-nationalist spirit of her household. Apart from this, the very tone of this conversation and the fact that she rapidly associates her use of the color blue with symbolic properties of colors give an indication of a more intricate play of signifiers at work. These data support the idea that her blue flag should be read as an act of significance rather than as arbitrary and meaningless.

Consider, for example, that when I ask her, "But why did you do it in blue?" she ties that act to the symbolic meanings of the color blue rather than simply remaining within the logical limits of 'because there were no red pens.' While the very process of attributing symbolic meanings to colors supports the meaningfulness hypothesis, the content of this process actually harkens back to a specific theme that she had indicated earlier, concerning the fate of intelligence in Turkish politics. Consider the following chain of associations: (1) For Senem, healing from her illness coincides with practicing freedom of thought. (2) She is afraid she might be taken to prison once released from the hospital. (3) She would be taken to prison because she has practiced the freedom of thought (and her twin Celal was also killed because he used 'freedom of thought'). (4) Her freedom of thought is exercised in drawing a blue flag instead of a red one. (5) For her, the color blue, which she picked to draw the flag, has to do with heavens, freedom, spirituality, and intelligence. (6) For her, the color red, which is the prescribed color of the flag, has to do with the republic, blood, and war and is associated with a "bloody rag" (which she also burned on her balcony).

Perils of a female subject: the Quran in a flag

The previous set of associations reflects the way private subjective issues of mental illness, hospitalization, and recovery are organically tied to larger questions of nationalism, politics, and 'freedom of thought' in Senem's system of discursive references. But they also put in more concrete terms a discrepancy that runs throughout her discourse. The flag, this symbol of Turkish nationalism, republican progressivism, and freedom of thought also stands for blood, violence, and shameful stains. The subjective state of being that Senem is experiencing in her psychotic illness, in other words, coincides and merges seamlessly with the collective experiences of her environment as expressed in social and political formulations of power (authority, the state, social norms) and the local history. A further, bitter aspect of Senem's predicament as a female subject is the implicit but powerful way she is located at the meeting place of two otherwise antagonistic discourses: religion and tradition, on one hand, and nationalism and modernity, on the other. Consider the following for example:

P   We've made the moon and star and sent it up the pole! Our flag is very high, ours is very beautiful. I mean that's why I told my sister you wrap the holy Quran inside a flag. I said a Turkish flag be my wedding gift and that's how it was too.

I   Hmm.

P   And she did as I said, she put the holy Quran in a beautiful Turkish flag and decorated it with beautiful ribbons.

I   What is the meaning of that?

P   What is the meaning of that? I am getting married today, I begin a new life, and that means that in my new life too I will have my flag and the holy Quran on top of my head for eternity, that's what it means.

I   Hmm.

P   I mean it is something like a vow, a promise I mean.

I   OK, I understand . . .

The flag and the Quran, eternally "on top of her head" coincide here with her wedding, a wedding that signifies subjugation to a powerful male authority for her in more than one ways. The bitter irony of her explanation of the meaning of a Quran wrapped in the Turkish flag may be subtle but difficult to miss: "we've made the moon and star and we've sent it up the pole! Our flag is very high. . . ." But let me be more specific. As both Senem and her mother agreed, her life changed drastically after she married. While as a child she had grown up with much freedom in a family where she had had full respect, her married life was quite different. Consider the following conversation:

P   Me and my older sister grew up together. Our family, we were raised like men. They allowed us freedom to do everything. What I want to say is they did not put limits on what we wanted to do. Well, they had waited for a long time longing to have kids . . .

M   They grew up with much freedom and comfort . . .

P   [slightly raising her voice] Basically, we grew up like women as well as like men. When we wanted to work somewhere, we worked. We wanted to go to this place or that place, it was not a problem, we were allowed to go. My father helped us a lot, my father as well as my mother. We pretty much did anything we wished to do. I mean, we never said, "I wish I could do this too" . . .

M   But she got married, of course. After getting married . . .

P   [The mother and the daughter speaking at the same time; unclear]. After getting married, my life turned black . . .

M   After getting married, there was much more discipline in the new life, of course. And, you know, she was raised with much freedom . . .

P   I grew up very freely. [The mother talking at the same time; not clear]. I married into a very conservative family.

I   At what age did you get married?

P   I was 18 years old when I got married. I mean I got married and how much later? Sometime later I became 18.

I   Right . . .

P   I married at too young an age. I mean right now I have children who are older than me! I have a son, a daughter . . . My son is about to do his military service. Anyways, that's how it is. I had five kids. During this time my husband did not do, you know, I mean he did not show me a woman's worth, to be frank. We got married with love . . . But then my husband changed quite a lot. I mean he hung out with other women, he drank alcohol, and he gambled. He did all kind of shit. But when I left him, he certainly left me. Because of all these problems I left him a couple of times . . .

As clearly as the dramatic change in Senem's power and status is captured in the preceding excerpt, that was not yet the whole story. As might have been the case for you, I found it hard to avoid wondering about the nature of her choice of partner and her acceptance of the new status of inferiority and restrictions, given the liberal upbringing that she and her mother had described (and which I could easily believe, given the style of interaction I witnessed between the three generations present in that first interview). The age of marriage was also another point of ambiguity for me, especially because she had emphasized on a few occasions that she married too early, that when she married she did not have legal age yet, or that she married so young that now she has children who are 'older than herself.' I had resisted addressing my curiosity, hoping that I would eventually find an answer to that question, and I did. In the second interview, away from her mother and daughter, Senem told me more details about the traumatic events that surrounded her marriage and her first pregnancy. That information then helped me better understand not only the significance of her marriage for her illness or at least for some of its specific expressions but also her paradoxical stance toward power and loyalty and the sense of internal struggle that pervaded her world so deeply. Remember, for example, my early discussion of the term *eş* and its double significance as placenta or as partner, where I had suggested an implicit semiotic significance for Senem's use of the term in both senses. In the following segments, we see how the notions of 'birth' and 'partner' merge into what could be seen as the nucleus of her psychotic experience.

The quest

When at one point Senem spoke to me of how she has read an incredible number of religious texts, I was curious to understand the significance/relevance of that behavior. So I asked the following:

I   Why did you read all those [texts]?

P   I was interested, I mean, a voice from inside of me, a voice told me "read," I mean it told me "read!"

I   Did you have a question? I mean, were you looking for an answer to something?

P   Yes, I was looking for an answer.

I   What were you, what was the question?

P   The question was my son. I became friends with my husband and then I got pregnant. Just friends, fiancé [*nişanlı*: marked, engaged]. And I got pregnant. And I was a virgin [*bakire*]. I mean it's like that baby would have gone to Hell, and I . . . it was like . . . if anybody could save him, that would have had to be me. And by reading I thought I could find a way. Because we were friends, and we did the religious thing, and then he tried to rape [*tecavüz*: assault, violate, rape] me. But it didn't work . . .

I   What?

P   But he couldn't rape me. My husband [*eşim*] . . .

I   I see.

P   We got together [*beraber kaldık*: traditional idiom for 'we had sex'], I mean no, nothing happened between us, nothing happened. Only he, excuse me, he poured out the manhood water [*erkeklik suyu*] . . . after that I got pregnant, I became pregnant but I was still a virgin. And he would have married me anyway, we were fiancés, but then we had an imam's permission too, after that we got married. When we got married I was 7 months pregnant and I was a virgin. You know, it wasn't just me, that time there were a bunch of women that the same thing had happened to them, they came and talked to me, so we are like that too . . . they said, what is going to happen to these children? Will they go to Hell or what . . . Why, I said, why would they go to Hell? They [the women] also had the imam thing . . . I mean, a baby in the belly of a virgin mother?! A virgin mother having a baby! I took off from that point, and I did a lot of searching.

I   I see. Now did you find your answer?

P   I found my answer, but I can't tell you that.

I   OK.

This information, and what followed (discussed later) put much of the earlier content of her story in a substantially new perspective for me, including the baffling sense of discrepancy that had plagued me throughout the interviews. To begin with, this new passage explained to me why a woman such as Senem with such a strong character and sense of liberty and coming from the liberal family tradition in which she was brought up would opt to marry so early[16] and to a man and a family whom both Senem and her mother described as ultraconservative, rigid, and 'unsophisticated.' A tragic fact of life in more traditional environments in Turkey is that a young unmarried 'virgin' does not really have many desirable options beyond marriage to the man who makes her pregnant, whether she is raped by him or not. In fact the pattern that emerges from the various pieces of information here fits in a traditional local model known as *kaçırmak*, which refers to the abduction of a young maiden by a man. Even though quite repressed from the explicit discourse and daily consciousness of modern Turkey, the notion of abduction (*kaçırmak*) is deeply rooted in old Turkic tribal traditions, in which a young man would abduct a family's daughter as a way of assuring that the woman will be 'given' to him. The 'assurance' was provided by the cultural tradition that deemed an abducted woman by default spoiled or tainted (expressed by the verb *bozmak*: to break, defile, spoil, rape, stain). Once abducted, the young woman would become stained, regardless of whether she has been literally raped by her abductor, and the only socially-sanctioned face-saving models of behavior for her father or brothers would be to ensure the abductor marries their daughter/sister, or else the stain is cleansed by punishment of both the man and the woman, or at least the woman, typically by death (hence the term *honor killing*). This is a well-documented tradition of tribal Turks (see, e.g., Bates, 1973, p. 72f.; Meeker, 2002, p. 319f.; Elver, 2005, pp. 298–299; Starr, 1978, p. 186f.) the residual behavioral patterns of which among Turkish immigrants in Europe leads to occasional serious cultural clashes (see, e.g., Van Eck, 2003). In the case of Senem, the problem was even more serious, given the fact that not only was she tainted by premarital sexual intimacy, she was impregnated as well. The *kaçırmak* scenario explains a number of aspects of the story that would otherwise remain puzzling, including her liberal father's acceptance of their daughter's early marriage to a conservative family of lower social status reflected in this excerpt, for example:

M   They [Senem and her husband] got married out of love [*severek evlen-diler*], you know . . .

P   [interrupts her] Actually the truth is my family did not want him and his family did not want me [3–4 words unclear]. My late father, my mother's spouse [*eş*], was saying "I would never give my daughter to this man from Sivas" no, "from Kastamonu. I would sooner give my daughter to a Gypsy!" It was all empty big words [*buyuk konuştu*] though, he did give his daughter to the guy from Sivas . . . [pauses, 5 sec] . . . And his family did not want me either, because I was 'open' [*açık*, can mean liberal, open-minded, but also, a woman who does not cover her hair and body in a traditional way], I was the daughter of a simple [? unclear] family.

M   Very beautiful. Blonde and, like, very beautiful, you know.

P   And his family was very conservative [*mutassıp*: person of serious and sensitive traditionalist conviction, specifically concerning religious, social and gender issues]. Because I was an "open" girl.

M   And, of course, she raised five kids, has gone through lots of stress. And naturally, she has changed a little. But she was still doing all right con-sidering her condition . . . [unclear].

I   I don't understand. Her condition?

M   I mean, when Senem was a young girl, she was very beautiful, blonde, beautiful hair . . . and by now she has give birth five times. And there was also the stillborn baby.

The fashion in which Senem rushes to interrupt her mother and speak of the "truth" of the two families' unhappiness and the anger/disillusionment with which she remembers her father's "empty big words" clearly negate the mother's intended implication that the marriage was a happy one, out of a love relationship, and fully 'voluntary' in the modern sense of these words. When Senem insists that the families were in fact against the wed-ding, it can, of course, be interpreted to mean that the marriage was actually an independent act driven by love and decided by herself and her husband despite the families' disapproval. But her following remarks of frustration with her father and his empty words make it clear that she indeed would have wished for her father *not* to allow the marriage to take place. The point I am trying to drive home here is that in this story, Senem, her father, and the two families are all consenting to something they would not have normally wanted to do: she is getting married too young, outside of the norm (before her elder sister[17]), despite the wish of her father, and premaritally pregnant, to a man who has already "treated [her] like an animal" and who does not intend to love or respect her as a partner from a restrictive and traditional family that is drastically antagonistic to her cultural upbringing and does not particularly like or respect her ways of being. Something larger than the family's hopes and larger than a father's love and wishes has mobilized the decisions, that is, social power structures and models of meaning that predated Senem, her father, and the families.

Even though unspoken, the pattern and practice of *kaçırmak* is pervasive and sufficiently deep-rooted to have gained legal reality. It was as late as September 2004 that a revision of the Penal Code went through the Turkish parliament addressing the plight of Senem and many other women who suffered, like her, from the common problem of 'rape marriage.' When I interviewed Senem in August 2003, rapists still had a legal way of evading punishment in Turkey: offering to marry the woman they had raped. An Amnesty International (2004) report titled *Turkey: Women Confronting Family Violence* speaks of this problem and a proposed Penal Code revision draft that included abolishing the postponement of sentences for men who marry the women they abduct or rape. The report says,

> Men have used forced marriage to evade punishment for sexual assault, rape and abduction. The government has proposed removing from the draft new Penal Code the provision that has allowed men to escape or reduce their punishment for these crimes by marrying their victim. Contributing to the debate on removing this legal loophole, Minister for the Interior Abdulkadir Aksu reported in November 2003 that the law had allowed 546 men in 2002 and 163 men in the first four months of 2003 to receive reduced sentences after being convicted of "taking someone's virginity with the promise of marrying them"
>
> (p. 10)

The Amnesty International document tells also the story of a convicted rapist in the Black Sea region (Senem's family's place of origin), who "was released from custody and his sentence of nearly seven years' imprisonment was postponed after he agreed to marry the 14 year old girl he had raped" (2004, p. 10). The practice is in fact so deeply rooted in tradition that the new amendments (pushed forward thanks to pressure from women's rights groups and the European Commission) have faced deep resistance in various levels of the society, and the legal process has been severely bogged down. In April 2005, a BBC news headline reported that "Turkey has again postponed the introduction of a revamped penal code – just hours before it was due to come into force."[18] The depth of this influence is captured also in a report by the Turkish daily *Radikal* on October 23, 2003, which quotes Doğan Soyaslan, one of the members of the Justice Ministry Penal Code Sub-Commission (Adalet Bakanlığı Ceza Kanunu Alt Komisyonu) and a professor of Penal Law, as saying,

> No one marries someone who is not a virgin. If something like this [rape] happens to a family, then they will want the girl to marry the individual. To say otherwise is hypocritical. There are many men who would say, 'if someone kidnaps [*kaçırmak*] my sister and doesn't marry her I would kill him' . . . If I were a raped woman, I would marry the rapist. People get used to these things with time.[19]

It appears, however, that Senem did not quite "get used to these things with time," an idea further complicated by the distinctly suspicious circumstances of her child's disappearance, and the far-less-than-desirable treatment she received at home as a wife and mother of five children.[20] It is much less of a surprise, in the light of this new information then, to learn that the birth and mysterious disappearance of her rape child marks the beginning of a 'quest' for her (or the nucleus of a delusional system, as her clinician suggests – see the earlier discussion), and becomes a turning point in her psychotic illness. You may recall that her doctor confirmed that Senem never saw the body of the dead child, nor was she ever shown a grave where it was to have been buried, despite the fact that she originally saw the baby alive when he was just born. She (the clinician) said the following:

C   Ms. Senem sees her child alive after she gives birth. They told her that the baby has to stay in the incubator, but after going home, after two days, her mother-in-law said, "There is no child, forget your child, your child is dead." They didn't show her the corpse of her child, they didn't even show her her baby's grave. Therefore, this may be the source of her delusions . . .

You may also recall that Senem's mother at one point suggested that the infant was a stillbirth, to which Senem reacted rapidly and passionately, and then the mother withdrew from the argument. Even though we do not have concrete evidence, the apparently enigmatic fate of that infant may well be described in the words of Van Eck (2003), who writes in a section titled "Honor Killing of Newborn Babies" in his book on Turkish immigrants,

> Not only women and their seducers fall victim to honour killings. Other victims include newborn babies, generally children born out of wedlock. Because nobody must know of the child's existence, the baby is killed in secret to prevent injury to the family's *namus* [pride].

(p. 51)

Given the accounts of Senem's premarital pregnancy and her rape-marriage, her fantasies of a fate other than early and natural death for the

missing infant appear disturbingly more plausible than the paranoid ideations of a psychotic woman, even if the twinning and state-run kidnapping
accounts remain distinctly psychotic. Unaware of the full story surrounding
that pregnancy, the clinician said that she had recommended to the family
that they should at least take Senem and show her the baby's grave after
her discharge, believing that it would help bring a closure to her mourning.
As for me, however, I doubt whether such a grave ever existed, keeping in
mind the possibility that the infant might have been done away with through
adoption or more severe measures.

A new reading

It is justified now to reexamine some of the themes we have encountered, in
the light of this new information. Consider, for example, the pronouncedly
in-between status of the infant in question, well reflected in Senem's existential uncertainty of whether the boy shall be a blessed one or a cursed one. As
I have suggested, the actual scenario one could extract from these interviews
would be that when unmarried Senem became pregnant, she was under age.
That was why it was not possible for the families to manage the situation by
simply having her married to the young man. This explains, for example, the
involvement of an imam and the original shari'a-based *nikah* (as opposed
to an officially processed marriage). The imam had to be involved, because
in order for the father of the baby to escape the penalties of having impregnated an underage woman out of wedlock and for the family to save its
social face, she had to be married. As the mother said at one point, Senem
was legally married just about a week short of the legal age. Consider the
issues raised and the points of tension in the following conversation on the
theme of her giving birth to that baby:

M When [Senem] was a young girl, she was very beautiful, blond, beautiful
hair . . . and by now she has given birth 5 times. And there was also the
stillborn baby. She gave birth to it but it was dead . . .

P [interrupts the mother] The kid was born alive! [seems distressed, inhales
and exhales heavily]

M It died [note that she revises her conjugation from "was dead" to "died"].

P What do you mean? Wait a moment . . . [The mother and Senem talk
loudly at the same time, words unclear, mother backs down].

M It was born after 7 months [Again the two talk at the same time, 3–4
words unclear].

P Yeah, 7 months.

I [to Senem] What happened?

M [Starts to respond instead of Senem]

P [cuts the mother off, speaks loudly] Mom, can you be quiet please a little
bit? [brief pause] I apologize for saying that [to the mother].

M   But you were getting tired and for that reason I . . .

P   [cuts mother off again] I did not get tired, let me speak! We discussed this the other day with [my husband] too . . . I had pains, and it was a *Kandil* day, the birth day of our Prophet. We went to the hospital and the child was born exactly at 12 at noon . . . the child was born, and it was 4 thousand . . . 200 grams, I mean 4 kilos and 200 grams, despite the fact that it was born only after 7 months.

I   Hmm.

P   It was 53 centimeters, and apparently, as it was coming in reverse . . . doctors tried to remove it with forceps, his eyebrow, for instance, his eyebrow . . .

M   Nothing, nothing. There was nothing . . . Did you see the child?

P   Of course I did. She held it by the feet, shook it, and brought it and showed it to me . . . They told me that they were going to put the baby in an incubator. And they took it and put it into an incubator.

M   Yes, they did. But the child did not survive after that.

P   They put it into an incubator, but then later they told me that the child had died.

M   It died.

P   So they give a child to my husband, and he told me I buried that child, [he said] you are still thinking about it? But, he said, they gave that child to me [husband] and I took it and buried it. And my mother in law told me, we had arrived home [claps her hands once, quite loudly]. She said, "Your baby is dead. Don't think about it anymore, don't even whine and cry, it's over," and clapped her hands like this [demonstrates a clapping gesture that signifies the ending of an affair] "Your child is dead, the baby boy," she said. He was born well, though, and because he was coming in reverse all the doctors had gathered in the delivery room . . . and it was a miracle from Allah I mean, that this kid he was hardly born but he already had his eyes open and was looking around . . . they even told me so . . . and the midwife, the midwife who disinfected its belly . . . she lifted him by his legs and showed it to me, she told me, "Look, your child has this and that marks". . . and after that . . .one more day . . .

This conversation highlights quite clearly the great sense of frustration, pain, anger, confusion, and discrepancy in addition to the guilt, shame, and fear so fundamentally embedded in Senem's missing-child story. Shortly after this the mother and the daughter became involved in further argumentation over the truth of the baby's death, during which Senem persisted, saying "If he was dead, why didn't they show me his cold body? Why don't I know where he is even buried?" The mother, who did not have good answers to either question, simply insisted that the baby died later and was therefore buried and that there was no need to show her a dead baby and upset her even more.

Add to all this uncertainty the fact that Senem's pregnancy outside of marriage would have rendered the baby a product of sin and illegitimacy according to the shari'a laws, and then, while still pregnant, she procured the religious *nikah*; all of this recalls the theme of liminality encountered earlier. Consider also Senem's assertion (noted earlier) that, just like herself and her twin, this baby was also born at 12 o'clock. These new facts also lend new significance to her vision of being burned by villagers and their accusation that she has a stain, as well as her own obsession with burning objects with red color/stain. And it gave me a better understanding of another one of her visions, in which she saw her husband in the form a pig:

P   I didn't see my husband in the appearance of a human being.

I   What was he like, then?

P   He appeared to me as a pig.

I   Is that so. That must have been very scary for you.

P   I think so. Of course. Very scary . . . when he'd come to me, like this, on top of me, when he'd come on top of me, my hair would stand on its end, and [the thought of?] killing would run inside of me, can you imagine that?

The double bind

Senem explained at one point that the reason she had burned all that material on their balcony was "to break the spell": the spell that had made her have bizarre ideas and had made her husband look like a pig. In the larger picture, these references bring to light a new configuration of associations built around the early event cluster of her pregnancy, marriage, and child loss. Not long after telling me the rape story and her worries about that baby's fate, Senem explained how her anxieties eventually spilled over, so that she now worries also about her other children and their fate and whether they are believers (Muslims) or infidels. She shared with me the method she used to find that out: you rub dark fruit juice on your mouth's pallet and then press a piece of white paper against it – when you retrieve the paper you will find printed on it 'believer' or 'infidel.' When she ran the test on her children, it came out positive: the marks had printed the name of Allah, and so the children are fine. But with her firstborn, the missing child, the situation was more problematic. Senem (or, rather, her family) had been able to take care of the social, superficial stain of the events by marrying her rapist. But internally things were neither clearly cut nor easy to accept or 'get used to.' Senem, in other words, had been put in a terrible double bind by her 'culture': accept to marry her rapist or live with a stain, be a shame to her family, and perhaps never get married. So marrying her rapist 'resolved' the predicament by satisfying one side of the deal. The other side, however, did not go away, and she did not get used to it; she was too 'enlightened,' and her experience as a social subject too far shaped by the discourses of modernity and an open-minded family, to metabolize the problem by getting used to her status. From her account and her life story, the pregnancy and the baby that she had in her belly were the focal point: Was she a rape mother? Was that baby an infidel? Was he going to hell? Should she be burned at the stake in the village square? A major component of her psychotic delusions is explicable in relation to that core paradox. As she puts it so acutely, "I mean, a baby in the belly of a virgin mother?! A virgin mother having a baby! I took off from that point, and I did a lot of searching." In the absence of a socially endorsed model of reconciliation that would allow and alleviate her painful subjective experience, Senem's unsolvable paradox eventually worked its way down to her very sense of identity. She was engaged, one might say, in an impossible struggle demanding subjective legitimization from the unforgiving gaze of a traditional system of power and meaning that strictly othered her and accused her of impurity while denying her access even to her firstborn. It is in the light of this intolerable state of affairs then, that I understand her persistence, for example, that she was a virgin mother and that she repeatedly found *bismillahirrahmanirrahim* (Arab.: 'In the name of Allah, the merciful the compassionate,' a central signature of Islamic creed along with *la ilahe illallah*, 'no god but Allah') written on her pallet or, as her doctor related as a 'delusion of grandiosity,' the word *Allah* written on her body parts by varicose veins. It is possible to read many of her delusions as geared to resolving the internal discrepancy of a subject whose legitimacy is violated by the same system of meaning that makes her a subject.

Solution to a paradox

Not long after explaining her anxieties about her firstborn, Senem decided she could trust me and moved, without my soliciting, to disclose more about the 'answer' she had found to her internal impasse (the answer that she had said she could not disclose). She said the following:

P   Now, you see, Jesus was born without a father, one could perhaps start from that, but mine had a known father, a known mother, I mean that's why Jesus came to be Christian, he [my baby] came a believer [Muslim].

I   So you mean it was like Mary that you had had a baby while you were virgin?

P   Like Mary, except Mary hadn't been with anybody, that thing was done to her by Allah.

I   I see.

P   [Allah] had blessed her.

I   Right.

P   Ours was different. We were together [*beraber olduk*: had sex], I mean we were together and I felt his, excuse me, I felt his manhood water. So for that reason in our case there's a father, there's a mother. I mean our son wouldn't be Jesus, it would be a believer [*mumin*], and that's why I have done all that I have. I've been trying to find Jesus and Mary throughout my life.

I   OK.

P   And I found them too, and right here, in Istanbul.

I   You found Jesus and Mary?

P   Yes.

I   In Istanbul.

P   In Istanbul, yes. All the prophets that have come and gone that you could think of, all the believers, Muslims, they've all gathered in Istanbul.

I   What for?

P   It's like there's a life force that pulls them.

I   A force, hmm.

P   I mean there must be something that has called them [*cezbetmiş*]. Think about it, all the way from Erzincan [city in eastern Turkey] they get up and come to Istanbul . . . drops everything takes a 2,000-kilometer road and comes, moves to Istanbul!

I   I wonder what that power is? What is it that attracts them like that?

P   Like me, they are also searching for something, looking for an answer.

The solution she finds to the terrible and impossibly binding stigma attached to her and her pregnancy is ingenious: to turn it on its head so that bad becomes good, shame becomes glory, hatred becomes love, and pollution becomes purity. Not only does the baby not go to hell now, and not only does she not suffer from being stained, the child becomes a Muslim Jesus, a savior, and she a virgin mother. Let me be more specific. Consider the following statements made by Senem:

1.   "A virgin mother having a baby! I took off from that point, and I did a lot of searching."
2.   "[I was] like Mary, except Mary hadn't been with anybody, that thing was done to her by Allah."

When Senem searched to find a locally legitimate model to symbolize her personal experience, in other words, she found in the story of Mary a structure capable of giving an acceptable form to her predicament, her wishes, and the related discrepancies. At another point in the interview the parallel became quite explicit, when she spoke of a figure who was 'Jesus' but had a different name, and when I asked her how she knew that was actually Jesus, she replied as follows:

P   How do I know it's Jesus?! Because without marrying a father his mother has become pregnant!

Remember, however, that although Mary and Jesus are legitimate figures in religion, Jesus stands nonetheless for a traditionally despised enemy, the Christian world. But that was not an impossible problem to resolve. The difference that Mary's pregnancy was not attributed to a man, and thus, Jesus never ended up having a 'real' father is put to work by Senem to produce a significant distinction. Here is how Senem's argument is arranged:

3.   "Jesus was born without a father. One could perhaps start from that."
4.   "[But] in our case there's a father . . ."
5.   "For that reason, our son wouldn't be Jesus, he would be a believer."

To recap the logical structure then: just as Senem is like Mary, her son is like Jesus. But Jesus did not have an actual father, so he became a Christian, whereas Senem's son did have a father, so he became a Muslim, a Muslim messiah if you wish. You may recall our earlier discussion on the significance of the number 12 in Senem's discourse and the liminal 12th imam, the Muslim messiah. I will shortly come back to this idea to further examine its structural implications. But before doing so, let us look more closely into another interesting idea in the last excerpt concerning Istanbul.

As she told me shortly after that excerpt, Istanbul is a very special place, because "the world's heart is Istanbul, like the Quran's heart is Yaaseen." Her considering Yaaseen [the Quran's 36th surah] the heart of the Quran is a locally and culturally congruent idea. A hadith from the prophet of Islam says that "surely everything has a heart, and the heart of the Quran is *Yaaseen*." But the relationship can be traced to greater depth. Yaaseen [written as *Ys*] is one of the 29 surahs that begin with a cryptic code word, and in fact, it is a rare surah whose very name is one of those code words: *yaa* [letter *y*] and *seen* [letter *s*]. *Tafsir al-Jalalayn*, a well-respected Sunni exegesis of the Quran, simply says of this bizarre opening: "Allah knows best what He means by these."[21] According to Allamah Tabatabaii's seminal Shiite exegesis of the Quran, *Tafsir Al-mizan*, the Yaa-seen (Surah 36) should be understood as a continuation of the *Maryam* [Mary, Surah 19]. I should point out here that Senem also said in her interview that she had read many *tafsir* [Quranic exegesis] books in her quest. The running theme of Yaaseen is prophethood, and it consists of a series of arguments and warnings addressing the non-believers who deny the prophecy of Mohammad as a messenger of Allah. It is this theme of reasoning and warnings about a messenger that then links this surah to Maryam and the messiah, which also details the story of Mary and people's denial of her virgin pregnancy:

... [Mary] said, how shall I have a son, seeing that no man has touched me and nor have I been unchaste? [The Angel] said, Allah says it is easy to me, and we shall make him [your son] a sign to men ... so she conceived him and she withdrew with him to a remote place ... And she returned to her people with him ... they said Oh Mary, surely you have done a strange thing. Oh sister of Haroun, your father was not a bad man, nor was your mother an unchaste woman ...

(Surah 19, Ayahs 20–28)

The Quran, in other words, contained the answer for her dilemma in its network of associations. After all, this has been done before, and the last time around, the results were quite spectacular, and Mary's stain situation had turned out all good at the end.

Istanbul pilgrims

The world's heart is in Istanbul, says Senem, and the beating of that heart has attracted prophets and believers to travel to Istanbul from cities around Turkey, as far away as Erzincan. Incidentally, during my visits to Senem's ward I met a friend of hers, a young woman who had come all the way from Erzincan and in whom Senem had taken a special liking, according to the clinician. I have explained earlier how Bakırköy hospital is perhaps the best-known mental care hospital across the country and how people travel long distances to bring their loved ones to that hospital. Let us consider three other pieces of information that are relevant here: a piece of information from the clinician's interview, one from Senem's first interview, and then a closer examination of the term *cezbetmek*, which she used in the last quote to describe that which has brought all these 'believers' to Istanbul. Senem's doctor told me in her interview that Senem had a special interest in other patients, an interest that generally appeared in the form of taking care of them and speaking to them. Senem, according to the clinician, had suggested on a few occasions that certain patients (typically younger patients) were in fact her stolen children or their twins or were associated with them. In the case of the specific young woman from Erzincan just mentioned, for example, Senem claimed that the young patient was related to her lost child, and she paid special attention to that patient. Senem herself had the following to say about her fellow patients at Bakırköy:

P   [Addressing her mother] My God! Do you really think all these people in this hospital are crazy?! They are not! But most of them get treatment ... And I, I don't see myself as a crazy person either ... I just did not know what to use where ... once unstable, I became like this after that. We are exactly 42 people inside here. And you know, out of all these 42 people, maybe 3 to 4 of them are crazy. The rest are here because of too much intelligence, because they know too much ... There is music playing on

TV, for example, so we dance in a circle. And we see that all our feet move in sync. All with the same rhythm! We are playing name-city[22] with 6–7 people, and none of them makes a single mistake! They put their intelligence to work so really well . . . I mean, how can I call them crazy? They must be here because of the excess of their intelligence, something brings them here!

To put these two ideas together then, a number of people, at least some of whom are associated with her messiah-son, and most of whom are more intelligent than the average person, have traveled from various cities of the country to come to this hospital for a mysterious reason, "something brings them here," because they are very intelligent. The term she used to explain the idea that these believers are 'pulled' to Istanbul is *cezbetmek* (pronounced *jez-bet-mek*), a Turkified form of the Arabic infinitive *jadhabah*, which Turkish dictionaries normally translate as an attraction associated with the notions of 'charming,' 'beguiling,' or 'bewitching.' The term *cezb* (*jazb*, or *jadhb*, the noun form of *jadhabah*) refers to an important concept in Sufism. In Turkish Sufi terminology the word *meczub* (a person affected by *cezebeh*) is used to mean what might normally be translated as *crazy*, except for the technical connotation that the term implies a fatal attraction to Allah with the outcome of the loss of self [*nefs*] and the abandonment of the world of meanings [*fina*]. The term is employed with slightly varying nuances in different schools of Sufism, and it can have 'positive' (healthy, desirable state of selflessness) or 'negative' (associated with illness or possession) connotations from one school to another, but it always indicates a state that can safely be translated as 'madness.' Frembgen (1998), for example, describes the *majzub* as "a special, but many-faceted ecstatic who is at the wilder end of the sufi spectrum" (p. 144), and Werbner (2003) writes of a stage in the Sufi pilgrimage during which "the body and vital desiring soul are utterly purified," adding that

> this is called *jazba*, which means attraction, desire, feeling (*jazb*=sucking, hence he who is sucked in by God's love is *majzub*, a person who forgets himself and the world). It means being totally enveloped in the love, the *mahabbat* of God.
>
> (p. 203)

We can think here also of Katherine Ewing's (1998) chapter 'A *Majzub* and his Mother: The Place of Sainthood in a Family's Emotional Memory,' in which she presents an astute treatment of the local intricacies involved in the play of signifiers 'madness' and 'sainthood': "Though the *majzub* is explicitly associated with sainthood," she writes, "the same individual may in another setting be called *pagal* (mad) and be rendered powerless" (pp. 161–162).

The return of politics

What I propose is that a constellation of signifiers can be deciphered here representing an intricate process of social anchoring of private experience. I am suggesting, in other words, that the previous segments of semiotic, behavioral, and discursive investigation indicate the presence of an intricate body of associations mobilized to 'translate' and therefore to semiotically anchor Senem's experience of her mental illness within the cultural and political realms of meaning. You have noticed, in other words, that once we take the event cluster of rape–birth–marriage as the point of departure (as *her* point of departure at any rate), and once we consider the mechanism by which she has arrived at an answer to her quest (for meaning, for justice, and eventually for power), then the flustering question of internal discrepancy has found a plausible explanation. While the family's solution (marriage and possible sending away of the infant) took care of the social stigma and Senem's delusional ideas and novel associations addressed her painful problem cognitively, there are profoundly unraveling consequences that persist. Senem now has to deal with fundamental discrepancies that contaminate her very sense of being as a social subject to the most basic levels of experience. It is that contamination that I also experience, now as explicit discrepancy now as implicit paradox, as I try to cognize her accounts and fantasies, be that her private fantasies around marriage, pregnancy, and the nature of that infant or the collective ones ranging from neighborhood interactions to flag and nationalist love/hate and the village square witch hunt. The idea that the same semiotic pattern that is invoked in her rape pregnancy stretches all the way to the collective political arena is not just a conceptual product of interpretation, Senem made an explicit association between that account and politics. After she told me about her awareness that Jesus and Mary are both in Istanbul, the interview continued in this way:

I   So how did you find this out [Jesus and Mary being in Istanbul]?

P   Well I watch the TV regularly, I follow the news daily.

I   I see.

P   That's what it means "daily," I follow the politics, he is actually into politics.

I   Into politics?

P   Inside of it.

I   You mean, eh . . .

P   Jesus.

I   Jesus.

P   But his name is not Jesus.

I   Now how do you know that's him?

P   How do I know it's Jesus?! Because without marrying a father his mother has become pregnant!

I   I see.

P   And plus I saw him having some powers.

I   Where did you see that?

P   On TV.

I   On TV. Hmm, you mean . . .

P   When I want to see Jesus I turn my TV on, and then I see him I mean, in the news, it is sure to come on at some point during the day.

I   And what does he talk about?

P   Could be anything, could be politics, he himself is into politics in actuality.

Senem's doctor told me in her interview that Senem had developed a special interest in a TV series called *Sihirli Annem* (*My Magical Mother*)[23] and that she (Senem) believed her lost child or his twin was acting in that show. Unfortunately I do not know much about the show and its content, nor did I discuss that show with Senem, so I would not be able to provide a closer assessment of that interest. But I do know that the show's storyline is constructed around the theme of family relationships in a community of humans and *peri*s [*peri*: Pers., fairy, jinn]. More important than this detail, however, is the readiness with which Senem links her lost/stolen son-Jesus to Turkish politics (you may also remember that he was already associated with Nationalism by Senem, when we learned that he had been taken away at birth to ensure the survival of the Turkish nation [*Türklük*: Turkhood]). In a way we have now completed a full circle to find ourselves once again back with her own twin, Celal Bey, also a savior of Turkhood [*Türklük*]. Having embarked on a journey into Senem's more intimate world of associations, meanings and experiences, we now have another hero of 'Turkhood,' her son-twin, the Muslim messiah who has come to the world under birth circumstances as ambiguous as those of her own twin (the 12-o'clock birth and 'the placenta thing'), and whom she has never met, just as she has never met her own twin. This messiah is tightly associated with Senem herself in an immaculate conception, and like herself and her twin, he has been sacrificed to ensure the peace and survival of 'Turkhood.' We have come back again to the puzzling world of Turkish politics, but this time hopefully with a clearer idea of the integration of disparate pieces of the whole, from her twin brother to her twinned son, from the village square fire to her balcony fire, and again from Celal Bayar and the Republican politics to TV news and the current politics. Let me contextualize this in a more concrete way through a Turkish cultural/religious/political phenomenon known as the Nurcu movement.

Said Nursi and his legacy

Bediüzzaman Said Nursi, founder of the Nurcu Islamic revivalist movement in Turkey (*Nurcu* is pronounced *noor-joo* and literally means 'seeker
of light,' in addition to implying a follower of Nursi), was born in 1876,
witnessed the last decades of the Ottoman Empire and lived to witness
Ataturk and his Republican legacy well into the 20th century (d. 1960).
The Nurcu movement has been the subject of a number of analyses, and
its scope and significance stretches well beyond the limits of this text.[24] I
include a cursory reference to Nursi and his teachings here, because Senem
explicitly referred to that movement and because it provides a set of references that 'bring out' the relationship among a number of apparently
unrelated aspects of Senem's discourse. In addition to its central claim of
a return to Islamic moralities and cleansing of the spirit, and a Messianic
philosophy emphasizing the approaching end of the world and the pending
return of a Messiah, one of the defining features of the Nurcu movement
is its strongly pro-Western political stance, even though it has consis-
tently claimed itself uninterested in politics. According to Mardin's (1989)
analyses, Said Nursi himself, for example, considered communism a manifestation of the Antichrist, and he was a supporter of Turkey's early (1952)
NATO membership and its participation in the Korean war (1950–1953).
He was a devout believer of sciences and modernity. He differed from
Ataturk, however, in that he believed and advocated a seamless merging
of Islam and modernity, whereas for Ataturk such convergence was not as
simple. Kedourie (1999) writes of the *Nurcu* movement that "this particular form of collective action was actually of benefit to the Turkish state, for
rather than secretly undermining its stability, Nursi evidently encouraged
both Muslim faith and loyalty to the established political order" (p. 57).
In fact Said Nursi went so far with his ideas of a possible convergence
of 'East' and 'West' as to coin the phrase "Muslim Christian,' a phrase
applied directly in the context of his Messianic teaching:

> When the Messiah (PUH)[25] appears in the future, a community which
> Said Nursi calls "Muslim Christians" will emerge, who "will work to
> unite the true religion of Jesus (PUH) with the reality of Islam."[26]

The significance of this constellation to Senem's world seems clear
enough. I work our way to these similarities again through an example
from current Turkey, in the works of a prolific pop author who by most
accounts (including his own) is a contemporary Nurcu writer, and whose
works address for the most part lower social groups and less educated
believers (as opposed, for instance, to prominent Nurcu figures such as
Fethullah Gülen, whose discourse targets higher socioeconomic and more
educated circles).

Harun Yahya

Contemporary writer Harun Yahya[27] is a prolific producer of Nurcu texts with strongly apocalyptic and messianic content. While Said Nursi set his 'enemy' to be the 'irreligion' of communism, however, Yahya has singled out the 'materialism of Darwinism' and the evolutionary theory as the antichrist, a strategic adaptation that led to both a serious internal inconsistency and an intricate network of conspiracy theories not so distant from Senem's world. In fact one encounters in Yahya's texts a range of ideas that are strikingly relevant to Senem's story. Yahya puts great emphasis on his university education and scientific training, though his audience is basically the uneducated masses who are devout believers simultaneously of Islam, Turkish Nationalism, and the notions of 'modernity' and science. Even though Senem does not make any direct references to him, it is quite plausible that Yahya would be one of the 'scholarly' writers she so proudly insists to have read, as opposed to her 'unsophisticated' neighbors who, she noted, read texts by 'uneducated' imams and preachers.

Harun Yahya typically pays due respect to Said Nursi in his texts and locates himself explicitly within that tradition where (Western) science, Islam, and Turkish nationalism converge. My attention was first caught by his books when they were being sold in great numbers on a street vending cart in Istanbul. My eye was directed to their highly colorful and 'flashy' appearance. Most of Yahya's books have large-font cover writings embossed, in gold, and typically against a background of images loaded with strong yellows, reds, and blues. The two books that I bought on the spot were *Kıyamet Alametleri* (*Sings of the Doomsday*) and *Ahir Zaman ve Dabbetü'l-Arz* (*End of the World and the Dabbet-ul-Arz*[28]). True to the hallmark spirit of the Nurcu movement, Yahya is not only prolific, but also a seriously pro-media figure. The books that I bought contain references to Yahya's other works: hundreds of books, CDs, websites, and audiovisual publications, mostly concerned with issues of the end of the world, the returning messiah, and how to recognize him, death and the netherworld, and to be sure, Ataturk, Turkish history, Turkish nationalism, and, of course, creationism.[29] Among his numerous titles, two are of special interest to my analysis here: a book titled *Maryam [Mary] An Exemplary Muslim Woman* (Yahya, 1999a) that asserts Mary, mother of Jesus, is "the ideal Muslim woman" (p. 12), and another, titled *The Glad Tidings of the Messiah* (Yahya, 1999b), dedicated to the story of Jesus and the argument that close ties link the Muslim community and this chosen one.

Mary, the exemplary Muslim woman

The first book (Yahya, 1999a) is dedicated to the stories of Mary (Maryam) and her son, Jesus (Isa), constructed mainly around two of the Quran's surahs that we have already encountered, that is, 'Mary' (Surah 19, Maryam], and 'The Family of Imran' (Surah 3, Aal-i Imran). "Maryam," writes Yahya, withdrew from her society so that she could be in a psychologically peaceful environment and away from the hurtful behavior of people who could not comprehend her miraculous situation. . . Allah told her *not to grieve* and bestowed His grace and protection upon her. No doubt, there was much wisdom in this advice, just as there was in Maryam's withdrawal to a distant place."

(1999a, pp. 34–35, original emphasis)

The problem for Mary, he says, was that "her people could not comprehend Allah's miracle, and thus they accused her of indecency and slandered her . . . [even though] she had an immaculate character and always protected her modesty " (Yahya, 1999a, p. 49). Maryam thus refused to speak to people, and remained only in touch with Allah, and so "Allah made both of them [mother and the son] superior to all other people" (Yahya, 1999a, p. 52). Mary became "the role model for all Muslim women" through her "impeccable" life style, and as a result Allah solved her "difficulty trial." He "gave her a solution, supported her with His Grace," and "turned all hardship into goodness and beauty" (Yahya, 1999a, p. 52). Allah, in other words, reversed the very source of her difficulties into a source of pride and glory. The trope sounds familiar.

Jesus, the Muslim messiah

"Although God reveals the narratives of many Prophets," writes Yahya (1999b), "Jesus, whom God supported with superior wisdom, is set apart," and in fact he goes far enough to make the unorthodox claim (following Said Nursi) that the Quran actually "indicates strongly his [Jesus's] second coming" (p. 11). The book's eighth chapter is titled 'Badiuzzaman Said Nursi Delivered The Good News of Jesus's Second Coming to Muslims' (Yahya, 1999b, pp. 168–185). We read in that chapter that when Jesus returns not many people will be able to 'recognize' him for who he really is, except for a limited few who are 'close to him.' Yahya 'proves' this argument by bringing excerpts from Nursi's letter in which he wrote,

> When Jesus (PUH) comes, it is not necessary that everyone should know him to be the true Jesus. His elect and those close to him will recognize him through the light of belief. It will not be self-evident so that everyone will recognize him.
>
> (1999b, p. 173)

Still more intriguingly relevant to Senem's story of her quest and discovery, in that same chapter (again with reference to Nursi's ideas) Yahya claims that "Jesus will rule with the law of Islam and [will] adhere to the Quran" (Yahya, 1999b, p. 175). And as to how this might be, he explains, "the religion of Christianity will be purified . . . and will be transformed into

Islam" (Yahya, 1999b, p. 175), and furthermore, "following the Quran, the collective personality of Christianity will be in the rank of the follower, and Islam, in that of leader" (p. 178).

Nurcu discourse and Senem's story

It is possible indeed to trace more ideas in the Nurcu tradition that resonate with bits and pieces of Senem's beliefs. Given the earlier excerpts I provided of Senem's views on her rape baby, his conception, the social anxieties caused by that whole process, and the eventual solution of that problem, the relevance of a discourse such as that of Said Nursi or of Harun Yahya should be self-evident. It is obviously easier for Senem to make an example of Mary's success story within a tradition that has already solved the problem of Mary being a Christian figure for her, a tradition that while remaining strongly Islamist and Turkish nationalist, is also able to call Mary 'the ideal Muslim woman.' That same tradition also makes it easier to have an immaculate conception and give birth to a son who is a messiah right in the middle of a traditional Turkish community, because not only does it accept the existence of a messiah, but it also constructs the messiah as an 'empty' signifier that can be filled by Senem's own son. More significantly, the Nurcu Messiah is Muslim too, just as Senem has configured her lost-yet-present child. Built on the Nurcu discourse, Harun Yahya's model gives Senem not only a way of 'recognizing' her child as Jesus but also a means of resolving the issue that Jesus represents Christianity.

I should point out that the messianic content of the Nurcu belief system is at odds with the mainstream Sunni model, for whom the messianic strategy is a point of divergence, for example, from the Shiite model – recall as well my earlier discussion on this point, emphasizing the significance of the number 12 in Senem's discourse and the fact that the Shiite's 12th imam is a messianic figure.

In addition to surf-structural correlations, the Nurcu belief system also corresponds in a number of less evident ways with Senem's experience of her predicament. These less explicit patterns are perhaps even more important, because they not only anchor her experience in a specific discourse (Nurcu) but also give her the means of linking all that to the larger social and political network of meanings. Let me be more specific. Not long into the first interview, for instance, Senem spoke to me of her neighbors. She explained that she was teaching some of them how to read and write better and how to help their own children with their schoolwork. You may also remember her and her twin's roles as teachers in various occasions. Incidentally, 'teaching' is considered an important task within the Nurcu discourse, and a great amount of it is done through local community gatherings, to which there are a number of references in Senem's interviews. Immediately associating with this teaching role she spoke then of some of her neighbors who try to impose their own opinions on her (remember also earlier discussion of 'freedom of thought' and the practice of tolerance. Tolerance of all creeds and opinions is considered a central slogan of the Nurcu movement). These are the same neighbors she had described as illiterate and unaware of what they read. When I asked Senem to tell me what exactly she meant, it became clear that she was speaking of religious groupings. She was, in other words, speaking about neighbors who were believers in a 'traditionalist' view of Islam as opposed to a 'modern' one. This, of course, is a slightly different variant of the 'modern/traditional' division, in the sense that both sides of her division are believers of a return to Islam, so that in a broader sense they would both be categorized as 'traditional.' But the nuances on which she bases her division are significant and accurate. You recall that Senem said the following earlier:

P   I don't . . . [3-sec pause] I don't trust my neighbors . . . because each and every one of them has a husband, with beards like that . . . they do not do their daily prayers right. I told them, something like, we are such and such with a certain [political] party . . . they wear baggy trousers and gowns but . . . I was seeing who was coming in and out of their house, I mean not . . . they are blaming everybody. Everybody . . . me for instance . . . I mean, we have weekly Quran gatherings, we go and all, then they read, I don't, so then they don't like you . . . whatever I do is wrong according to them. As long as what I do is right according to me, let it be wrong according to you, what do I care!

The people with beards and baggy pants stand for the 'traditionalist' camp. Unlike the 'modernist' Senem, who reads the Turkish Quran, they read it in Arabic, and because she cannot do so along with them, she is marginalized in their circles:

P   I mean, I . . . how should I put it . . . I read . . . read the Turkish translation of the Quran. So naturally, uh, my books are very different from theirs . . .

    or

P   [T]hey recite [the Quran] in Arabic, I don't, so then they don't like me.

You may also recall it was at this point that she added, "I read books written by academicians, university graduates. They, however, they read books from here and there, about tea and hazelnuts." The circles she is referring to are associated with a highly political brand of Islam linked in turn to a highly political man, Necmettin Erbakan.[30] In fact she makes these links more explicit later on, when she says the following:

P   I mean, for example, they say this is Allah, that is the Prophet. Allah forgive my language. They say this is that, that is that. And they are trying to make you believe all that too. Why should I believe that? I have eyes, I can see everything myself, I follow the news . . . on TV, I follow the daily programs all the time.

I   Now, when you say, this is Allah, that is the Prophet, how do you mean, what does that mean?

P   They worship, I mean, how can I say it, they worship Necmettin Erbakan. They see him as God. Also, the person beside him, the one closest to him, they gave him the nickname 'the Prophet.' Meaning he is the Prophet, we should obey them . . . stuff like that . . . But then you have the Nurcus . . .

So the neighbors, the ones who don't respect 'freedom of thought,' who are not well educated, who read the Arabic Quran, and who want to impose their views on her, are followers of Necmettin Erbakan, whose ideas she then describes as a 'rival' to those of Said Nursi. Necmettin (pronounced *nej-met-tin*) Erbakan was the founder of a number of political parties, all of which were eventually dismantled by the Turkish state/military because of their strong Islamist stance. His first party, the National Order Party (Milli Nizam Partisi) was dissolved in 1971 following an ultimatum from the military. The military coup of the 1980 is also often associated to the political activities mobilized by Erbakan, and his National Salvation Party (Milli Selâmet Partisi). Following that coup Erbakan's party was also banned, and he himself was deprived of political activities for a period of 7 years. Later, however, Erbakan's third political party, Refah Partisi (Welfare Party) gave him the opportunity in 1996 to become famous as Turkey's first 'Islamist' prime minister of the Republican era, through a coalition government. This, of course, did not last long either, once again with the military's intervention he had to step down and his Welfare Party was dismantled as well. As even this cursory introduction highlights, Erbakan stands for a brand of highly political Islam in secular Turkey, in contrast not only to the secular spirit of the Republic but also to the apparently nonpolitical stance of the Nurcu community. Erbakan and his followers advocate a 'return' to what they consider traditional readings of Islam, which they identify as Ottoman Islam. The Nurcu school claims to be both highly pro-modern and nonpolitical, even though the Nurcu community also advocates a return to the Quran and Islamic principles. The subtle yet pragmatically significant differences between these schools of thought are reproduced in Senem's daily reality, as in the differences she describes between herself and her neighbors. When I asked Senem at one point to tell me who the *Nurcu* are, she said the following:

P   They are the owners of STV [seh-tee-vee],[31] *Samanyolu* TV [tee-vee], and the Flash TV [tee-vee]. . .

I   Ah.

P   And a lot more things . . . in Turkey they have a lot . . .

M There you see, by constantly watching that television she picked them and put them in her head. For example, how come I don't know any of them . . .?

P What should I do? Whoever calls himself Allah is shown on television . . . the channels, they recite Quran on the television. Am I wrong? The Samanyolu TV belongs to the Nurcus, the Flash TV belongs to the Nurcus, to Fethullah Gülen. The other, uhh, Kanal D belongs to Necmeddin Erbakan, they are competing with each other . . .

Fethullah Gülen, whom she here sets against Necmeddin Erbakan, is considered the contemporary leader of the Nurcu community (sometimes referred to as neo-Nurcu). Gülen is a reclusive leader who lives in the United States (another witness to the Nurcus's pro-Western stance) and leads his followers through a wide range of media communications, from the Internet and newspapers to recorded audio taped and videotapes, radio and TV stations, books, and pamphlets. Senem's reference to the Nurcus's extensive media ownership was in fact quite accurate, and it continues to be the case.[32] The Nurcu concept is so identified with the 'West' that when I told Senem that I didn't know who they were, she was surprised and did not seem to believe me; she insisted, "I bet you already know them!" and when I persisted, "No I don't know them," she said, "They are in the United States . . .," implying 'since you are familiar with the West, then you *must* know who they are.' Senem then told me a bit more about 'what kind of people' the Nurcus are:

P [T]hey are, they are not like the followers of Necmeddin Erbakan. They are always clean [shaven], properly groomed. And they don't wear that stuff like robes and baggy pants and all that . . . they are dressed normally, like us. I mean, they are more progressive-minded . . . I have some books published by them, because they always publish books written by academics. They publish the works of people who are professors or experts in their fields. I buy their books, I have lots of those. I buy them and I read them. They have monthly magazines too, I buy those too.

M You see what I mean, then all these readings give her too much brains . . .

The Nurcu are "progressive-minded," "like us." "Us," of course, was a reference to herself, whom she had already established as a progressive, intelligent, and well-read woman, and to me, who represented the Western educational and medical systems. Here Senem is once again locating herself as a well-read person who has studied scientifically sound 'modern' texts. She is constituting herself as a subject within a socially accepted and politically endorsed discourse of 'modernity,' 'progress,' and 'science,' of shaving the beards as Westerners do and wearing Western-style clothes, as opposed to growing beards as they would in the Eastern tradition and wearing baggy pants as they did during the Ottoman period. This is only a basic instance of the way a range of otherwise divergent concepts from religion, science, and politics are arranged together into a pattern that proves useful for giving sense and expression to Senem's experiences, while also affording her a voice as a legitimate social subject. Not only does she recognize herself in progressive and noble signifiers such as Celal Bayar, who fought for freedom of thought and Turkish Nationalism and who, incidentally, was the exceptional Turkish president who showed a positive regard toward Said Nursi (as reflected in their correspondences; see Çelik, 2005), but she is simultaneously able to locate and identify herself as a special and valuable subject within a discourse that offered her the Muslim Mary and Jesus signifiers. By 'calling on' the Nurcu discursive ensemble, in other words, Senem is procuring herself a specific multidimensional semiotic constellation in which to legitimately exist as a subject and to reclaim a status of value and power for herself and her lost son, statuses which she is so deeply deprived of in her daily life within the community and underneath her husband. That uniquely formulated 'constellation' actually allows her to achieve another fascinating semiotic reversal: it allows her to live her very illness in terms of a struggle for 'freedom of thought' and against patriarchy in its various forms, from social and religious fundamentalism to domestic paternalism. It is in that same formulation, for example, that her madness is so often referred to as a result of the overabundance of intelligence, as in the preceding excerpt, in which the mother complained, "You see what I mean, then all these readings give her too much brains [and she goes crazy]."

Let me produce further evidence for this reading. In that same line of semiotic mobilization, Senem makes the ironic turn of attributing her illness to a hoja (*hoca*: local religious healer; see the earlier discussion). This I call ironic, because in an unusual move, here the religious and spiritual figure is set up to represent not the healing magic of faith, but the destructive power of black magic. She spoke of a hoja who would come to Quran recital gatherings, in these terms:

P   He was coming to my mother's place and doing stuff . . . He made all these religious gestures [*töbe estağfürüllah çekiyordu*]. Tea was brewed, women prepared tea . . . it was very crowded. Members of his followers came from other places as well. First of all . . . that man . . . is the man of . . . He is a man of Necmeddin Erbakan. And if he is not telling his name openly, in my opinion he's up to no good . . . Why is he keeping his name secret? Is he some kind of a criminal or something? You keep talking about him all the time, and you go to his meetings, but he is hiding his name. He should tell his name openly, my name is such-and-such, with courage and pride . . . and after that they go and recite one or two things, prayers, that we already do by ourselves. And after that they say bad things about Ataturk, or the president, or whatever, the prime minister.

Ataturk at the time fought like lions with courage and pride, with a gun in his hand for years, without sleeping on a bed in peace. And why? So that the Turkish nation can reach a certain point, isn't it so? And still they keep demeaning him. They are able to behave and talk like this in this country thanks to the order that was established by Ataturk . . . isn't it so?

I   Why are they demeaning Ataturk? How do they demean him?

P   I mean, they say things like "they buried Ataturk in the soil but the earth did not accept him and threw him out." Also, they call him devil . . . Can such a thing be? Ataturk, may God forgive what I say, Ataturk left them the kind of good things that their own parents could leave them . . . to say the least. He left them the right, the opportunity to live freely, naturally. And I see very often here and there, they break the head, the bust of Ataturk in school gardens.

I   Is that so?

P   Yes, I saw it, I saw it with my own eyes.

I   Why do they do such things?

P   For what reason? They call Ataturk devil.

I   Why??

P   Because Ataturk gave the women their rights.

M   I have not heard such things from anybody before . . . [she goes on to deny the breaking of Ataturk's busts or the insults].

What has just happened is that Senem has once again made clear the distinction between herself and the 'traditionalist' ignorant followers of Erbakan's anti-secular (i.e., political) Islam. She identifies with Ataturk, and women's freedom, while her illness is caused by a hoja who is "a man of Erbakan's," who hates Ataturk, and who recites the Arabic Quran, a hoja who makes a veritable icon for the rigid tradition that has marginalized her, deemed her stained, and taken her liberties away from her. The theme resembles closely the village square event. Like the village crowd, here is a group of people whom Senem declares in earlier excerpts are less educated and more traditional and who have marginalized and outcast Senem because she cannot recite the Quran in Arabic, the same group of people whom she has been teaching how to read and write Turkish. Significantly, when her mother objects to her remarks, saying, "I have never heard such things from anybody!" Senem retorts quickly:

P   Yes, I have heard it, Mother, I have! I . . . long time ago, when I was in that place, was it like that? When I was in a village . . . when . . . I wasn't like this [unclear] . . . In this country nobody considers anybody a friend, all because of these brotherhoods [*tarikatlar*]!

We do not have any 'hard' evidence for this, but I cannot help associating these remarks about a village story with her village square vision, where she was being burned despite the fact that she was a friend of the people. In these apparently disjointed remarks, uttered with a sense of urgency, Senem seems to be trying to convince her mother that she has witnessed an extraordinary event that proves a problem with the society. For me the remarks harked back to her village square vision, especially because there were no other mentions of any other village-related events in her account. Also significant here is the fact that she then links that same thread of traditional masses destroying their own 'friends' (as they did, we have learned, to Ataturk's busts, Celal Bayar, Celal Bey, or Senem herself) directly to her illness: I was struck by that traditionalist hoja. Note also that here she claims 'brotherhoods' are the reason people reject their own friends, and remember that hojas are quite strongly associated with those brotherhoods in Turkey.

Senem's mother then objects, saying that by speaking negatively of those people Senem is insulting people who have "read" (*okuyan adamlar*: people who read), referring to those with a traditional religious education. Senem says in response:

P   Well, those who [can] read [*okuyan adamlar*] should be educated properly . . . And also . . . those . . . hojas are like this . . . let's say you [to me] were a hoja, I cannot simply pass by your side like this, I would be struck [*çarpılırım*]. For example, I . . . that's the door there, right? And I walk through here like this, and you are the hoja, now I came here, like this [demonstrates] . . . I offer you your tea like this . . . and then I am supposed to walk away backwards like this . . .

I   Why?

P   [Otherwise] he would strike me!

I   What do you mean?

P   One is not supposed to turn one's back to hojas and walk away.

I   Who would strike?

P   The hoja!

I   Would he, really?

P   Well, apparently he would, judging from my situation [laughs, with an air of sarcasm and/or resentment].

M   Now all you are doing is demeaning hojas. Now talk about other things with the doctor, why don't you talk about something else?

I   So you mean this is what happened to you? Are you saying a hoja struck you?

P   Yeah, I think that's what happened.

Senem was struck mad by a man of religion, because she 'turned her back on him.' This scenario, of course, does not make a lot of local sense, as far as I know. It is not an acceptable behavior for a hoja to strike people mad simply because they have turned their back after having served him his tea. What this means, then, is that the problem between Senem and the hoja is more serious at some level, more meaningful. You may recall from earlier excerpts that the same hoja had also refused to tell her his name. At one point she complained to her mother, "You [plural] are always saying his name, but he wouldn't even tell me his name." The hoja, in other words, is known and familiar to the mother and the rest of the crowd, but not to Senem, this woman of freedom who has turned her back on him. Not only conventionally but also based on the specific details in Senem's discourse, the hoja stands here to represent a certain group of people and a certain concept.

Earlier when I had asked the family if they had any plans to visit a hoja (that was before I knew any of these details), the mother had said that she was thinking about it. Senem, however, had insisted quite anxiously, "Mother! Please stop thinking that. I am doing well now, and if you go to a hoja, you know, I would be here [hospital] for one more year. Please don't think about that." And she then had continued to explain, "the stuff that the hoja would read to me, I myself have already read 40 times . . . and plus, imagine he would read that in reverse!" Reading in reverse here is a strong, if implicit, reference to the fact that the hoja would read the prayers in Arabic, which is written from right to left, rather than left to right like modern Turkish. The hoja who can cause Senem to remain in hospital for another year, in other words, stands for a group of people of a certain level of sophistication and a specific sociopolitical milieu. Once again, the hoja signifier highlights Senem's sense of marginality and otherness, but also once again, it does much more than that. This cause of her madness represents multiple layers of signification: politically he signifies Necmeddin Erbakan, religiously he signifies militant Islamic fundamentalism, socially he signifies ignorance, culturally he signifies tradition, and privately he signifies an abusive husband – a matrix network that then allows Senem the subject to religiously signify Said Nursi, to politically signify Secularism, to socially signify enlightenment, to culturally signify modernism, and to privately signify rebellion, dignity, and 'freedom of thought.' For all practical means and purposes, Senem's intricate semiotic apparatus is a successful attempt at procuring a suitable sense of identity for a subject in distress, mind you, an 'insane' identity.

Another achievement of this semiotic maneuver that deserves attention is the identification of violence (rightly, I may add) with a space where political patriotism, religious morality, cultural paternalism and domestic abuse converge to deprive Senem not only of selecting a lifestyle of her choice and a sense of respect, but indeed of a *voice* even, with which to speak her deprivation as a victim. The same notion that is conveyed so succinctly through the 'Quran wrapped in the flag' imagery is also staged (indeed 'lived') through this larger scale and more detailed semiotic conglomerate in which a range of smaller preexisting arrangements are put together to form a unique map that would correspond to her unique lifeworld. In the magical realm of semiotic transformations, the violence she has lived privately is duly deposited back in those whom she holds responsible for it, ranging from the fundamentalist priest who puts a spell on her because she has turned her back on him to the state that puts her in jail because she has painted the flag in the color of intelligence and life or because she has used her freedom of thought, to the ignorant masses who burn her on the stake because she has a stain on her, and, perhaps most important of all, to the cruel man at the root of all this wretchedness, the husband who aptly turns into a pig on top of her.

Thanks to her ability as a 'subject' to produce new semiotic links and associative conglomerates, Senem has arrived at a narrative that affords her the selecting and tying together concepts and associative patterns from various domains of meaning in her environment. As a result she now has a working delusional system wherein otherwise divergent characters and concepts are 'logically' associated: the husband has become a pig under the spell of the hoja, and to break that spell she has to burn a red-ink Quran, a red Turkish flag, a red means of entrance (doorknob), and last but not least a stained hygiene cloth . . . This is the amazing story of a 37-year-old woman who has arrived to subvert and put to work, through semiotic appropriation, the very headquarters of paternalism, the Bakırköy mental hospital and its thinking men, toward gaining a 'voice' with which to speak to resist and to defend her dignity and freedom of thought, even if that is the crazy voice of a madwoman. "Look now," she said, "I burnt all that stuff, and now again he looks like a human to me!"

Notes

1 This is a very specific meaning of the word *imam*, referring to a number of divine-selected descendants of the family of Mohammad the Prophet who are endowed by superhuman qualities including direct relationship with Allah and innocence from error or sins.
2 I have spoken elsewhere of the prominent relationship between purity and fire in Sufi meaning system. See, for example, the case of Emel.
3 Remember that Turkish third-person pronoun *O* can refer to *he*, *she*, or *it*.
4 *Zaman*, "Gülen's Warning," October 29, 2005. Available online: http://www.zaman.com/?bl=columnists&alt=&trh=20051113&hn=25850.
5 *Zaman*, "TITLE," August 6, 2014. Available online: http://www.todayszaman.com/national_31-officers-suspended-as-several-referred-to-court-for-questioning_354754.html.
6 Gareth Jones, "Bombing Throws Spotlight on Turkey's Deep State," Reuters, November 18, 2005. Available online: http://today.reuters.co.uk/news/newsArticle.aspx?type=reutersEdge&storyID=2005–11–18T103511Z_01_NOA838082_RTRUKOC_0_ANALYSIS-TURKEY.xml.
7 Stephen Kinzer, "In Turkey, the Novelist as Lightning Rod," *New York Times*, October 23, 2005. Available online: http://www.nytimes.com/2005/10/23/weekinreview/23word.html.
8 Sarah Rainsford, "'Deep State Plot' Grips Turkey," BBC News, February 4, 2008. Available online: http://news.bbc.co.uk/1/hi/world/europe/7225889.stm.

9   *Tafseer Al-Mizan*, aka *Al-Mizan fi tafsiri'l-Qur'an*, is one of the main Shiia Muslim exegeses of the Quran. The 20-volume book is written by Allamah Sayyid Muhammad Husayn Tabataba'i in Arabic. An English translation of the book is available online: http://www.almizan.org/.

10 From question and answer by Almizan publisher, available online at http://www.almizan.org/new/8Q&A.asp.

11 Ben Arnoldy and Owais Tohid, "Why Koran Is Such a Hot Button," *Christian Science Monitor*, May 17, 2005. See also section under heading "*Quran Translation*" in the *Routledge Encyclopedia of Translation Studies* for relevant information (Baker & Malmkjaer, 1998, p. 200f.).

12 The Turkish flag is held in such respect that in July 2002 a case was filed by the Istanbul chief public prosecutor against Hulya Avşar, a famous actress, singer, and talk-show host, for insulting the Turkish flag. The following text, directly from a July 27, 2002, news article in the *Turkish Daily News Online* (www.turkishdailynews.com.tr), captures the sensitivity of this issue:

> The indictment against Avşar and her co-defendants was brought in connection with an episode of the Hülya Avşar Show that aired on a private television channel on April 27. A video of the episode reviewed by the Prosecutor's Office showed Avsar trampling on balloons that were printed with a moon and star, the main elements of the Turkish flag. Several newspapers had also printed photos showing Avşar, the host of the variety show, kicking the balloons as she saw her guests on and off of the programme. The indictment also named the Izmir firm Lateksan, the producers of the balloons, Ali Bitis, owner of an Istanbul toy shop who had placed the order for the balloons, and Fazli Altintaş, employee at Bitiş's shop where the balloons were sold. Sony Music and Art Inc. Assistant Manager Karin Kazeryan, who bought the balloons, and Med Production Television and Film Inc. representative Mine Ozturk, who granted permission for the balloons to be used on the program, were also mentioned in the indictment.

13 This sense is reflected, for example, in the word *hastane* (hospital; pronounced *hass-taa-neh*) or in the lingering, infamous 19th-century description of Turkey as *Avrupanın hasta adamı*, 'the sick man of Europe' (e.g., Çırakman, 2002; Swallow, 1973). Etymologically, *hasta* comes from the Persian *khasteh*, which can mean 'tired' or, in its more archaic use, 'injured.'

14 As in English, for example, in Turkish the phrase 'a sick man' could be used to speak of a man with the flu or a man with a deranged mind.

15 The taboo sense of this expression was so strong that my Turkish transcriber in Canada was unable to write it down. The transcriber had left a blank space for the phrase 'bloody rag' (*kanlı* [. . .] *affedersiniz*), and I had to review the tape to find and fill in the blank. Of course, both recording quality and speech clarity were flawless.

16 "I married at too young an age . . . I mean right now I have children who are older than me!" We also know from the family interview that when she got married she was just below the legal age, and the clinician also spoke of her getting married "quite young."

17 The urgent and inevitable nature of this marriage is also reflected in the locally uncommon fact that Senem got married earlier than her significantly older sister did. In her own words, "I got married, got kids and all, but my older sister [*ablam*] got married after that. I mean, she gave her turn to us, to me I mean."

18 Jonny Dymond, "Analysis: Turkish Penal Reform Woes," BBC News, April 1, 2005. Available online: http://news.bbc.co.uk/2/hi/europe/4400993.stm.

19 Quoted and translated in Amnesty International (2004, p. 15).

20 It was confirmed during the family interview that the husband has a drinking problem, gambles too much, spends his nights out till the late-morning hours, and travels regularly. In Senem's own words, "my husband did not do, you know, I mean he did not show me a woman's worth, to be frank . . . I mean he hanged out with other women, he drank alcohol and he gambled. He did all kinds of shit." These comments were reluctantly confirmed by Senem's mother as well, though she insisted that because the husband provides regularly and because the children need a family, Senem ought to be able to forgive him and return to her life and her responsibilities as the mother of the family.

21 An online version of *Tafsir Al-Jalalayn* is accessible here: http://www.altafsir.com/Al-Jalalayn.asp.

22 *Isim-şehir*, a pen-and-paper game based on one's knowledge of Turkish words including names of cities, persons, objects, animals, plants, and so on.

23 "Sihirli Annem," in *Wikipedia*. Available online: http://tr.wikipedia.org/wiki/Sihirli_Annem.

24 Interested readers would be referred to a wonderful book by Şerif Mardin (1989) titled *Religion and Social Change in Modern Turkey: The Case of Bediüzzaman Said Nursi*.

25 'PUH' is a convention used in Islamic texts when referring to prophets, stands for 'Peace Upon Him.'

26 Mustafa Abu Sway, "Said Nursi and the People of the Book" (paper presented at the Fourth International Symposium on Bediuzzaman Said Nursi, Istanbul, September 20–22, 1998). Available online: http://www.saidnursi.com/symposium/s21e.html.

27 Harun Yahya is a pen name used by Adnan Oktar. I continue to use this name, however, because it is the more publicly known name for the author.

28 *Dabbet-ul-Arz* is a Quranic term generally used without translation. Etymologically it could mean 'that which crosses the earth with difficulty.' See, for example, a discussion of the meaning of this term here: http://www.endoftimes.net/02signsofdoomsday10.html.

29 See, for example, one of his English websites: http://www.harunyahya.com/.

30 Necmettin Erbakan (1926–2011), politician and academic, served as the prime minister of Turkey from 1996 to 1997.

31 She pronounces STV as *Seh-Tee-Vee*, delivering a hybrid of Turkish *se* (S) and English *tee-vee* pronunciations. This is not an altogether uncommon practice, and as my Turkish assistant pointed out, it is typically used to locate the speaker somewhere 'in between' those who would use the fully English pronunciation (*Ess-Tee-Vee*) and those who would say it all in Turkish (*Seh-Teh-Veh*).

32 The following website, for example, provides links to some media websites belonging to the Nurcu community: http://nurcu.org (last accessed August 15, 2014). See also the website of Nurcu author Huran Yahya, mentioned in note 29, as well as Joshua Hendrick's 2011 informative report titled *Media Wars and the Gulen Factor in the New Turkey*, accessible through the website of the Middle East Research and Information Project (MERIP): http://www.merip.org/mer/mer260/media-wars-gulen-factor-new-turkey (last accessed August 29, 2014).

5 Love, loss, and a language for madness

The story of Ahmet

This chapter is dedicated to the psychotic illness of a 27-year-old man whom I call Ahmet. I met Ahmet in the Balıklı Rum Hastanesı in Istanbul shortly after his arrival there (Balıklı Rum Hospital, aka *baloukli* or *valoukli* [Grk.]). I had two separate interviews with Ahmet, once 4 days after his arrival at the hospital, and then about 2 weeks later, shortly before his release. Ahmet was a young restless man from an upper-class family according to Turkish standards as I discerned from complaints that his parents would not let him spend time sailing in the Mediterranean or let him drive his car and go on a vacation by himself and not least because he was hospitalized in a private hospital such as Balıklı Rum. These constitute clear indices of an upper socioeconomic status in Turkish society today. But my classification falters because Ahmet's family is a Turkish immigrant family of the working class in Switzerland where they live, and they are not counted among the higher socioeconomic echelons there. Like many other families in their situation, Ahmet's family had come back to Istanbul to take care of their son's illness. And like many families in their situation, they had selected the Balıklı Rum Hospital because it is private and because it has a reputation of knowing better how to deal with European Turks: Turks who have grown up in Europe. The 'private' part is attractive because the hospital is a (much) more luxurious establishment than state-run establishments such as Bakırköy. It is cleaner, has shinier equipment, offers private rooms with showers and Television sets, affords better paid, better rested, and better groomed staff, offers psychological consultation and even creative art therapy, and not the least of all, though generally unspoken, it has a strong Western 'spirit' to it, a spirit that goes beyond money and luxury, or technology and the practice of psychiatry, or even the 'modern impersonality' of the atmosphere. This spirit comes with the very land on which the hospital is made (see the following discussion). For all these reasons, Balikli, listed under 'foreign hospitals' in Istanbul (in the same sense, of course, that Istanbul Jewish and Armenian hospitals are also listed as 'foreign' hospitals[1]), is preferred by the richer and more 'modern' families with sick members, especially those who have Greek ancestry or, like Ahmet's family, who have lived in Europe.

The analyses presented in this chapter are based on interviews, as follows. As I mentioned earlier, I had two separate occasions to speak to Ahmet: shortly (4 days) after his arrival, and shortly (1 day) before his departure. In addition, I had a chance to speak to Ahmet's parents in an interview that could be broken into three segments both dynamically and content-wise: a first segment with his mother alone, then a second part with both his mother and his father, and finally a last segment where his uncle, the mother's brother who had organized Ahmet's hospitalization, joined in to throw his authoritative weight into the discourse. Furthermore, I have used content from three separate interviews with clinicians in Ahmet's ward. Two of the three interviews are with the clinicians, a psychologist and a psychiatrist, who worked with Ahmet (when I interviewed the psychologist, Ahmet's psychiatrist was on vacation for a week or so), and in the third interview I focused on the ward itself with a clinician who had introduced the establishment to me.

Ahmet

Ahmet is a 27-year-old man, brought to the hospital all the way from Switzerland because of what his family describes as his being "obsessed." His is a very specific obsession: he is "love obsessed," he argues and his mother and his father agree. This interpretation is not explicitly shared by the medical staff at Balıklı Rum, it is too modern a place for that discourse to be endorsed formally. But even there the story is well known and not altogether rejected. The clinicians speak of his unrequited love as something that 'triggered' a psychotic reaction, rather than being the cause of his psychosis. According to one of his clinicians, he is diseased, and his disease is schizophrenia: "we first thought he was depressed . . . now we believe he has schizophrenia." The second clinician largely agrees, even though she adds that Ahmet's childhood difficulties and later social problems such as failure to adjust to the European culture are also important factors.

Ahmet himself does not find the psychiatric diagnosis or discourse convincing as far as I could tell, nor was the family's accounting for his state altered by the hospital's medical view, although they were in agreement that social difficulties did not help their child. The same clinician who said "he has schizophrenia" also complained, "I tried to explain that these hallucinations are symptoms of schizophrenia but I am not sure that they [the patient and his family] completely understood." She has a point. The family has a list made of ideas about what Ahmet's problem is, and 'schizophrenia' is not close to the top of that list. As for Ahmet himself, let me quote what he thought of his problems in the first interview, four days after his admission:

Interviewer (I)   So, do you know why you are here?

Patient (P)   I know. I am here because I am distressed [*rahatsız*].

I   What is your distress [what makes you distressed]?

P   As I said I have a psychological distress.

I   What kind, what kind of a distress is that?

P   When I say distress, I mean majnun [*mecnun*], I mean constantly my mind, my brain sticks to that woman [*takılıyor*]. Because it's stuck with that woman, because I haven't gotten that *emanet*[2] back, it's always like this, and meanwhile it is tough. And it comes and goes. I mean if I could just see her and talk with her myself for one or two hours, I'm sure I would find peace [*huzura kavuşurum*]. Whether she loves me or if she doesn't, either way at least I can have my freedom [*özgürlük*] back for myself. So long as I don't have my *emanet*, my freedom will never be realized [*hiçbir zaman özgurlüğüm doğmaz*].

And here's how he put it in the second interview, the day before he was released:

I   So remind me, why did you come here?

P   Well they said there was a hospital here.

I   Who said?

P   My uncle, my uncle said.

I   OK, your uncle.

P   He said I know a place. He said if you want, maybe you can stay there for a while.

I   Why? What was bothering you?

P   There was a woman that distressed me.

I   In Switzerland?

P   In Switzerland. Somehow it wasn't fated [*nasip olmadı*], we couldn't be together [*kavuşamadik*: we could not unite]. It mixed me up good . . .

I   I see, because of that . . .

P   Because of love.

I   Are you better now?

P   But there are still hang-ups [*takıntılar*]. I mean when I think [about it] it makes me uncomfortable.

I   Bothers you. So what will you do after you are released?

P   I would go to her. Now she has mixed things up. I left an *emanet* with her, it would be good if she gives that *emanet* back. Then I can perceive the world normally again.

I   What *emanet* is that?

P   There was a pack of cigarettes, and there were 10 francs.

We will come back to investigate the fascinating content of these excerpts and many similar statements by Ahmet. For now, however, these excerpts serve to demonstrate his own perception of his illness, an understanding that remains basically unchanged after a few weeks of hospitalization and exposure to the deeply medical discourse, treatment, and social-behavioral organization of the private hospital.

Ahmet was born in Eastern Turkey to a Kurdish family. His experience of growing up in Turkey was that of an outsider, because when he went to school he could not speak Turkish; his mother tongue was Kurdish. He was born in a village around Erzurum.[3] His difficulties started, he says, when he moved to Erzurum to go to school at the age of 6 or 7. He learned how to read and write Turkish "by force," and he continued in that Turkish school until Grade 5, after which he moved with his family to live the life of a 'Turkish immigrant' in Switzerland where his father had been working for a number of years. After a series of moves, the family finally settled in a small town outside of Zurich, and Ahmet continued and finished his education, in German, in a vocational school. "But I never actually started a career," he insists. Instead, he took a series of short-lasting jobs, from a publishing house to textile industry and restaurant work to finally a job at the same factory as his father, "anyway, it went like that for 8–9 years, until I met a Swiss woman." That meeting was about 1.5 years ago, the same time his difficulties started.

Ahmet's account of his travel to Switzerland is replete with details, names of people, names of places, kinds of houses and apartments they lived in, and even the names and types of buildings near the homes they had, as if a strong sense of nostalgia colors his earliest memories of traveling to Switzerland to join his father, or as if these markers somehow give him a sense of located-ness, dreams of an anchor in a night of storms. Ahmet's father insisted that Ahmet was his dearest child; he liked him more than the other three children. For Ahmet, however, not many things could be farther from reality: "My father left us 25 years ago and went to Europe," he says, and he constantly spoke of his father's death wish for him or, even more frightening, his father's shadowy relatives following him around with the plan of eventually killing him. Ahmet is the second child of four; his older brother is married and has his own family, works in a factory and lives in a town not far from the suburbs of Zurich, where Ahmet lives with the rest of the family. The two younger siblings are girls, one a university student and the other a high school student. Ahmet's mother is a housewife, and his father is now retired; he used to work in a factory in Zurich where he had been employed ever since he left his family when Ahmet was only 1 or 2 years old.

Ahmet's behavior and his appearance do not contain anything specifically striking beyond a sense of overall gloom, apart from the fact that he seemed anxious in the first interview. He experienced his anxiety in terms of a desire to leave the hospital where he feels "repressed"; he wanted to step outside "to get some fresh air." The staff, however, was against that idea; it was out of question. Ahmet linked a sense of inability to speak to this experience of suffocation and repression. "Oh," he said, "if we were outside, I'm sure I would really feel like talking much more! But I feel so pressed here, I don't really feel like talking." When I suggested, after another similar remark, that if he was too tired we could stop our conversation, he nonetheless continued to speak, implicitly refraining from ending the interview, and so we continued. That urgent need for leaving the hospital seemed less pronounced during the second interview, which took place in one of the doctors' office, perhaps because he had already received the good news that he was to leave the hospital the following day, or perhaps also as a result of his treatment. He was leaving the hospital after about 19 days, during which he had received nine treatments of electroconvulsive therapy and a heavy dose of antipsychotics, injected into him for the first few days and continuing now in the form of pills that he swallows voluntarily, including Akineton (biperiden; "3 pills a day," i.e., 6 mg?), Largactil (chlorpromazine, which he was no longer), Zyprexa (olanzapine, 10 mg), and Norodol (haloperidol, 15 mg). The last day before Ahmet's release, the psychiatrist in charge of him spoke of the hospitalization and treatment effect in these terms:

Clinician (C)   Right now the patient does not remember anything. Before he had auditory hallucinations, now those have disappeared. The delusions have disappeared, there are no delusional persecution references. The patient does not remember any of these. The idea that he had a relationship with Satan or Allah seems comical to him now. He doesn't remember such things. People are not following him anymore. When he first came his affect was very limited and his expressiveness was very low, but now he is much better, for example, he can now smile when he hears humor; and his thoughts are more straightforward, he answers questions asked, gives meaningful answers. Apart from that, the grandiosity delusions, persecution references, he does not speak of those anymore. That is to say the patient has responded to the treatment very well. So tomorrow he will get out.

I   Tomorrow he will leave for sure?

C   Tomorrow . . . he is supposed to leave, yes, because his ECT finished yesterday. He got his nine ECTs, yesterday it finished. I believe he will leave us tomorrow.

You may have noticed a special emphasis in the clinician's discourse on 'not remembering' or 'forgetting' as a sign of recovery. It is worth pointing out in passing that 'forgetting' has in fact an old history as a practical treatment and a sign of recovery, specifically to those suffering from various forms of love pathologies, including love madness. Ahmet himself emphasizes a number of times: "[I]f I could only forget her, then I'd be fine. I would go get myself another woman, and everything will be normal again." In Lacanian terms or specifically Kristevan semiotic accounts of subject development, a child's initiation into the symbolic order can also be understood as a 'forgetting' or at least a way of 'replacing' the lost object with signs, and the comfort of a symbolic system, an 'identity.' I will come back to Kriteva in this analysis, because I find her theory of melancholia specifically relevant to the case in hand. But here I point out this issue of 'forgetting' for another reason, to speak of a common understanding of the effect of ECT treatments: it works because it makes the patients forget. They do not just forget the person they loved; indeed, they "forget their symptoms." As to how true this is, I would not be a good judge. Of the patients that I interviewed, all with the exception of one had received varying numbers of ECT treatments. I encountered this systematic use of ECTs regularly in Bakırköy and Balıklı Rum hospitals, though significantly less in ÇAPA. So far as my interviews reflected, even though often after their treatment sessions the patients showed significant signs of confusion and an air of compliance, the symptoms were hardly 'forgotten.' Ahmet's story is a good case in hand. I had interviews with him both before and after his treatments, and in both interviews he spoke of the exact same delusional ideas, although in the second interview he was less anxious or less able to act out his anxiety. Ahmet is not an exceptional patient in receiving such heavy treatment package of ECTs and psychotropics. This heavy-handed treatment is part of what makes such private institutions 'efficient' apparently and thus are even more popular among a more 'modernized' clientele. Despite the systematic use of ECT, one may say the treatment package in public hospitals such as Bakırköy is somewhat 'lighter,' chemically at least, due to the heavy cost of medications.

Balıklı Rum Hastanesi

Balıklı is a large establishment in Istanbul with a wide range of medical services advertised on a large sign at the main entrance of the hospital. Publicly it is best known as a rehabilitation facility. When the media wish to address drinking and driving, for example, they come and speak to the head of the Anatolia clinic at the Balıklı Rum Hospital, because he is most qualified to speak to drugs and their abuse, specifically alcohol. The hospital's oldest service segment has been its alcohol abuse program. Now the hospital provides treatments for all drug abuse problems: I even met a man who was hospitalized for marijuana addiction, which, my guide explained to me, is much more dangerous than people think and "really needs serious treatment." Even though the psychiatric clinic has a building of its own, I was told that the borders are permeable, since drug abusers may show psychotic symptoms and psychotic patients may have substance abuse comorbidities. The psychiatric ward consists of two floors of a building marked 'Anatolia 2,' with the top floor for women and the ground for men. Each floor can accommodate roughly 30 patients. There are altogether four 'Anatolia' clinics in Balıklı Rum: Anatolia 1 for alcohol dependence, Anatolia 2 is psychiatry, Anatolia 3 for substance abuse, and Anatolia 4 provides service to chronic substance abusers who can afford to stay over longer periods. The psychiatry clinic is also involved, along with Bakırköy hospital, in an important nationwide substance abuse research program known as AMATEM.[4]

As legend has it, one hot summer day a young prince found an old man dying with thirst outside the city of Constantinople. As he started to search for water to save the old man, the prince heard a female voice call him to a bubbling spring, and the old man was thus saved from death. The voice, it was reckoned later, was that of Virgin Mary, and the young man, who was to become the Byzantine emperor Leo II, decided to dedicate a shrine to Virgin Mary on that spot. When later, in the 11th century, the strange illness of another Byzantine emperor, Justinian, was also healed by the water from that same spring, he built a big church on that spot that became famed as 'the Life Giving Spring.' To this day Greek and local Christians have kept alive the ritual of visiting the life-giving spring, a spring that is no longer really a spring (if ever it was). The area is now called by a Turkish title 'Balıklı Rum' (though the Greek continue to refer to it as Zoodochus Pege, the Life-Giving Spring) and includes the lands on which the hospital is built as well as a nearby Greek Orthodox church by the same name (*Balıklı Rum Kilisesi*: Balıklı Rum Church). The term *balıklı rum* signifies an association both with fish (*balık*), the powerful symbol of Christ in Greek culture, and with Christian Europe at large, represented by the word *Rum* (Roman or Greek[5]). The more recent history of the hospital (and the church, the Balıklı establishment at large) is also of interest here, because due to its strong symbolic function it has been a locus of tension between Islam and Christianity, on one hand, and Turkish and Greek nationalisms, on the other. Establishments such as Balikli Rum, traditionally run by minority communities and their own institutions, were gradually taken away in the post-Ataturk era to be run by the state through Islamic endowment foundations known as *vakıf*.

As even my cursory examination here reflects, Balıklı Rum Hospital holds a special if implicit place as an iconic point of religious, political, and historic reference. It is in the continuation of this story that one can understand why this hospital, whose entire staff and clientele are Turkish and in whose yard is a grand statue of Ataturk with the attribution "the greatest man in the world," is listed nonetheless under 'foreign hospitals' of Istanbul. Not unlike Ahmet and the many other Turks who are now citizens of or at least long-term residents in Europe, Balikli Rum has the place of another within: it is Turkish yet Greek, Muslim yet Christian. Although lands have always marked what is home and what is not, Balikli Rum has the unusual status of being a piece of land in exile. The trivial fact that the buildings inside the hospital are all named 'Anatolia' is in fact a telling sign: Anatolia 1, Anatolia 2, and so on. Consider this sequence:

Inside Istanbul, there is a hospital that is marked as 'foreign' and is called 'Rum' to strengthen its foreignness, its 'Westernness.' Now inside that hospital, every single building is called Anatolia, a term with direct reference to things 'Eastern' [Grk. *Anatoli*: East], specifically the Asian part of Turkey, land-wise and heritage-wise. But the buildings are not called *Anadolu* (Anatolia in Turkish), they are called *Anatolia*. When on my arrival one clinician kindly showed me around the establishment and its buildings, I made the mistake of referring to them by the Turkish term *Anadolu*. She was quite quick to correct me: "No, not Anadolu! It's *Anatolia*," while spreading a smile over a fleeting shade of discomfort. So the 'language' in which these buildings are named 'Eastern' *was* important, and that language, it so happens, is Greek, Western. This quality of juxtaposing inner and outer, this lack of finality, this continuous chain of others within and exiles at home, I suggest is inviting to people such as Ahmet or his family. It gives a person such as Ahmet comfort, perhaps, to be in a place that, like himself, has never arrived at integrating fully within one or another symbolic order, one or another nationality, one or another language, one or another religion – one or another system of power and meaning. Let us look now more closely at Ahmet's story, where it will become apparent what I mean by the similarities.

Tracing the story

I was introduced to Ahmet by the ward's psychologist as "a doctor from Canada here to work with us." Once we were left to ourselves I made it clear that I did not 'work' with the hospital and that I had no allegiance to the medical establishment; the information I collected was not to be shared with the staff and would be used only for my research. Ahmet was weary of the tape recorder at first and questioned why I had to record the interview. I explained to him that I was interviewing many people, and this was the best way for me to accurately remember the content of all those interviews. "All right, I understand," he said finally, seeming convinced that I was harmless. He raised the same concern at the beginning of the second interview, though not as seriously, and he ultimately decided that the recording would be acceptable again. This was one indication to me that he did not have a clear memory of our earlier interview (ECTs do make people forget *some* things after all). After I reminded him of the earlier interview, he was then curious to learn what we had or had not spoken about the first time. Every once in a while he would ask me, "Didn't I talk about this last time?" But in either case, he was convinced for a second time that he did not have a problem with me recording the session, and so we started again. I start my analysis with the first interview; however, given the utter similarity of the contents in the two interviews, I have not found the need to 'locate' each utterance in one or another exchange and therefore treat the two as one continuous text.

Once the tape recording question was resolved, Ahmet was quick to open up and started the conversation in response to my question, "Tell me about yourself":

P   Now . . . my place of birth is ***, Erzurum's district . . . Erzurum's village. I went to school in Erzurum until fifth grade. Because I left the village late, when I was 7–8 years of age, and because I didn't know Turkish, I went to a Turkish class from first grade to fifth grade.

In this basic introduction Ahmet has already located his sense of identity in an experience of 'otherness.' In his first years of social life outside the family, in other words, he already had to live the life of an outsider who does not speak the language, not to mention the great social tension implied in the fact of being a Kurdish village boy in a Turkish city school. Here is how the conversation continued:

I   You didn't speak Turkish?
P   I didn't speak Turkish. We used to speak Kurdish.
I   I see. You spoke Kurdish.
P   Yeah. I mean for a while we had a good deal of beatings from the teachers. That's the way it is anyway. So, I speak Kurdish, but people around me are all Turks. I'm the only Kurd. Then they taught me the alphabet, by force and by beating me. My grades were very weak because I couldn't understand, so I had a real hard time. They treated me like I was lazy [*tembel*]. After that I got the fifth-grade diploma with a lot of effort. And then, our father was in a foreign country himself, in the Switzerland state. He's worked there for 25 long years. And then he came back, he took our papers and we brought them to the consulate. We got the permission to exit and our visa from the consulate . . .

As disturbing as the forced alphabet imagery is, it was not just the question of language that would have made life difficult for Ahmet in that elementary school. Two overwhelmingly powerful forces would have been part of the institutional ideology and would have influenced the young child's sense of being, undermining him as a social subject in Turkey: nationalism and modernity. While the Turkish Nationalist discourse, so strongly present in the practice and social-behavioral organization of Turkish schools, would ensure this young child grows with a problematic stance toward his Kurdish background, the modernist ideology makes it clear for the village boy that it is his duty to move as far as possible from the unsophisticated Eastern Anatolian village culture, toward a more 'civilized' mentality and lifestyle.

Two unmistakable themes of loneliness and otherness, on one hand, and inefficiency and wastefulness, on the other, can also be discerned in this early excerpt from Ahmet. When he speaks of his father, Ahmet puts it this way: "[O]ur father too was in a foreign country himself." The terms *too* and *himself* here are not coincidental figures of speech, they were employed to convey a thematic similarity that runs throughout the story: father and son, they were both in 'foreign' lands. After what one might arguably consider an early trauma of losing his father, the second traumatic event seems to have brought home the point still more explicitly, that Ahmet is alone and that little support is to be expected from the environment.

Two of those early experiences are still present in the discourse that surrounds Ahmet as a subject, they have gone all the way to Switzerland and come back once again to Turkey to be pronounced now by his father, on one hand, and his psychiatrist, on the other: that he is lazy and that he is not intelligent. His father's idea was quite explicit: "[I]f he wasn't lazy, if he was interested in getting out and working or do something positive, he wouldn't be having all the problems that he has." This, of course, is not a rare reaction to children with mental illnesses, specifically on behalf of fathers in Turkey. I was told about the prevalence of this idea by a psychologist in Turkey, and I personally encountered this suggestion a number of times. The idea that Ahmet was not intelligent became explicit in the interview with the psychiatrist, who even suggested Ahmet might be mentally retarded, despite the fact that no tests have ever been made, and despite the difficult educational trajectory he had survived. The clinician put it in these words:

I   What do you know about his life?

C   Well, at the age of 14 they have taken him from Erzurum to Istanbul, I mean, to Zurich[6]. His father was a laborer there, now he is retired. They are four siblings, his mother and father and the four siblings live together. Our patient has studied till . . . eh, he finished secondary school. At school he had difficulties. Maybe his mental capacity is deficient. We don't know, we haven't had a test of his intelligence. But his mental capacity is likely defective, because apparently there, in Zurich, he had a hard time learning the language too. He studied for 4 years and he didn't go very far. After leaving the school he had to take more language courses. I mean right now despite all that and despite the fact that he stayed there for such a long time he still doesn't speak the language very well, that's what they say.

We have already seen what Ahmet's own understanding of his not doing well at school is, and the way he links that with the questions both of identity and of language. It would be imprudent of me to evaluate the clinician's judgment, but neither her presentation of Ahmet's mental 'deficiency' nor the evidence she presented for that struck me as sound, specifically given my knowledge of his difficult childhood of forced language learning and otherness, a story to which both clinicians appeared impervious. Indeed, Ahmet never was either a good Turk or a good Swiss. He was apparently deprived of the luxury of a 'final' symbolic system, in other words, to which to defer his identity as a social subject. The 'father' was absent in a number of senses from his life, and language never seems to have developed to fully 'format' him or cut him away from the agonies of being between worlds: a Kurdish Turk and a Turkish Swiss, or is that a Turkish Kurd and a Kurdish Swiss . . . "I don't speak any of the languages now, I can't speak anything! See what they have done to me, brother?"

As he continues to put his life story in a nutshell for me Ahmet piles up in front of me fragments of names and places that represent an effort at locating himself somewhere in his memory. But simultaneously, and likely counterproductively, they also seem to produce a formless heap of memory fragments, places, faces, and names that do not have any real or concrete place any longer, either in reality or even in that moment of his existence as a remembering subject. Consider the rest of his account:

P   . . . We got the permission to exit and our visa from the consulate. Later on when we went abroad there was a woman called *** who worked there in the *** factory, my father knew her, so we stayed with her for 3–4 months. Then I started school. This was outside the town of ***, near Zurich. We stayed with them over there for a while. It was not bad, we got along all right [that lady] was nice to us. Then we moved to our neighbors' place, Mr. and Mrs. ***, and stayed with them for about 2 months. Then we had to move away again because their aunt, aunt ***, was coming to stay with them, so we went to their neighbor's place. Someone they knew, his name was ***. We stayed there for 2–3 months, and then moved to another place behind the church, where we stayed for one-and-a-half months. Then my parents began searching for another place and they found one next to our old neighbors Mr. and Mrs. ***. That's the way it continued for a while. Then later I started a vocational school in ***, though I didn't actually start any career after that. I was around 16 then. After school ended I started to work in a printing house, I worked there for a while. Then I worked in *** textile workshop, then in a restaurant, and a glass factory. So, 8–9 years went on like that. Anyway, then there I met a lady, a Swiss lady. Mind you I had met a German lady before that too, but later on I met the Swiss lady. We talked, we were nice to each other, chatted . . . now in the restaurant, over there, there was one other person. He was Satan [*Şeytan*] . . . Roki.

I   What was that?

P   Roki. He himself was Satan I mean. I mean a nation worshiping Satan I mean. I mean the Christian world.

I   I see.

"That is all," as he often puts it. As far as Ahmet intended, this account captures his whole life, all the way up to the moment when it all 'changed' because he met the Swiss woman and Satan. Besides the intriguing array of names and location references, this brief account captures also a strong sense of unsettledness. The account contains more details about the first year or so of the family's trajectory of moves and transitory residences than the more than fifteen following years altogether. The bulk of what he has kept in mind, what he deems significant to recount, and by inference, what he selects to ground his sense of identity on, is a collection of transitory moments, faces, and locations, rather than the family, the town near Zurich where they have lived for the past 15 years, or even the village where he was born. And then there is his new self, the one who encountered 'the Swiss woman,' and Satan himself, in the Christian world where they worship the devil. Ahmet's basically coherent discourse suddenly takes a distinct turn for less understandable and more 'psychotic,' as soon as he gets to the encounter with the Swiss woman. Here's how he continues:

P   Well, from there on unhappiness [*kırgınçlık*: resentment, disappointment] fell between us. There was a glass of whiskey in his hand. He threw one, I got out of there. We worked together in our friend's work place and he [or she][7] . . . He mixed up our nights and our days. Probably took [it/him/her] to [his/her] bed I wonder, or took [it/him/her] to [his/her] room, I don't know . . . I wanted one thing from her . . . Either you love me or you don't love me. She wouldn't say either. If she had, then I wouldn't have gone after her. Because I left an *emanet* with her I need to get that *emanet* back from herself, *from herself* [emphasizes]. Because of the fact that she doesn't love me. I got out of the hospital, then basically things repeated. I fell into the hands of doctors and I couldn't get away to my freedom. I went to psychologists I went to doctors, to prison.

The shift in clarity and flow of Ahmet's discourse is striking, though not surprising given the importance of this love story to his conceptualization of his psychotic experiences. Unhappiness falls between him and the beloved in the form of Roki, Satan himself impersonating a fellow factory worker. Satan enters as the archrival, and the story then culminates in an unfinished business with *emanet*. I have decided to use the original term, *emanet*, because I was unable to find an English word that would represent the notion. None of the common Turkish–English dictionary definitions of *emanet* – usually 'trust,' 'deposit,' or 'escrow' – capture the sense of the term. Literally, an *emanet* is an object left to a person, or, rather, entrusted to a person, and for which that person is thus charged with a certain responsibility. But *emanet* does not have to be an 'object.' When you borrow a book out of a library, that book is an *emanet* with you, and when your neighbor who is traveling to Mecca leaves his family to your custody, that family is an *emanet* with you. But one's children are also *emanets* left to one by Allah, as is one's 'life' an *emanet* from Allah. To complicate things, there is also the Quranic usage of the word [Arab. *amanah*], referring to something vague and open to interpretations, something that is simultaneously a terrible load and a privilege. We will come back to this.

The scenario Ahmet hinted at in the last excerpt, and obsessively repeated throughout both interviews, is a conglomerate construct. That is, it is possible to unpack the elements of this scenario into a number of distinct themes borrowed from local meaning systems and fused into each other. Similar to the cases discussed earlier, Ahmet's scenario constitutes a significant point of semiotic and discursive reference, and as such, important features can be distinguished in it. First, it is densely packed with indices and references: discrete cultural, religious, political, and historical allusions that converge to form what may best be described as a semiotic knot. Secondly, the so-called knot helps construct a semiotic space in which the subject can claim experiences in locally familiar terms, assuring that private experience and collective meaning systems interface at some level. Finally, the construct represents a central story or theme built around a deeply disconcerting abyss or lack, as if to cover, to deny, or to give an outer 'form' to the formless irrationality and chaos that is the hallmark of their 'experience.' What the psychotic subject experiences is an existential horror, not simply of disorder but, more accurately, of annihilation. These 'knots' represent the subjects' efforts to cover and patch over the gap that lies behind and between any two signifiers, the gap that the 'nonpsychotic' manage to deny or ignore regularly and with ease. While nonpsychotic social subjects are able to assume or imagine the existence of a central logos from where to then build away webs of signification; the unfortunate psychotic patients I interviewed generally seemed unable to tell themselves that basic starting lie. It is in that sense of 'experience' that I speak of a central disconcerting experience: an 'experience' only insofar as one could ever symbolize that which is born of the encounter of the experiencing subject with the abyss that underlies the subject's very experience of being. When the psychotic look at the center of their existence they only see the horror of nonbeing, and they are unable to delude themselves with a fantastic 'beginning point' to which they would then attach the loose end of their thread of meaning, as nonpsychotic subjects do. It is therefore in an effort to cope with the destructive force of that absence, I am suggesting, that the patients I interviewed have all opted for such conglomerate narratives, made of bits and pieces of meaning systems and fragments of various maps. While theoretically this process is not necessarily different from the 'normal' process of subjectivity, the main difference lies perhaps in the final success of it. Whereas non-psychotic subjects are able to select and adjust their working meaning systems to fit and match those of their environments (i.e., local common sense), the psychotic subject falls short of that final 'capacity' of putting together fragments of meaning using the blueprints of collectively endorsed common sense.

Let me clarify the previous abstract remarks through a closer examination of Ahmet's world. I will start with a few more instances in which he tries to put into words his disturbing sense of a lacking object, and of a universe fundamentally 'flawed' as a result of that which is missing – an 'experience' he tries to capture through a simple semiotic structure: that a woman he loved has something of his and she refuses to give that back. Not long after the introduction of the *emanet*, Ahmet said the following to me:

P: We went here and there then we went on leave, but I couldn't get a reply. The lady was no good for me. She constantly caused pain, pain after pain; she made me run after her. Since then I've been after the *emanet* I left with her. If I can get it back from her then maybe . . .

I   Hmm.

P   What I am trying to say is that maybe millions of people know about it, but, of course, the son of Adam [*insanoğlu*: fr. Arab. *bani Adam*] cannot understand this. But when I get it back, then everything will become normal. That's the way it seems to me. I mean the world will return to its normal standard state, it seems to me. Because as long as I don't have that *emanet* back, I can never find peace of mind.

I   Hmm.

P   Also, the people around me have also started to become restless. The environment, people that I know, and strangers, they are mixed [into each other: *birbirine karıştı*]. Whatever I do, I can neither see, nor find my *emanet*. That's all.

On another occasion when he brought up the *emanet* issue again, I tried, naively, to become more direct about that question and to see if I could get a clearer idea of what it was about:

I   There is one thing that I can't quite understand and I want to ask you. You said if you get your *emanet* back, then everything will be straightened out.

P   Yes everything will be straightened out.

I   How will everything be straightened out?

P   It all becomes normal then. In my view everything will become normal. But as long as she has not given it back, nothing will come to its normal state.

I   Yes, for example, what will become normal?

P   Life, life will become normal

I   For instance?

P   For example, life, people always do things together, they talk, work, struggle together. There are factories, I go back to my own work, I work in the factory, I do this, I do that. Then it's normal. But when the *emanet* isn't there, my environment the surrounding that I face, is not right, it breaks down. When I say breaks down, my environment gets disordered, and the nation breaks, no one remains peaceful. No, there is nothing, none. All sorrow, depression, pain. It all piles up on top of each other. But once I get my *emanet*, I will gladly love, from the depth of my soul. We'll say thanks to Allah we are saved, we are freed from this *emanet* thing. After that everything will be fine, I mean good, I mean really normal . . . I will find myself another woman. Understand?

I   Understand.

Note here that he speaks of being free from the *emanet*: "we are freed from this *emanet* thing." This is not contradictory with the spirit of the way he constructs the story. His discourse around the *emanet* and what it is and who it really belongs to have a tendency to become ambiguous at times: it is possible for example to hear him identify himself alternatively with the elusive 'beloved,' with an omnipotent 'Allah,' or with a frustrated young man. The terms of identity and object relations become fluid in the flow of his psychosis, but more specifically such shape-shifting seems to take place around this notion of *emanet*. Here, for example, it manifests itself in Ahmet's sudden switch to a first-person plural point of view from a first-person singular "we are freed." *We* would be an appropriate pronoun here in the sense that a number of the subjective spaces he can identify with would be 'free' if the *emanet* story is settled. I expand on this later, but for now, keep in mind this changing subjective stance, this fluidity that I suggest, is necessary in order for the semiotic process of bringing threads of ideas from different discursive domains (e.g., social, and religious) into a novel formation corresponding to the unique psychotic experience for living of which no preconfigured models exist. The next excerpt contains another instance of this fluidity. Not long after having explained this concept the preceding excerpt, Ahmet speaks again of the Swiss woman and his unreturned *emanet*, thus describing the stage on which the drama took place:

P   I left that *emanet* to her, saying maybe one of these days she will return it to me. I knew actually what was going to happen to me, I said . . .

I   You knew?

P   I knew, of course I knew, brother [*ağabey*]. Then I went near Satan, we hang out a bit, this and that . . . Then, I said, I said I leave *emanet* with you this pack of cigarettes and ten Francs, here take this and get lost, I don't love you anymore. *Ich liebe dich nicht.* I don't love you. I'm sorry, I have friends and family, leave me free from shame and humiliation, and I will be pleased with you. But that *emanet*, give that to me, that is something very valuable, I mean it constantly distresses me.

I   Why is it so valuable?

P   When I say valuable [*değerli*], it is because I left it as an *emanet* with her. I said, one of these days I will be in a hospital, either a hospital or a prison, I will escape the factory. That was on my mind. Then from there I ran off to Satan. He took the things I left.

Notice how easy it is in this excerpt to confuse the voices and identities of the characters involved, that is, Satan, Ahmet, and the Swiss woman. To start with, when he speaks of his conversation with Satan and then moves to apparently speak of his beloved, the transition is ambiguous and linguistically unmarked. It is difficult not to assume that he has left his *emanet* with Satan when he says, "I went near Satan, we hang out a bit, this and that. Then I said I leave *emanet* with you this pack of cigarettes and 10 francs." We understand from the more frequently repeated version that he has left the pack of cigarettes and 10 francs to the Swiss lady, despite the structural ambiguity of voices and identities in his speech. But then again just after he speaks of Satan in the excerpt above, and we decode the ambiguity with the 'logic' that Satan is not the Swiss lady, suddenly the narrator, the first-person singular speaking in the interview, is now the party who is rejecting, namely, the Swiss woman. The narrator starts even to speak German, in a first-person singular voice, asking the one who is pursuing to leave him or her alone. Of course, once again, knowing the story and being a 'reasonable' listener we 'appropriately' interpret this switch and say, "Now he is telling us what the Swiss woman would or could have said." But the fact is that Ahmet offers no linguistic hints here that the speaker is about to switch or that he is going to 'quote' the Swiss woman. Nor are we given a sign as he rapidly then comes back to assume the voice of Ahmet himself. Subtle and ambiguous maneuvers like this take place in a number of occasions primarily associated with his repeating accounts of the *emanet*.

A major challenge in a case such as Ahmet's is that there are a number of good excuses listeners may use to avoid the difficulty posed by these semiotic and linguistic events. First and foremost, Ahmet is a psychotic patient. His utterances are hardly worth pondering at micro-analytic levels because psychotic discourse is generally understood not to follow a reasonable course of unfolding. This is perhaps the most common approach to the discourse of a psychotic individual. I would like to add, however, that this is also an intellectually irresponsible and socially violent approach to psychotic discourse. It is irresponsible because it consists of a rejection of an urgent and challenging problem due to a sweeping generalization with no scientific basis. There is simply no reason to consider Ahmet's discourse inappropriate for structural analysis. The thousands of sentences I collected in interviewing him indicate no deficiency in his ability to use language to communicate with me. If this is true then, that the semiotic content produced by Ahmet as a speaking subject in Turkish is to be taken as expressive of his subjectivity just as the discourse of anyone else would be, then the challenge to structural analysis disappears.

Another problem that might be specifically raised in Ahmet's case is the challenge suggested by his psychiatrist: his difficulties with language, which she then extends to question his intellect as a whole. While I tend to agree with the caregiver that the question of language is significant in that Ahmet has not gained full mastery of Kurdish, Turkish, or German, I am convinced after having spoken to Ahmet and his parents that the problem is more nuanced than an intellectual disability. Before elaborating, let me argue also that even if I agreed that Ahmet's 'language problem' has a simple explanation like intellectual deficiency, I would have a difficult time explaining why the main ungrammatical issue throughout his interviews concerns the confusion of 'voices' and identities. True, Ahmet does not use a wide or 'sophisticated' vocabulary as he speaks and it is true that his use of the language is limited. But those limitations are not generally reflected in his syntax; they appear primarily in the form of a limited vocabulary, the trend of confounding identities, and a tendency to not distinguish between metaphoric and concrete usage of ideas. Ahmet's apparently limited vocabulary is also intensified by another issue, that is, his obsessive determination to speak ceaselessly in reference to the *emanet* and the Swiss lady who is supposed to have it with her. The scope of Ahmet's language use is limited, yes, but not necessarily because he is intellectually deficient; in fact I would like to propose a relationship between Ahmet's linguistic deficiency and his psychosis, one which may best be expressed in Kristevan terms of 'asymbolia' than in cognitive deficiency as such. Let me explain myself.

Le soleil noir de la mélancolie

Borrowing the title from Gérard de Nerval,[8] Kristeva (1989) dedicated her book, *Black Sun,* to developing a semiotic theory of a specific kind of depression, a kind that corresponds with Ahmet's story quite closely. My use of the terms *depressed* or *melancholic* in what follows reflect Kristeva's own ambiguous usage to refer to "a composite that may be called melancholy/depressive" (1989, p. 10), whose borders are blurred and run across conventional diagnostic categories, including the psychoanalytic one of psychotic versus neurotic. In fact, regardless of what Kristeva might have had in mind, my reference here is quite specific; I have in mind the case of Ahmet, the one so filled with melancholia that his clinician clarified, "[W]e first thought he's depressed, but then we realized it was schizophrenia." Kristeva herself dedicates too brief a section to this question, but even so she clarifies her interest in a specific form of illness and she suggests that she will "try to bring out, from the core of the melancholy/depressive composite, blurred as its borders may be, what pertains to a common experience of *object loss* and of a *modification of signifying bonds*" (1989, p. 10, original emphasis).

Kristeva's model is especially relevant since it offers a semiotic conception of the deeply melancholic experiences so prominent in Ahmet's account, and can serve us as a useful backdrop as I continue the synchronic and diachronic investigation of the various local layers of signification involved in his story. I start with the notion of the *Chose* (Thing) as Kristeva proposes, a notion helpful in addressing the mysterious *emanet* so central yet so incomprehensible to all around Ahmet. "Let me posit the 'Thing,'" says Kristeva (1989), "as the real that does not lend itself to signification" (p. 13). As opposed to our daily objects, which are typically conceptualized, signified and cognized within the realm of the symbolic, the 'Thing' belongs to the pre-symbolic (and pre-imaginary, if you are thinking in Lacanian terms) realm, it stands for none but the 'real,' the 'no-thing,' and as such it eludes signification, it is unspeakable. This concept, the 'Thing,' is central to melancholia in her semiotic analysis, because all that the depressed subject can be conscious of is "the impression of having been deprived of an unnamable, supreme good, of something unrepresentable that . . . no word could signify" (Kristeva, 1989, p. 13). She elaborates on the relationship between the depressed subject and the Thing in these words:

> Unbelieving in language, the depressive persons are affectionate, wounded to be sure, but prisoners of affect. The affect is their thing. The Thing is inscribed within us without memory, the buried accomplice of our unspeakable anguishes . . . The Thing falls from me along the outposts of significance where the Word is not yet my Being. A mere nothing, which is a cause, but at the same time a fall, before being an Other, the Thing is the recipient that contains my dejecta and everything that results from *cadere* [Latin: to fall] – it is a waste with which, in my sadness, I merge. It is Job's ashpit in the Bible.
>
> (Kristeva, 1989, pp. 14–15)

Here is how it all works for Kristeva, in my simpler words. Derived in part from Freud, Klein, and especially Lacan, Kristeva's theory of melancholia connects it to the process of integration of the subject within the symbolic order, within language. The human newborn is fated to deal with the task of growing apart from the original oneness with the mother, if it is to develop into a distinct human subject. An essential part of this objective takes place by the mediation of the 'name of the father' as a signifier of an 'external' system of law and order that 'cuts' through the original unity in a process that amounts to initiation of human subject into the symbolic order (and here, by the way, is precisely where the fundamental role of meaning and power as merged parameters becomes involved). The human child, in other words, moves to symbolize, understand, use, be, and apply language and other symbolic means to 'communicate.' The symbolic system, specifically as represented by language, is then not only a means of achieving an anchored sense of identity, but perhaps more essentially a means for the child to process (or as I suggested earlier, to 'forget') the early loss associated with being torn from the bliss of unity with the 'original object': "upon losing mother and relying on negation, I retrieve her as sign, image, word" in the symbolic realm instead (Kristeva, 1989, p. 63). Put in other words, the subject learns to speak in order to forget the abyss of disintegration that opens in developing from a selfless extension of the mother's body into a 'separate' human subject. Now it is easy to see what the problem might be, if the integration into the symbolic order does not take place as it should, which is the case with the 'melancholic' subject, proposes Kristeva. The melancholic subject is therefore disinvested in language, at a loss in describing his or her experience, and suffering from a chronic 'asymbolia': "I shall call *melancholia* the institutional symptomatology of inhibition and asymbolia . . ." (Kristeva, 1989, p. 9). Once the original initiation within the symbolic order fails to reach a certain level of completion/closure, then various losses may trigger crises and lead to a collapse of the subject's anchor within the symbolic order. In Kristeva's words,

> Melancholy persons, with their despondent, secret insides, are potential exiles but also intellectuals capable of dazzling, albeit abstract constructions. With depressive people, denial of the negation is the logical expression of omnipotence. Through their empty speech they assure themselves of an inaccessible (because it is 'semiotic' and not 'symbolic') ascendancy over an archaic object that thus remains, for themselves and for all others, an enigma and a secret.
>
> (1989, p. 64)

The fittingness of Kristeva's model of melancholic disorder for the case of Ahmet is clear. Ahmet grew up to show distinct signs of a failed initiation into the symbolic realm. Young Ahmet grew to be a boy in the absence of the father, whose major developmental role, according to Lacan's notion of *nom/non du père*, would have been to introduce the structured organization of the symbolic order of meaning and power into Ahmet's psychic world.[9] He then continued to show his deficient 'assimilation' by developing a distinct inability to partake of the symbolic order represented by the ruling laws of Turkish and later German languages.

Ahmet's 'deficiency' traveled with him as he went from one exile to the next, finally coming to the ultimate crisis with the love-loss trigger of the Swiss woman and the disturbing 'Thing,' for speaking of which he has found the notion of *emanet* as a 'partial object,' this mysterious thing the significance of which nobody including himself could understand or describe.

Interestingly enough, Ahmet's parents explained to me that when they arrived once at convincing the alienated and frightened Swiss woman to actually come to Ahmet and bring him back his *emanet*, he refused to have such a meeting saying that he did not want his *emanet* any longer. Yet he was only to pick up the *emanet* discourse again shortly after, once that literal possibility no longer existed: "[T]hey assure themselves of an inaccessible . . . ascendancy over the archaic object that thus remains, for themselves and for all others, an enigma and a secret" (Kristeva, 1989, p. 64). With this cursory discussion of a Kristevan reading in mind, let us go back now to Ahmet's case and the way his *emanet* functions at the center of his story, indeed at the center of his being as such, as a gaping well from or around which his psychotic reality seems to have spread its branches.

Later into the interview, speaking as usual of the Swiss lady and the enigmatic *emanet*, Ahmet associated that account directly with the notion of identity, specifically as related to issues of otherness and language. He said the following:

P   Now I am taking medication, waiting to get a response. If it comes out I will get out of here. I will go back to the foreign country. There again from the doctors' hands . . . [seems to change his mind about what he was about to say] . . . I will make a special trip . . . It will go on I mean . . . Except until I tear that *emanet* away from that lady's hands [*elinden o emaneti koparana kadar*].

I   Hmm.

P   That is very important. If I don't have it, inside me there will never be peace. I mean that's it, there is nothing more to speak about. I mean I've always had this pain, it's nothing new. They were talking Turkish and I didn't understand because I was a Kurd. I had a hard time learn-ing Turkish. So we learned a bit abroad, a little at school a little bit with friends. So I learned Turkish, but then my Kurdish is weak I can't really talk Kurdish. They made me forget [*unutturdular*], I mean no more Kurdish anymore I mean. At home we are four siblings, a father and a mother . . . [gives list of family members, where they live and what they do] . . . he [brother] works about 25 kilometers from home. So I mean there's not much else to say, that's about it. But if I manage to take that *emanet* back from that woman, it would be good. If I do, I would find peace. If I don't have it that gives me misery and pain. It's really a small thing, a pack of cigarettes and 10 francs, I mean something like 5–6 dollars. When I have that *emanet* I will be OK. That's the whole problem.

After finding a chance to get out of the hospital he is going to the 'foreign land' again. There really exists no home out there for Ahmet, no place that he would feel 'arrived' and 'at home,' geographically, politically, psycho-logically, or linguistically. I pointed this quality out earlier when speaking of the way he puts together elements of his life to form a narrative. When he speaks of making a 'special trip' after his release here, this is significant, both because he calls it a 'trip' and because of the specialness he attributes to that trip. It is significant in the sense that his phrasing attributes a distance, an otherness to the place he should otherwise be calling home, after living there with his entire family for so long. Not only is he calling Switzerland a foreign country, but he is also calling his homecoming after release a 'special trip' defined not in terms of returning home and joining his family but in terms of a quest for the thing that is missing.

In Ahmet's discourse there really is no 'home.' This becomes clearer as he continues in that same excerpt first to say again, as he says so often, that 'there is nothing else to speak' and then immediately to tell me this is related directly to earlier traumatic experiences of selfhood and the unspeak-able agony of growing as and into the 'other' trapped inside of essentially hostile symbolic systems: a Kurd in Turkey and then a Turk in Switzerland. Notice also that he is putting all this in terms of 'language.' Not only does he insist again and again that there is nothing speakable about his experience, that language in a way has no capacity for describing his missing *emanet*, but he also directly associates his agonies with 'language' as such. He speaks of the way he has been unable to become assimilated in any languages: his Kurdish, they "made [him] forget," and his Turkish and German never flourished. All this is now compacted into the vague and hard-to-understand concept of *emanet*, a notion I examine in cultural and psychological terms. One last invocation of Kristeva could help recap Ahmet's excerpt above in terms of her semiotic melancholia, before I resume the cultural investigation. Consider the language and identity difficulties just discussed in the light of Kristeva's remarks, that such (melancholic) subjects

> experience difficulty integrating the universal signifying sequence, that is, language. In the best of cases, speaking beings and their language are like one: is not speech our 'second nature'? In contrast, the speech of the depressed is to them like an alien skin; melancholy persons are foreigners in their maternal tongue . . . the dead language they speak, which foreshadows their suicide, conceals a Thing buried alive. The latter, however, will not be translated in order that it not be betrayed; it shall remain walled up within the *crypt* of the inexpressible affect,"
>
> (1989, p. 53)

Thus, the *emanet* continues as the centerpiece of Ahmet's discourse to represent a deeply unsettling history of un-coagulated identities and incomplete symbolic assimilations. The question of language is not limited to the idea of formal languages; it is an 'existential' problem of assimilation in the symbolic order as such. Ahmet is suffering from a lack of final comfort in *la langue*, to take this back to de Saussure (1959). He feels short of the means of 'speaking' as such, and specifically of symbolizing that which is missing, the *emanet*. There are direct associations in Ahmet's discourse of his melancholic love loss, his agonizing asymbolia, and a painful trajectory of uncompleted identifications. When at one point he asked me if I could help him, for example, the conversation unfolded as follows:

P   I mean, can you help me in any way?

I   I want to understand you, would that help you?

P   Of course . . . to understand . . . it would be good to understand, or to arrive at a situation, a position where one could understand [*anlamak bir duruma, vaziyete gelmek iyidir*]. If I were outside now, I would speak from A to Z, I mean that would have been no problem to speak I mean. But as it is, I am depressed [*sıkıntı basıyor*: tightness is pressing], I get very depressed, I am closed in and I cannot speak. Forgive my shortcoming.

Again, conveying a similar sense of frustration and aphasia, at another point he said the following:

P   I can't talk any more.

I   You can't talk?

P   No, I have nothing else to say.

I   Ah, OK. So then maybe I should not disturb you anymore.

P   It's just that there isn't much else to say. I hope that there will be in the future. If I go back to Switzerland then maybe there will be something to say. If I get the *emanet* back, then I can talk to the whole world . . .

The *emanet* is of a liminal nature in many senses of the word. It is located somewhere between reality and fantasy, between symbolic and real, between self and other, 'both and.' In part for that reason, it is persistent. Because it does not refer to any specific object yet it assumes the semiotic guise of a 'thing,' it cannot be grasped and described, and for the same reason, it cannot be erased and forgotten either. He laments a number of times:

P   [I]f I could forget that *emanet*, that would be so nice! If I forget, it will be good for me, but I can't even forget that.

In the second interview, after all his chemical and electrical treatments, Ahmet still 'remembered' the *emanet* story, in the exact same terms as in our pretreatment interview. When I asked him why he was in the hospital, he responded, "[B]ecause of love." And when I then asked him if he was feeling any better, he went on to explain the same old problem once again. Even though the discourse is more or less the same, let me quote this segment in some length because it contains important notions for further discussion. He said the following:

P   I still have some problems. When I think about things, it bothers me.

I   It still bothers you . . . So what will you do after you are released?

P   I will go to her. She has mixed things up quite well for me! I left an *emanet* with her. She needs to return that to me, then I can finally perceive the world normal.

I   What *emanet* is that?

P   It's a pack of cigarettes and 10 coins.

I   I see.

P   When she returns that, the world will normalize again. Of my ill fate, the world is turning in reverse. I mean nothing is in its place for me.

I   I see.

P   That really makes me uncomfortable.

I   If she returns it . . .

P   If she returns it everything would come back to normal. But as long as I don't have that back, the world constantly trembles.

I   What do you mean, the world trembles?

P   I mean as long as I don't have that *emanet* the world turns in the opposite direction.

I   I don't understand this idea very well.

P   And for me too it is hard to explain.

I   Of course, of course, I understand that.

P   Say I leave an *emanet* with you for one or two years, but it's constantly in my mind. I am always waiting for it, but she herself cannot come, cannot return it, or maybe she has forgotten, I don't know. But when I get this *emanet* back I will say, "Done!" I will say, "Thank you Allah." But as long as I don't have it, I am agitated. At least if I could find out if she loves me or not.

I   OK. Now let's go back to the world. I don't really understand that, and I guess you don't understand it yourself either. But what happens? You said the world turns in reverse.

P   When I say in reverse I mean when I don't have that *emanet* my world turns in reverse. It will all be corrected once I get back . . .

I   So there is something wrong with the world?

P   There is something missing [*eksik*].

I   Missing.

P   Something is missing and it's that *emanet*.

There is hardly any need for me to reemphasize the fit of this discourse within Kristeva's theory of the melancholic and his missing Thing. But having that model in mind, let me now start a closer investigation of all this from different points of view, first by opening up the main storyline. Earlier I suggested the storyline, while distinctly simple and obsessively isolated, can nonetheless be read as a conglomerate construct. What the excerpts examined so far have demonstrated is an emptiness, the blank space of a missing object. We have seen that the closest Ahmet has come to naming that missing object is by employing the signifier '*emanet*' and by anchoring that signifier within a short and rudimentary narrative of a beloved who has betrayed that *emanet* and thus 'caused' it to become a missing thing, an emptiness. This basic narrative that Ahmet has managed to conjure as a semiotic ground on which to situate the *emanet* signifier can be read as a conglomerate of a number of locally available themes and associative networks, or at least fragments of such networks. Earlier I termed these conglomerates semiotic knots and suggested that they seem to function as 'covers' or tropes for denial of a gaping abyss. As evident also in other cases discussed in this book, psychotic subjects often resort to collecting from their cultural environments narrative constellations or fragments of meaning that they mobilize to build transitory identities captured in chimera narratives. These constructs function 'for' reality, where the collectively endorsed consensual 'reality' fails to offer the subject the comfort of a full-fledged self-identification within that meaning system.

Of interest to my analysis is the process through which this secondary identification takes place, the process, that is, whereby the psychotic subject struggles to construct himself or herself a semiotic 'home' from the bits and crumbs that he or she can salvage from the devastated landscape to which he or she is exiled by the 'illness.'[10] In the remaining analysis of Ahmet's discourse I address some of the locally legitimized semiotic constellations from which Ahmet seems to have borrowed for his account of who he is and what is happening to him. To begin, let us consider the two main themes of this story, love and *emanet*. These two concepts are not completely distinct and separate; in fact, love may indeed *be* the *emanet* in some sense or in some contexts. Let me begin then with the notion we have encountered also in other case analyses, love.

Love and madness

You remember the earlier excerpt where Ahmet asserted that he is hospitalized "because of love," not to mention the general theme of the story, which is constructed into the model of madness due to unrequited love. The idea of love as a semiotic trope for experiencing and expressing psychotic states in Turkey emerged in the case of Emel, whose discourse semiotically articulates a brother figure and a lover figure in a motif shared by the patient's family, physicians, and the larger cultural milieu and therefore making her experience 'readable' in the local symbolic system. Love is indeed a common signifier in cases of psychosis in Turkey for both male and female patients, although the central model for this process (*Mecnun* or Majnun; see the following discussion) is a male model: he falls in love with Leyla, and as the love proves impossible, he becomes mad. Not only did almost every interview that I conducted around psychotic cases (including those with patients' relatives) contain a causal reference in one way or another to the notion of love; indeed, almost every other interview that I had about madness with nonpsychotic individuals also included references to love. One young female psychology student in a highly Westernized English private university in Istanbul (Koç University) revealed in a group interview that she had personally experienced the madness of love and that she knew what it would be like to become Majnun. When I pointed out that Majnun was male, she said, "Well, I know. Perhaps there is something like 'Leylahood' [*Leylalık*] to explain my situation." When I recently discussed this fact with a Turkish psychiatrist, she was surprised to learn that I considered that idea interesting or unique in any way, and to hear that 'love' is not as regularly involved in the construction of psychosis in Canada or the United States, for example. For her, it was a matter of fact that a great number of cases with psychotic (as well as nonpsychotic) illnesses in Turkey are associated with love. Love does not lead to madness as a rule but can lead to madness when lost or unrequited in the case of human love, and it leads to madness when consummated in the case of divine love. In either case, control is beyond the human subject; it is governed by divine fate. As Majnun, the primordial archetype of love madness in the Islamic and the Middle Eastern world complains,

> Oh my friends, by God, I have no control
> Over what Allah ordained for Leyla and for me
> He predestined her for another man, and tested me with her love
> Why does He not try me with something else?
>
> (Khairallah, 1980, p. 72)

So does Ahmet, who says the following:

P   Allah is the one. What Allah is doing, putting me in prisons and hospitals, making life so miserable for me, getting injections or taking pills, this all seems very wrong to me. My heart would not be content with this, what is this fate?

Or elsewhere more specifically in terms of a 'test,' he complains:

P   . . . as for humans [*insanlar*], a test has happened to all of them, things have happened, accidents and things, realities, love and pain, they are all tests done by Allah Himself.

The test of love has befallen him, as it did Majnun. Love, of course, is much more than a test in this tradition, it is a 'terrible gift' that, on one hand, can mean an attainment of the greatest joy of all, while, on the other hand, it can spell miserable madness, an utter loss of the world order. This is precisely the special double significance of love and madness that makes possible a powerful playfulness in Sufi literature, where Rumi (1984) can write,

> Oh Lover! Quit reason and become crazy, become crazy!
> Come, throw yourself into the fire, become a moth, become a moth!
> Alienate your self from yourself, destroy your home,
> And only then can you come, come and live with those who are in love!
>
> (*Ghazal* 2131, p. 799)

In Ahmet's story love takes a specific form. His love story begins the 'usual' way, complying perfectly with the Majnun model of unrequited love.

Ahmet falls in love with a woman who ends up proving unattainable for him, and he becomes progressively distressed, depressed, obsessed, and ultimately psychotic. Apart from the 'cliché' unfolding (or, rather, arrangement) of the story's basic elements in terms of the Majnun tale, the specific form that Ahmet's obsession takes is also significant. His narrative of the *emanet* contains an allusion to the Islamic theme of *emanet*, a theme regularly discussed and explained in religious texts, in Sufi texts, and even in the Quran itself, though perhaps with somewhat different implications in each context. Even so, his specific obsession was not understood as a common phenomenon by his clinicians because it combines familiar content into an unfamiliar configuration. Ahmet produces, in other words, an exclusively private story out of collectively developed elements, with the advantage that this story simultaneously 'works' for him as a mode in which he can experience and express his unusual state of being, while remaining within the realm of speakability and semiotic legitimacy. The larger narrative is culturally legitimate, while its details are personally relevant and viable. In what follows I examine how culturally produced signifiers such as love and *emanet* are built into the story of his madness in a process of consensus between the patient and his family. Subsequently I examine the wider implications of this process as a constructive effort employing social and private strategies of selfhood and subjective legitimacy.

Love and madness: *Mecnun*

The concept of becoming a *mecnun* [majnun], 'going crazy' because of love, was quite present throughout the interviews with Ahmet and his parents. Let me quote a few instances. When I asked him why he was hospitalized, for example, he responded as follows:

P   As I said, I have a psychological distress.
I   What kind, what kind of a distress is that?
P   When I say distress, I mean majnun [*mecnun*], I mean constantly my mind, my brain sticks to that woman [*takılıyor*]. Because it's stuck with that woman . . .

At a later point Ahmet told me of a dream of his. Not surprisingly, that dream was also constructed around the notion of *emanet*. In his dream he ran out of money and could not take out the woman he loved (same Swiss woman) and her parents because someone close to him betrayed his trust and did not return his *emanet*. He then went on to add:

P   That's it, that's all. So my dreams came true. I am a majnun [*mecnun*], and that because of the love of this woman! If it wasn't for her I would have a great life now. Oh, she could have told me that she didn't love me, that she didn't want to be with me, that she had someone else, or anything . . . But she didn't, she just turned away and turned me into this crazy majnun [*mecnun*] that I am . . . my illness is all about this, that's all!

Similarly, in the parents' interview, when I started by asking the mother to tell me the story, this is how she put it:

Mother (M)   It's been a few years now that he's been uncomfortable [*rahatsız*], I mean. I mean, how did it begin? Let me say, let me tell you, in a restaurant, in Switzerland . . . he is always thinking about that I mean . . . there is this woman . . . she comes up to him and says to him, "Why are you thinking so much, I want to help you." And this [he] says, "Come, come be my friend." She's said hello, she's talked to him, and in his head it's though the woman loves him.

I   A Swiss woman?

M   A Swiss woman, but she lived in the same area as we did.

I   So there was an actual woman.

M   There is a woman. This [he] says no, the woman gave me cigarettes, talked to me, sent me a message. But right from the beginning, maybe the woman answered him, meaning like being friendly, not with bad intentions. But then he comes home and he is a majnun [*mecnun*] already, he became crazy [*delirlendi*], became ill tempered, cried, threw things around. He was all love-crazy.

As the uniquely central signifier of love and madness in Turkey (as in much of the Islamic Middle East), Majnun [*mecnun*] is the signifier in which two very important themes of madness converge: the jinn and love. The *Online Babylon Dictionary Mecnun* as follows: "1. crazy 2. madly in love, Love-crazed 3. mad, insane, crazed by love."[11] My other dictionary gives only one meaning: "madly in love." This more or less accurate definition does capture the sense of the word *mecnun* in modern Turkish, superficially at least. Similar to most of the Islamic world, almost anybody in Turkey knows that, beyond the dictionary meaning, as a proper name Majnun refers to the hero of love who became insane because of the love of beautiful Leyla. Majnun, says the great poet Nizami, is the "King of love." Technically speaking, Majnun is a nickname for a character by the original name of Qays; however, that is not how he is known to the average person. I noticed during my stay in Turkey that a classic film depicting the story of Majnun and his love is rerun occasionally on different TV channels. The story of Leyla and Majnun is a pre-Islamic tale that has been told and retold by various narrators through time, and so it comes in slightly differing versions (see, e.g., Khairallah, 1980). But some core elements are constant: a young man meets a young woman, falls in love with her, and she proves inaccessible to him. In pain and frustrated, as he loses access to the beloved so does he lose all bounds of reason. Majnun abandons all signs of 'order,' within and without: he becomes 'mad,' and he quits home, family, and town to become "king of the wilderness," associated and able to communicate only with wild beasts. There is a large literature on the stories of Leyli and Majnun, consisting not only of numerous works of poetry and prose that capture one or another version of the story, but also many works of analysis and interpretation (for detailed reviews and discussions see, e.g., Dols, 1992; Khairallah, 1980; or Seyed-Gohrab, 2003).

Although the original story did not give a 'positive' regard to madness, it eventually was appropriated and loaded with spiritual and religious connotations in the emerging Islamic mystical tradition of Sufism (see, e.g., Dols, 1992, p. 320f.). Today Majnun stands for a vastly undifferentiated notion of 'love,' all the way from the spiritual or religious love for Allah to the masculine love for flesh-and-blood females. What remains once again constant across these otherwise polarized domains of signification is the sense of resistance to 'reason' and a glorification of pain, frustration and the ultimately destructive power of love represented in 'madness.' It is in madness that the 'problem' of 'self' is fundamentally 'resolved' and Allah and the flesh finally unite. An interesting detail is the contrast between the way madness is arrived at in the two domains: whereas with earthly love it is a loss of the love object that leads to madness, on the heavenly side of the coin madness marks the consummation of the quest and the union with, or at least being touched by Allah (see the following discussion on love and the fate of the self).

Love and madness: the jinn

Semiotically speaking, the word *majnun* has another important sense that is no longer explicitly present in the semantic geography of modern Turkish, but which continues nonetheless to have its full effect through invisible associative networks that can only be explained in a diachronic examination. That explicitly absent yet implicitly present sense comes from the word's original Arabic, a sense probably more readily accessible to the 'pre-Roman alphabet' Turkish speaker, that can be translated as 'affected by the jinn.' The jinn, as I mentioned earlier, are special creatures in Islamic and Middle Eastern cosmology understood at multiple levels to constitute an alter ego for the human subject. The jinn defy final identification, not simply because they are invisible but also because even within the well-defined Islamic order of the universe; they are in-between creatures, simultaneously Man's equal and his double but also somewhere between man and beast, on one hand, and between man and angels, on the other. They are Man's equals and his double in the sense that a Muslim child growing up in the Middle East is taught often and again that the jinn, though invisible, actually look very similar to humans; have social hierarchies and organizations, families, clans and tribes; have their own sultans and queens; have prophets sent to them from Allah; can be male or female, believer or nonbeliever, violent or gentle; and may even be educated or not (see, e.g., Al Hariri-Wendel, 2002, p. 59f.).

The Quran also makes numerous references using the phrase "al-jinn wal-ins" (the Jinn and the Human) as a fundamentally associated pair. The two groups are addressed by Allah simultaneously as he warns of Hell or gives hopes for Paradise. In Surah 55 (Ar-Rahman), for example, Allah taunts the twin communities in these words:

> Soon shall We settle your affairs, both you worlds . . . You assembly of jinns and of humans! If you think you can pass beyond the zones of the heavens and the earth, then pass [if you can]! But no, not without [my] permission will you be able to pass!
>
> (Ayahs 31, 33)

But also in the Quran, the jinn are described as creatures made neither of flesh and 'mud,' as Adam has been, nor of pure spirit, as the angels are. The jinn are made of fire, smokeless fire, which ranks somewhere between matter and ether, thus between man and angel. As in many other occasions, in Surah 15 (Al-Hijr) Allah explains: "We created man from sounding clay, from mud molded into shape. And the Jinn race, We had created from the fire of scorching flames" (Ayahs 26–27). And finally, the jinn are quite regularly imagined as occupiers of a demi-level between Man and the beast, specifically insofar as questions of flesh and desire are involved. Like humans, they eat and drink, they reproduce and have sexual activities among them and could at times become sexually involved also with humans to give birth to half-breeds. They are animal-like because they have hooves instead of toes, and a small tail. The animal association is reinforced in the belief that frequently the jinn take the form of animals, often domestic ones but also non-domesticated animals, such as panthers, jackals, or dogs (e.g., Al Hariri-Wendel, 2002, p. 60).

The jinn indeed find even further significance in Ahmet's story in two respects: the way they are associated with Ahmet's Kurdish ethnic identity and then, not unrelated to that, the fluidity and mystery with which they are identified. When it comes to a 'Kurdish identity,' as Ahmet explicitly attributes to himself, the jinn association is dramatic. Anthropologist Margaret Kahn (1980), for example, has picked up this association in her study of the Kurdish people. "Centuries ago," she writes in her book about Kurds, titled *Children of the Jinn*:

> Solomon threw 500 of the magical spirits called jinn out of his kingdom and exiled them to the mountains of the Zagros. These jinn first flew to Europe to select 500 beautiful virgins as their brides and then went to settle in what became known as Kurdistan.
>
> (p. xi)

Ahmet's own travel to Europe and his quest for his own virgin, however, were doomed to fail. And as for the jinn, not only did they not aid him in fulfilling his quest; in fact, they also became the causes of his failure by helping his archrival in love, Satan.

The fluidity of the jinn is reflected, as poetic tragedy, in the apparent failure of a Kurdish 'nation' to coagulate[12] and captured 'concretely' in the idea that the jinn are made of flaming fire. This fluidity is also part of the reason why they do not have a final 'location' in the universal hierarchy. This 'unknowability' is closely associated with the fear-inducing aspect of the jinn and thus quite relevant to the horror so often evoked by madness in both patients and people around them. Fluidity is also powerfully present in the Arabic etymology of the term *jinn*, whose less noted sense includes 'wanderer,' 'absent,' 'invisible,' or 'unstable.' In fact in this sense *jinn* becomes once again the alter entity of the word used in the Quran to refer to Man, namely, *ins*, which has the etymological traces of 'stable,' 'sedentary,' or 'present.' It is not difficult to see how this aspect of the term is linked with Ahmet's story, from the angle of identity and the chronic experience of otherness that he expressed in terms of ethnicity, language, and endless periods of moving and change and from the perspective of loss and lack, as associated with Satan and his role in the Islamic story of creation. Not only does Ahmet refer to himself as *mecnun*, but he also describes his madness as being "all because of love." His family strongly believes that the jinn are at work in this story, and the person who Ahmet insists has brought all the misery and alienation to him and his love is Şeytan [Satan; pronounced *shey-taan*], the most infamous jinn of all. When at one point Ahmet spoke of Satan, I asked him if or how he recognized Satan when he saw him, and he told me the following:

P   I have basically known him [*Şeytan*] for a long time, of course, I recognize him.

I   But are you certain it is him?

P   Yes I am certain. I actually went up to this spiritual journey, that's when I learned about it.

I   What spiritual journey?

P   I went up to the world of the spirits. Up. When I say the world of spirits, I mean I went all the way to the top floor of heavens. There I saw myself. There were angels and stuff, they tied me up though, the angels didn't like me up there very much.

I   Didn't like you.

P   Didn't like me because of Satan, over Satan. And he has all these helpers too, these jinn that work things out what he wants. I beat them up once, because they think they can tell me what to do. They are actually the ones that took her away

I   Took who away?

P   The Swiss lady I mean. Satan caused pain between us.

I   What did he do?

P   Well, Satan was actually not to blame maybe. He ran away. In front of the restaurant, we were looking together, I wonder, I said, I wonder if he was trying to rape the friend, or whether the woman herself, did she desire that in her heart [*gönülden*: from the heart], and of course I can't know.

So Ahmet's knowledge of these events has a cosmic source: he learned it in a *Mi'raj* (this is an Islamic term for heavenly visits achieved by selected individuals/saints). What is special about Ahmet's *Mi'raj*, however, is that unlike the prophet Muhammad or Ibn Arabi or other mystics who have been there and done that, his wasn't a pleasant trip; he was pushed around and tied up by angels, despite the implied fact that he was truly the One himself: I went on a *Mi'raj* and up on the top floor of heavens I saw myself! I will come back to this identification with Allah shortly, because it is significant as an element in Ahmet's story and is yet another signifier of convergence where the cultural and the private, the collective and the narcissistic merge to give expression to a specific experience. What one witnesses in his *Mi'raj* is in effect what he has been trying to tell me repeatedly: that the order of the universe is broken, in fact reversed, and that the world is turning in the wrong direction. The angels, who are supposed to be Allah's helpers, have turned into the helpers of Satan, and this already in addition to the fact that Satan has his own helpers here on earth, jinns in red hats. We will come back to this scene later.

To recap then, the jinn are implicitly involved in the notion of love sickness. The association is implicit because modern Turkish syntax sees no grammatical links between the terms *cin* (jinn) and *mecnun* (*majnun*), but the association holds nonetheless, because, in addition to the diachronic etymological ties that remain implicit, in people's accounts love madness and the jinn are almost always associated synchronically, for no explicit reason. This idea fits well within the typical accounts of madness I have encountered, in which both love and the jinn are simultaneously invoked to explain the madness or its onset. In the case of Emel, for example, whose story was constructed around the loss of a lover/brother, one feature mentioned but not explored in detail was her suggestion that she became psychotic because she was struck by the jinn. The jinn, she explained, had 'struck' her when she made the mistake of throwing hot ashes and burning coal over a spot where a jinn family were having their dinner. Even in that scenario there is a tight association between the jinn and her lost love. The jinn are also invoked indirectly by Senem, whose theory of the cause of her madness concerned the wrath of a hoja and the spell he had put on her. In fact the more precise term for the hojas who write such spells is *cinci hoca*, or 'jinn-worker hoja.' The association is direct: they do what they do by taming and putting to work one or more jinns.

Love and madness: a local model for subjective transformation

In his examination of Sufi themes, Sells (1996) speaks of the two concepts of "love-madness" and "perishing" as "key Sufi motifs," which were, in turn, "combined by Sufis with the bewilderment of reason on contact with ultimate reality, and the annihilation of the human in mystical union" (p. 69). The themes often become key motifs in cases of psychosis, specifically in male psychotic experiences organized around a love story in the Turkish context. I shortly give evidence of this in Ahmet's story, but first I introduce an excerpt from another case of love madness that I have no space to explore in detail. This was the case of Yusuf, a young man also from Eastern Anatolia but much poorer than Ahmet and hospitalized at Bakırköy, the state-run hospital. In Yusuf's psychotic experience the family of the woman he fell in love with had converged with the Turkish secret police to condemn him to a horrific space of fear, persecution, and ceaseless 'psychological torture.' This young passionate man offered me the gift of a poem he had written for his beloved (the clearly inaccessible daughter of a rich Turkish family who lived in Europe and came home for summer visits), and I share that here, partly because it is in direct relation to the issue in question but partly also because it is a eulogy to Yusuf's tortured spirit, which left his body not long after our interview. He finally arrived at his many-times-attempted objective of burning himself to death to put an end to the ruthless and unbearable horror of life as the subject of constant persecution. At some point in his interview, Yusuf asked me if I wanted him to recite a poem he had written. I told him I would be honored to hear his poem, and he recited the following to me:

Yusuf (Y)   I lost myself on the shores of Istanbul
Neither the goblets in my hand, nor the girls I deceive,
Nothing fills your emptiness [*boşluğunu*]
After you, my one and only [*birtanem*], my name was written in memories as Curse [*bela*]
My left hand is lost
I am in the police station
My crime: not being able to make myself be loved [*sevdirememek kendimi*].
I don't know how to describe how I love, should I say like crazy [*delice*]?
Bush flower!
If I put my heart into your hand, sigh, and revolt, then the smile will come to your lips.
What was that, as if you couldn't understand?
But I knew well what had been fated for me
You had tied me to yourself, with the appearance of the angel
You wrote on my heart those curses of words
The day you become Majnun [*Mecnun*],

When you cannot hide from Majnun [*Mecnun*] by writing poetry,
When your blood freezes, and you revolt against exploitation
[*sömürülmeye baş kaldırdığında*]
Remember me the day,
When you realize you've been taunting Allah, not one of his creatures!
[brief silence]

I   You wrote this poem?

Y   I wrote this poem. I really had a crisis. I really wanted to die, so many times. Now I'm not like that, I'm very calm now, right now, I am really not like that, I am very calm. These people followed me a lot, they caused me to throw gasoline on myself. I say to him, brother, shoot me! He doesn't. I ask [myself] she loves me, she loves me not, she doesn't love me, and she doesn't love me. I just don't know. They neither find me very strong, nor do they kill me or do something. I say if you're going to do something to me, just pull it [gun] out, tak, tak, tak, tak, shoot me and go on, and I'll say bless you [*helal olsun*]. But they don't . . .

Even though a meaningful appreciation of the tragic story of Yusuf is impossible from an excerpt, the segment here speaks powerfully on its own. Yusuf's immediate concern with self and identity is explicit. I should also add that about 40 minutes later in that interview I asked Yusuf to recite me that poem once again, and he did. The two versions are virtually the same, confirming that this was a preconfigured rather than a spontaneous production. The fact that his poem begins with an expression of the loss of the self sets the overall tone and theme of the poem. The themes packed into this segment are strikingly similar to those of Ahmet's case, not simply in terms of explicit references to Majnun and his fate of love madness but also in other details like the loss of the self; the agony of an emptiness that cannot be filled by anything; the strong sense that in the style of a 'curse' the love of this woman has caused his very 'name' to be associated with disaster and misery (*bela*); and, associated with that, the theme of revolt against the society and a 'knowledge' that one is destined to police stations, prisons, and hospitals: "my crime: not being able to make myself be loved." Also recognizable here is the overall sense of this being a 'fate'– "I knew well what had been fated for me"; a sense of utter confusion and uncertainty about whether Yusuf is loved or not – "loves me, loves me not"; and, finally, a grandiose sense of omnipotence reflected in involvement in cosmic scenarios where visits are made, wars are fought, and negotiations are made with Allah (as well as Satan in Ahmet's case) or other powerful entities of high heavens – "remember me the day when you realize that you've been taunting Allah, not one of his creatures!"

I have introduced some and will present more instances from Ahmet's account of themes shared with those of Yusuf's poem, but consider now the last of these details, that is, a delusion of grandiosity in the form of identification with Allah "Himself," in both Ahmet's and Yusuf's experiences. I offer some instances from the interviews. The first time I encountered the sense that Ahmet identified with Allah was not long into the interview, when he spoke of the many things that he has to say but that he cannot articulate. Here is how he put that:

P   . . . I mean the truth is that there are a lot of things that I could be telling, except that being in the midst of these [people] I cannot speak all that easily.

I   Why can't you speak it?

P   The fact is nobody wants to understand either

I   Who doesn't want to understand?

P   I mean the humans [*insanlar*: humans, people] here, I cannot speak my thoughts to them. I say look, let's go outside into a park, or take a ten-minute, fifteen-minute fresh air. They say no, the doctor doesn't give permission. And the doctor says I gave permission before, says you can go out easily, no problem. But these humans [*insanlar*] here, unfortunately they think I am their enemy, they think Allah has a problem with them.

I   You don't think Allah is upset with them?

P   No, why would I be upset with them? I say let there be all kinds of nations, all kinds of people. They may be friends of Satan, they may be nice people. But why would I make a problem for them?

It is possible to attribute Ahmet's interchange of *I* and *Allah* to a slip in communication or a semantic error, but the identification is already implicit in his suggestion of a qualitative difference between him and 'these humans' or his suggestion that 'these humans' are not nice to him because "they think I am their enemy, they think Allah has a problem with them." But he also reproduced this sense. Later into the interview he said again that he couldn't really 'speak,' this time because he was tired. He said the following:

P   I'm tired, I'm tired. I can't tell the story [I can't narrate: *Anlatamıyorum*], otherwise I would say it all.

I   But maybe you can speak to me, you know, I am also a Muslim.

P   Of course, my dear, we're all Muslim, but I'm saying that for Allah the creation is different. Some of the created things need to develop. You will not compare one country to another, leave that to the creator. He may also be Satan, he may appear friendly . . . all humans are capable of reaching peace.

I   Now, I am not sure I understood what you just told me.

P   Of course not. This means Allah knows everything. I mean, He Himself
     is the creator. There is no power above mine. The books are full, the
     Quran is full of these issues. You don't understand me, and you will not
     find a power over mine either, can't be found [*benim gücümün üstüne
     başka güç yoktur, bulunmaz*]. I am the only being [existence] in this
     world [*bu dünyanın tek varlığı benim*], and there shall not come another
     being beside me either.

This notion was also confirmed by Ahmet's parents. First, before the
arrival of his father, his mother spoke of it when telling me the course of
Ahmet's psychotic illness and his hospitalization in Switzerland:

M   So they took him to the hospital. He stayed there for two months, the
     police talked to the woman, they said, "Come, we will also talk to you,
     what did you do with him? Why did he fall in love with you like that?"
     The woman didn't come to the hospital.

I   Why not?

M   She said she had a boyfriend, she had changed her phone number, she
     didn't want to see his [Ahmet's] face . . . they had deceived my son to
     begin with, had told him she's rich, you'll go out with her and you'll be
     this you'll have that . . . But then they said this is illness, she's not rich,
     she's a waitress . . . at the end the woman turned out to be like that and
     he ended up in the hospital . . . Now he still goes to be checked, but he
     sometimes gets strange still [tone of voice drops suddenly, almost starts
     to whisper now], he talks and says things now, he says I am Allah, I am
     this I am what . . .

I   How do you mean?

M   [clearly anxious and not interested in speaking more about this topic] He
     says he is this and that, that he has powers and things . . . There's nobody
     listening to us, is there?

I   No, nobody is listening, and this tape is for my research.

M   [changes the topic] And his father says to him don't go to work, stay at
     home and get better. . .

I decided not to push Ahmet's mother further into the obviously discom-
forting direction. She herself, however, made a rapid reference to the issue
about 10 minutes later while speaking of Ahmet's behavior at home:

M   . . . and doesn't talk to anybody, since then [the Swiss woman incident]
     he's all alone by himself

I   Friends and . . .

M   No, no. He used to have friends, now there's nobody left . . . one day
     I had invited a neighbor over. He threw everything out of his room,
     started to shout. I looked and he's all of a sweat, he shouts, "I'm very
     good, I am the boss, I am everything there is," he shouted and he
     shouted, "I am this and that, you are nothing." And then he says,
     "Sometimes I am this and that, I am Allah, the boss," he says. We just
     don't know.

When the father joined us, he reported separately that his son had claimed
Godhood. Similar to the mother, Ahmet's father was disturbed with their
son's claim of being Allah and was unwilling to get involved in a discussion
of that claim. I respected that anxiety. Here is how he worded it:

Father (F)   . . . about 1.5 months ago, 2 months ago, I can't tell you the situa-
              tion of his room, doctor. [Turns to his wife] Did you tell the doctor
              about that? [The mother nods] He was saying blasphemy: "I am
              Allah, I am this and that. So far I've listened to everything you've
              said, now it's my turn, now you will kneel in front of me." He is
              seeing some creatures, he says they are wearing red hats, he says,
              and the things in his room he says he is throwing at them, until
              now, he says, "You made me like this, now I will make you listen
              to me he says to them" . . .

The creatures with red hats (described occasionally also as having red
heads; redness of the head or eyes is a common attribute of the jinn hinting at their 'fiery' origins and their association with desires, among other
things), a hoja tells Ahmet's parents later, are the jinn trying to disturb their
son. They are Satan's helpers (*Şeytanin elçileri*), according to Ahmet himself.
The two accounts are not contradictory for as noted Satan himself is a jinn.
So here again we encounter the jinn at the very center of a love-madness
story.

Of more immediate interest to us, however, is Ahmet's claim, his blasphemous claim, of being the godhead. While such grandiosity could at
first go unnoticed and be considered typical, certain nuances of this claim
and experience of godhood warrant a 'cultural' unpacking. Ahmet's claim
fits within a network of associations that are distinctly local in a number
of ways. To begin with, the story is clearly a Turkish and Islamic one
despite the Swiss setting, as Ahmet is claiming godhood in order to fight
the redheaded jinn. Secondly, the grander plot within which this claim is
staged can be understood best in local Turkish and Islamic terms. By 'plot'
I refer to the overall story about a rivalry between God and Satan over the
love of mankind and to the cosmic struggle in which Ahmet experiences
himself as involved. Finally, Ahmet's godhood is also Turkish and Islamic
in that it resonates closely with a Sufi model of selfhood and subjective
existence.

Glory to me!

The stories of Yusuf and Ahmet share not only a common sense of confusion and loss of self in the context of love madness, but both entail an identification with Allah. While I cannot be certain to what degree Ahmet's or Yusuf's specific brand of grandiosity is common among psychotic individuals suffering from love madness in Turkey, I do know of the existence of a powerful vein across a number of Sufi traditions advocating love, madness, and, ultimately, an identification with Allah as the true themes of a Sufi's quest. To be sure, such claims are critiqued by the 'pious' community and formal guardians of the religion, the *ulama*, but they are nonetheless recurrent. The famous Sufi Mansoor Al-Hallaj is a well-known example. Hallaj was so strongly in love as to achieve the state of unity with Allah, and to make his famous claim, "an-al-haq" (I am *Haq* [*Haq*: the ultimate Truth, Allah]). He was consequently prosecuted and sentenced to death for his blasphemous claims (see detailed accounts of the life and views of Hallaj in Massignon, 1922, or Mason, 1995). The agony of Hallaj in his experience of unification was so unbearable that another phrase of his has also become well known: "I wish for my self freedom from your love" (*arju li-nafsi bara'an min muhabbatik*; e.g., Mason, 1995, p. 82). Hallaj stands along with Majnun as the archetype of the loss of the self and reason within love. While Majnun's 'unreason' manifested in, or was interpreted as madness, that of Hallaj took a more directly political twist in his social context and was thus identified as heresy. He wrote, for example, "I am the One whom I love, and the One whom I love is me. . . . If you see me, you see Him, and if you see Him, you see me" (Lewis, 2001, p. 65). The following verses from Hallaj bring together the association among love, loss of the 'ego,' and identification with Allah in these terms:

> Your spirit is mingled with mine
> As wine is mixed with water!
> Whatever touches you, touches me
> In all the stations of the soul, you are I
>
> (Lewis, 2001, p. 64)

Hallaj's 'infidelity' was crystallized in his claim of godhood. Similar claims by Ibn Arabi concerning his oneness with Allah continue to be interpreted as blasphemous by Islamic religious scholars, so much so that his books were burnt in one of the main centers of Islamic scholarship, Egypt (see also Knysh, 1999, p. 203f., or Lewisohn, 1995, pp. 148ff). To give another brief example of this trend in Sufi tradition one could also think of Bayezid Bestami, who is considered one of the main figures that have established Sufism as an integral aspect of Islamic thought. Bestami was an early advocate of the subjective dissolution of the self in love, or *fena* (Arab. *fana*, lit. annihilation). A phrase by this Sufi became famous and remains controversial within Islamic scholarship: *subhanee!* (glory to me!). *Subhan* is among the adjectives used exclusively in reference to Allah, as in the two important moments of the Muslim prayer, *salat*; the moment of bowing, *rokuu'*; and the moment of prostration, *sujuud*, when Allah is 'glorified' with this adjective. "Is such an utterance blasphemy, insanity," asks Sells (1996), "or is it, as Bestami's many defenders would have it, simply the deity speaking through the tongue of Bestami, who has passed away in mystical union?" (p. 212). I do not have an answer in the cases of Bestami or Hallaj, though Ahmet's is considered insanity. The point, however, is that no matter what it might be called, here is a transformation of subjective experience that follows a culturally sanctioned path, even if the 'sanctity' may be highly conditional or marginal. Elsewhere in the same book, Sells (1996) speaks of " the ecstatic utterances of Bestami" in terms of a "bewilderment of identity caused by the annihilation of the ego-self in mystical union." He goes on to elaborate how this path of self-loss and bewilderment follows the "Majnun tradition" and how these transformations should be understandable "in terms of love-madness, when the beloved becomes the sole object of existence, as in the case of Majnun and Leyla" (Sells, 1996, p. 69).

The similarities between the Sufi formulation of divine madness and the folk experience of psychosis are too clear and too frequent among Turkish patients to be treated as coincidences, and in Ahmet's case the 'pattern' is present in many ways and instances. By pointing this out, however, I do not mean to imply 'sameness' of the Sufi experience of *fena* and the psychotic loss of self. Even though semiotic and structural similarities are striking, I am not arguing that the phenomenological and/or existential dimensions can be identified as the same. It is possible to argue, for instance, that fundamental differences remain between Ahmet's psychotic loss of selfhood and the spiritual/philosophical state of selflessness reported or advocated by Sufi mystics and thinkers. The point to be stressed, however, is the significance of culturally available configurations of meanings and associative patterns for the formation of private discursive and experiential dimensions of selfhood in a case of psychosis. Of interest to me here are structural and semiotic registers of experience, rather than the phenomenological register.

Consider, for another instance, Ahmet's treatment of the figure Roki, whom he persistently refers to as 'Satan' rather than 'Roki.' Roki plays a double role in Ahmet's story: on the one hand he is a love rival, on the other, 'Satan himself.' This specific combination of signifiers would not strike a Muslim as strange or incomprehensible: not only is Satan God's rival in the 'biblical' sense of the story; Satan is also referred to as 'rival,' literally, in Sufi literature. In that context Satan is a love rival of Man, a rivalry that started on the cosmic stage where Allah made Man, and Satan refused to prostrate in front of Man, citing Man's shortcomings. Some schools of thoughts within Islam, including the Yazidi Kurds and certain Sufi groups, consider Satan the 'true' lover of Allah, because he selected eternal damnation over prostrating to anything other than Allah.[13] The 'cosmic' division of romantic roles was thus decided in that moment according to Muslim literature: Şeytan, the jealous Other (the term *Gheir*: 'Other' is indeed used in Sufi literature to refer to Şeytan, as is the term *Raqib*: rival] refused to submit to the will of the newly arrived Insan [Man; pronounced *in-saan*], because he felt entitled to being the companion of Allah and superior to Insan. When Allah punished him by sending him away from His court, Şeytan struck a conspiratorial deal with Allah, and thus managed to make Insan lose his unity with the Beloved, Allah. Insan was rejected by the Beloved and 'exiled' from the presence of The Real (as Allah is so often referred to in Sufi literature), but before being rejected he was given the 'gift' of *Emanet*, a gift that was both a curse and a privilege, and it took madness to accept that (see the next section). The cosmic romance continues today with Insan's ongoing quest for reunification with the Beloved and Şeytan's eternal plotting to prove that Insan is not truly worthy of Allah's love nor a true lover of Allah. That Ahmet's story dynamics and characters fit strikingly well with this scenario can hardly be understood as a coincidence. The elements are all present, in varying orders, all the way from Allah and the Beloved to Satan and the *Emanet*, and the theater of his story is of cosmic proportions.

Emanet: love and madness on the cosmic stage

The cosmic scene that Ahmet points to is central to the construction and maintenance of his narrative. His cosmic drama includes a description of the trip he made to the top floor of the heavens, usually the residence of Allah himself, where a reversal in the order of heavenly things caused Ahmet great disillusionment. Satan, the rival, is revered by the angels, and Ahmet, the lover, is rejected and put in chains. And the notion of *emanet* is also playing a central role. Let me unpack this in more detail. As I indicated earlier, the term *emanet* is of Arabic origin, and the literal meaning associated with it in Turkish is the same as in its original Arabic, concerned with trust and trustworthiness and signifying 'that which is committed to one's care.' Now the term *amanah* (Turk. *emanet*) is used repeatedly in the Quran, including Surah 3 (Aal-i Imran), Ayah 75; Surah 33 (Al-Ahzaab), Ayah 73; Surah 8 (Al-Anfaal) Ayah 27, and so on. Ayah 73 of Al-Ahzaab is likely the best-known instance, possibly due to its ambiguous usage of the term. In many cases, as in the first example here (3:75) the term is used in the common sense of an object left to another's care. Here's a partial translation of Ayah 75 of Surah 3:

> And among the followers of the Book [*i.e.* Jews and Christians] there are some such that if you entrust [*amanah*] them with a heap of wealth, he shall pay it back to you; and among them there are some such that if you entrust them [*amanah*] with one Dinar he shall not pay it back to you except so long as you remain firm in demanding it . . .

In Al-Ahzaab, Ayah 73, however, the term is used to refer not to material wealth, but to an ambiguous, unnamed concept:

> Verily We offered the *amanah* to the heavens and the earth and the mountains, but they refused to bear its load and were frightened by it. Man [*Insan*] accepted the load. Surely he [Man] is unaware and ignorant!

In addition, or perhaps due to the ambiguity inherent in this confession-like statement by Allah, this passage has become well known because it has been referred to frequently by Sufis and the *ulama* alike. Each group interpret the ayah to its own interest, of course: according to one it refers to *Wilayah* [Trk. *Vilayet*, representativeness], and according to the other it refers to *Ishq* [Trk. *Aşk*, love]. The *Wilayah* interpretation, more in line with a 'religious' reading of Islam, understands *emanet* to consist of a set of responsibilities and ethical duties that Insan [Man] has on his shoulder insofar as he represents Allah on earth. The *Ishq* interpretation, more common among those of a spiritual/Sufi inclination, interprets the *emanet* as 'love,' love that "makes man great beyond the seven levels of the heavens" (Rajai-Bokharai, 1986, p 82). Man, in this reading, is the only one crazy enough to take that *emanet*, because neither angels nor animals are capable of love – or craziness. It is remarkable the way Ahmet's construction of his story centered on the *emanet* corresponds with the cosmic drama staged by the Quran, on one hand, and with the Sufi reading of *emanet* as something the acceptance of which is associated with love and madness, on the other. The fact is, I might add, that even the less 'creative' reading of religious scholars, where *emanet* is that which makes Man ethically responsible, is congruent with Ahmet's narrative. In that reading what makes Man responsible is that he 'stands for' Allah (*wali*). This semiotic reference is in fact central to Ahmet's experience where he represents Allah with a high degree of similitude (see the following discussion).

There are frequent references in Sufi texts to the 'moment' of *emanet* described by Allah. Rumi, Attar, and Hafez, and many others, have made references to this incident in their poetry. Hafez alludes to the same Ayah I just discussed in the following *ghazal*:

> Last night I saw angels knock on the Tavern's door,
> They sifted Man's dust,[14] and mixed it then with wine.
> Those residents of the precinct of secrets and sanctity in high heavens,
> Were drinking wine, intoxicated, with me, the homeless one.
> The heavens were unable to take the load of *emanet*,
> So the lot fell upon me, the crazy one.
> <div align="right">(<i>Divan of Hafez</i>, Ghazal 338, my translation)</div>

The associative network mobilized in this poem is relevant to Ahmet's world in a number of ways. Not only does the *ghazal* speak of the *emanet* and links it directly with intoxication and madness, but it also embeds and associates that process with potent images such as *Mi'raj*, an intrusion into Allah's own private 'precinct of secrets and sanctity' and an affair with his women (angels)[15]; and the cosmic scene of creation, where angels mix dirt and wine to make the mud from which Man's clay is to be molded by Allah. Let us consider Ahmet's report of his own *Mi'raj*, where he said,

P   I went up to the world of the spirits, up. When I say the world of spirits, I mean I went all the way to the top floor of heavens. There I saw myself. There were angels and stuff, they tied me up though, the angels didn't like me up there very much.

It is tempting, and perhaps fruitful to read Ahmet's trip in a traditional (Freudian) psychoanalytic language of rivalry with the father and an oedipal struggle because the overall construction of Ahmet's story, including his childhood memories and his 'psychotic' perception lends itself well to an oedipal scenario. Both Ahmet and his father told me of his conviction that his father wishes his death. Ahmet also said at one point, "My father made his son crazy by squishing him," and he believes strongly that his father's side of the family follows him in the darkness with the intention of harming him. But what interests me is not the satisfaction of 'formulating' Ahmet's story psychoanalytically, even though partial formulations obviously take form throughout my analyses. What I am interested in achieving is simply the analysis itself, with the contention that the medium here *is* the message. My goal is simply to demonstrate how a multilayered and multidimensional reading of a case of psychosis can reveal culture busy with its 'work' (Obeyesekere, 1990) in fluid and non-static ebbs and flows, taking place in multiple simultaneous layers of meaning and associations from various registers of life, and merging various historical references into a timeless whole. A psychoanalytic reading, or at least a traditional psychoanalytic reading, might be able to offer the comforting sense of a 'closure' here, but it is precisely such notion of a closure that I am out to challenge in the course of these analyses.

Let us return to Ahmet's *emanet* and its trace in Islamic and Sufi meaning systems. I noted that, like Ahmet, Hafez associates the story with a certain cosmic grandiosity. Apart from the obviously cosmic dimensions of Ahmet's heavenly journey in which, unlike Hafez, he fails to seduce Allah's women, his struggles against the jinn, his fights with Satan, and the *emanet* itself can be read as further elements of this cosmic drama. At one point he explained to me that in fact it is Satan who has caused the Swiss woman to either forget the *emanet* or just ignore her responsibility about it. I asked him what the significance of that situation was to him. He responded as follows:

P   For me it is just too difficult to lift. A load like this is quite a heavy one to bear and carry. I just can't carry such a load . . .

I   Where does the load come from?

P   Of course, it's obviously because she doesn't respect the *emanet* that I have given her!

The fact that he should associate that *emanet* with an 'unbearable load' makes sense in light of the Quranic verse that I cited earlier (33:73) and the network of ideas that surround that story. Remember that the Quran suggested that "[w]e offered the *amanet* to the heavens and the earth and the mountains, but they refused to bear its load and were frightened by it." In another occasion, when speaking of his father, Ahmet repeated that his father "acts like he hates his own child . . . tries to crush his child, he tries to drive his child mad." So I asked Ahmet why he thinks his father does so, and here's how he answered:

P   Well, he would slap or he won't give his car or money . . . I mean, he tells me to live like everyone else. But Allah gives everything, no? Allah gives everyone their own load. If He has given me a load then I must carry that load and live my life accordingly. But if He hadn't, then I would be like everyone else. I would work at the construction sites, I would be a garbage man. Allah has given everyone a load, and if you prevent that, it wouldn't be appropriate.

The *emanet* here gains an uncanny resemblance to that of the Sufi tradition or indeed the Quran itself. It is a load, a source of pain and difficulty, but simultaneously, it is also a signifier of uniqueness and special value. It is precisely that 'load' that makes Ahmet not be like everyone else, not be a construction worker or a garbage collector (considered lowly jobs). Here again what we are witnessing is that apparently irrelevant pieces, characters, concepts, and narrative fragments in Ahmet's highly psychotic discourse, gradually begin to resemble pieces of a larger 'story.' Not a story that Ahmet has necessarily ever thought of, heard spoken or told others about, nor is it a story that would make a lot of 'sense' in its entirety. But a story nonetheless, at least insofar as it has characters and a plot, a story also in the sense that it is a conglomerate of parts and parcels already present in Ahmet's cultural environment, though presented by him in an idiosyncratic combination.

Like the other cases presented in this book, Ahmet's story is a highly 'private' story, the way concepts, events, and characters of his life – real or fantasized – are put together leads to a unique and personal narrative, so unique as to be considered psychotic by people around him. But at the same time, and again like the other cases presented in this book, Ahmet's private story can be unpacked into a sea of associative fragments and meaning configurations that are unmistakably local and collective. The same story can be read at various levels of meaning. It is a common Muslim belief backed with a number of hadiths, that the Quran has many layers of meaning, often referred to as the '7 layers of meaning' (see, e.g., Madigan, 2001, p. 79f.). While I certainly do not want to be accused of speaking heresy, yet I do nonetheless propose a similar quality for psychotic narrative, in fact for all cultural subjective productions, speech being one of them. The simple fact is that all texts, psychotic or nonpsychotic, are semiotic cultural productions and, as such, are capable of being unpacked into more basic culturally produced 'units' constituting fragments of associative maps and meaning networks. It is precisely due to this quality that I have advocated a meaning oriented method of understanding the relationship between culture and psychosis.

I have further tried to examine through my analyses the process through which subjectivity comes to 'take form' within the existing systems of meaning and power. Once we conceptualize human subjectivity as a semiotically constituted representation of an elusive yet undeniable driving force – to avoid using the notion of 'agency' – the question of how exactly such subjecthood is produced becomes central. Accepting that what happens in the process of initiation of the human subject within the symbolic order is not a completely passive process, that there is something 'individual' that enters an interaction with the local systems of meaning and power, then one is led to ask first, 'What is that force?' and, second, 'What kind of an interaction does it become involved in?' The first question lies beyond the scope of this book, but the latter constitutes an important aspect of what I have been examining throughout, implicitly and explicitly. One simple yet intriguing finding of these analyses is that psychotic discourse and psychotic subjectivity are constructed somewhere 'outside of,' yet for all means and purposes 'within,' the local semiotic space. In an important sense, that duality is a feature that makes psychotic content specifically useful for studying the processes of subjectivity as such. It is certainly important to try to understand the way a story, a private story of subjective experiences, is put together using local raw materials. But still more important is to understand the way the process of construction and the resultant structure unfold in an interaction with the systems of meaning and power to negotiate a subjective 'voice' for the force that claims that narrative: a process whose implications go well beyond the question of psychosis to apply to the very notion of subjecthood, a process best understood in the framework of political subjectivity.

Notes

1 See online directories such as www.about-turkey.com/guide/frgnhospital.htm (Accessed August 15, 2014).
2 *Emanet* can be translated as 'something entrusted to someone else's responsibility to be retrieved later.' See the following detailed discussion.
3 Note also that the word *Erzurum* means 'The Roman Land,' a meaning that can gain specific significance in the context of this story (see the following discussion).

4 Alkol ve Madde Bagimliligi Arastirma ve Tedavi Merkezi (Alcohol and Substance Abuse Treatment and Research Centre).

5 Even though etymologically the term *Rum* is obviously associated with Roman origins, in Turkey it is more commonly understood to denote a Greek origin. The first meaning for *Rum* in many dictionaries is in fact 'of Greek origin and Turkish nationality.'

6 Ahmet was actually 11 years old when they moved to Switzerland.

7 Third-person pronouns in Turkish do not specify gender, nor do they distinguish humans from animals or objects.

8 'The black sun of melancholia.' These are the last words of the first quatrain of de Nerval's poem 'El Desdichado' ('The Unfortunate, or The Unhappy'), which appeared in a collection of poems titled *Chimère* (1853).

9 See Lacan's (1993) elaboration on the notion of *nom du père* in *The Seminar of Jacues Lacan, Book III: The Psychoses, 1955–1956.*

10 As complex a term as *illness* might be, including the overall historical, political, social, cultural, familial, private, and biological forces that have to converge to give form to a psychotic illness.

11 See http://translation.babylon.com/turkish/to-english/mecnun/.

12 This remark is by no means to be interpreted as my taking lightly the obvious geopolitical sources of the fate of this victimized group of people. Kurds have been one of the main receivers of the 'collateral damage' caused by postcolonial regional politics and the British-imposed geopolitical configuration of the Middle East.

13 See, e.g., Awn (1983, specifically p. 122f.) for detailed discussion.

14 *Geleh aadam*: the dirt of which Adam is made.

15 *Harameh setr-o efaaf.* Notice that the word *haram* has strong connotations not only of sanctuary and piety but also of privacy and privilege. In the king's court, for example, the haram (aka harem) was the section where his wives would live, and no strangers, certainly no male strangers, were allowed. The fact that Hafez enters Allah's haram and drinks wildly with Allah's angels here can be read to have strong oedipal undertones.

6 Conclusion

Milan Kundera once said that the way to "liquidate a people" is to erase its collective memory. "Destroy its books, its culture, its history," he wrote, "then have somebody write new books, manufacture a new culture, invent a new history. Before long the nation will begin to forget what it is and what it was" (Kundera, 1980, p. 159). One cannot say whether Kundera had Turkey in mind as he wrote these lines. But one thing is clear: if he did, or even if he did not, he was wrong. He was wrong in the way he thought of such concepts as a nation and its memory or culture and its erasure – and more significantly, he was wrong about where politics and history are stored. The scenario is familiar, of course. When Ataturk changed the alphabet, the history books, and so many other things Ottoman, he literally tore a nation away from its past. The average Turkish person today is unable to read texts written more than 90 years ago in his or her country or any of the elegant calligraphy that decorates so many old buildings and monuments. All Ottoman documents, books, newspapers, literary works, and original religious texts including the Quran and prayer books have been inaccessible to the average Turkish person for about a century now. New books have been written, a new history has been invented, and yes, perhaps in a certain way the nation has started to 'forget' what it was. But here is precisely the point: only 'in a certain way,' and I am tempted to say in a certain superficial way – one that has been clearly undermined or at least seriously challenged over the past 12 or so years with the popular return of the century-old specter of a pro-Islamist neo-Ottoman agenda in the form of the AKP government and the strong figure of Recep Tayyip Erdo an.

Culture, meaning, and power systems were not inside the Ottomans' heads or their headgear. They were not stored simply in their books and their alphabet either. What this book, and most prominently the case analyses of the three psychotic patients, has hopefully driven home in a strongest sense is that culture, meaning, and power systems have obscure genealogies written in an elusive alphabet invisible to the eyes of the beholder and running in veins impervious to the blade of the truest bottom-up revolutionary, let alone the command of the top-down ruler.

Among other things, the case studies have demonstrated that the past can never be simply 'erased' from the present of nations or of individuals. Modern Turkey, after almost a century of concerted state efforts to do precisely what Kundera proposed in precisely the way he suggested, does not represent a brand-new system of meaning fundamentally different from its Ottoman roots and "founded on the latest results of science," as Ataturk (1929, p. 723) once hoped possible. While the impressive project of social engineering applied by Ataturk has made Turkey a uniquely suitable site for examination of political subjectivity and modalities of intergenerational transmission of memory, meaning and affect, however, the significance of these findings reaches well beyond Turkey and its culture or history. That the kind of fundamental break anticipated by Kundera and hoped for by Ataturk has not taken place, or the robust process of intergenerational transmission of political affect brought to light in these case studies, provides facts about the nature of human subjectivity as such. These findings underscore the culturally and historically embedded nature of subjective experience and, more specifically, the fundamental role of local patterns of meaning and power in constructing subjectivity and shaping subjective experience through a set of processes whose 'location' lies well beyond the reach of assigned meanings and whose persistence we can observe in the form of various implicit 'continuities.' Above all else, what these basic findings demonstrate is the way in which subjectivity is fundamentally inextricable from systems of meaning and power, rather than being in a simple interaction with such systems. Subjectivity, in other words, *is* in many ways a manifestation of such systems as they interact with the basic human processes of desire and self-consciousness. It is in this sense then that politicality is not an acquired quality but an aspect of the social subject, and it is in this same sense that the notions of continuity and intergenerational transmission of political affect have to be understood.

Building on the four principles I outlined in Chapter 1, and based on the body of data presented in the case analyses, we can consider the idea of continuity in three basic modes, namely, the mutual continuity of private experience and collective meaning, the continuity of symbolic systems (and thence of culture and of subjectivity) in time, and the continuity of psychotic and nonpsychotic modes of subjectivity. These dimensions of continuity converge in turn to lend strong support to the formulation of human psychological and affective processes in terms of political subjectivity.

The first mode of continuity, the mutual continuity of individual subjectivity and collective system of meanings, maps directly onto principle one discussed in Chapter 1, "inseparability of the notions of subject, culture, and meaning system," while drawing strongly also on principles 3 and 4 (heteroglossic and composite organization of meanings and narratives) and finding conceptual support in principle 2 (synchrony/diachrony). This mode of continuity was most visibly illustrated throughout the three analyses. In the case of Emel, pattern recognition exercises unearthed such 'continuities' so abundant and so striking as to lead me to write a conclusion to that chapter warning against attribution of 'final meaning' to the patient's discourse. In her narratives of experience and identity Emel cleverly incorporates collectively shared semiotic patterns such as love and madness, pollution and cleansing, wholeness and dichotomy, and mobilizes signifiers of power such as Ataturk, Turkish blood, nationalism, modernity, or East/West dichotomies. We saw similar processes in the cases of Ahmet and Senem. Ahmet's narrative produced superb instances of conglomeration; manifolds of meaning and semiotic patterns borrowed from the cultural environment were packed into new arrangements. Ahmet's case offers also a unique illustration of the third and fourth principles highlighting the heteroglossic and conglomerate nature of private associative networks containing bits and pieces of collectively produced narratives and patterns of association. The analysis unpacked his narrow private storyline into a multitude of smaller fragments derived from the collective realm, discrete cultural, religious, and political allusions that converge to form a semiotic knot. Ahmet's notion of *emanet* creates a window opening on a host of cultural patterns of meaning that hold together his story of loss and melancholia, unrequited love and madness, and extraordinary encounters with Allah, Satan, angels, and the jinn, all mappable directly onto local models of meaning and power relations abundantly present in religious and literary texts. In the case of Senem, she borrowed powerful implicit and explicit tropes of duplicity (in both senses of the term) from her cultural environment and specifically from political and historical narratives to form her uniquely private reality. Her deeply power-oriented narrative incorporated associative patterns from discourses in her society including the political and historical accounts of modernity, nationalism, and Islam. Indeed, the idea of continuity between the collective and the private systems of meaning and experience, and specifically the deeply political nature of subjectivity as such, becomes so explicit in the unpacking of these stories that no need seems left for further elaboration.

Lest we forget, the continuity discussion is not an altogether new or revolutionary claim. This notion of 'continuity' resonates for instance with what Clifford Geertz (e.g., 1973, p. 93) proposed decades ago in his conception of symbolic systems that function as models both 'of' and 'for' reality. If this study has anything new to say about that notion, however, it is in the fashion in which it differs from Geertz's conception of continuity and, more important, in addressing the serious implications of these facts in terms of the fundamental politicality of the subject and of subjective experience. Whereas Geertz's 'continuity' refers (or at least has been read to refer) primarily to a synchronically conceived interactivity of the subject and the symbolic system (see, e.g., Sewell, 2005, pp. 175–196, for a discussion of synchrony in the work of Geertz), I have developed here a diachronic model that accommodates change over time without breaking systems into conceptually unrelated planes of interaction that can and should be studied only synchronically. It is in this diachronic model of continuity that Kundera's (1980) idea of erasing a culture and replacing it with another becomes impractical, if not impossible. While the atemporal (synchronic) reading of the subject in the symbolic system can conceive of that system and that subjectivity as susceptible to erasure given an intervention of sufficient force and scale (such as Ataturk's reforms), the diachronic formulation of meaning systems and the subjects in/of those systems renders the entire apparatus too intricate, manifold, and multidimensional for such 'erasure' to ever take effect. The diachronic model locates structures of power in the very subjectivity of the subject of meaning, and combined with the basic pan-temporality of meaning systems and subjective experience, the very nature of the issue in question shifts into a new modality.[1] And it is within that modality that the idea of intergenerational transmission of (political) affect needs to be understood.

Apart from the common appearance of locally legitimized associative patterns, the three case studies illustrated that discourses of psychotic patients and their families also produce models of associations that can only be matched with patterns from past contexts of meaning, including fables, myths and historical events, or even linguistically 'extinct' associations that no longer have an explicit presence in the formal or 'conscious' linguistic system. In the case of Emel, for example, we saw her identification with the legendary she-wolf Asena and her repetitive use of the word *kimya* in associative formulations no longer active in modern Turkish. Emel's identification with Asena symbolizes an experience of *extimity* through manifolds of contemporary and historic associations of that term, ranging from politics, history, nationalism, and Ataturk to motherhood, Islam, and purity of the blood. Asena, in other words, worked in the form of a 'temporal hub' (or a 'wormhole,' if you like) that collapsed into each other layers of significance from various points in time and from different systems of meaning, not all of which could have possibly emerged in a synchronic formulation/analysis of her utterances. Also in Emel's story, we encountered a network of associations between apparently unrelated terms such as *purity*, *Urfa*, and *fish*, as well as the singer Ibrahim Tatlıses, that reproduces powerful mythical associations such as the burning of the prophet Abraham, among others, by linking new signifiers into original configurations modeled after the mythic event. Only a diachronic analysis was capable of demonstrating the fact that each of those 'new' signifiers referred to a different element from the 'old' story in such a way that Emel's otherwise absurd set of associations 'made sense.' A diachronic point of view, in other words, provided 'meaning' for a semiotic configuration considered simply meaningless when viewed exclusively in synchronic terms. In all three cases a diachronic analysis revealed simultaneous presence or juxtaposition of patterns from apparently distinct synchronic systems of meaning. Recall Ahmet's connection of the notion of jinn to fluidity and a lack of stability, on one hand; to love and madness, on the other; and simultaneously to deception and rivalry. There, too, only diachronic analysis was capable of revealing an 'outdated' etymological relationship between the words jinn,

madness, and fluidity, as well as a semiotic association between the signifier jinn and deception and rivalry, associations that no longer exist in the
modern Turkish language. Senem associated the idea of *eş* (placenta) with
doubling and duplicity reflecting a historically viable concept also no longer
present in current Turkish systems of associations. Senem's own nonpsychotic mother, for instance, emphatically denied the possible logic of any
relationship between the notion of *eş* and a twin or a duplicated entity of any
nature. Similarly, a large portion of Senem's hallucinatory experiences and
characters and delusional networks of ideas and events are 'recognizable' in
terms of preexisting patterns when analyzed in the context of past historic
events such as Turkish politics of the past century.

Finally, consider the third modality of continuity across psychotic and
nonpsychotic modes of subjectivity, which brings us still closer to a full
appreciation of the essential role of power and the political in the construction and the workings of subjective experience. A difficult yet unfortunately
relevant metaphor in understanding the impact of schizophrenia on subjective experience would be a city ravaged by an earthquake. I think of the
difficulties and challenges faced by a schizophrenia patient somewhat similar to those of a person thrown into the aftermath of a terrible quake who
now has to make sense of what is going on there, or perhaps to rebuild a
whole town. It is a terrifying task, even to simply make sense of the blocks
and pieces and the structural foundations of buildings and to try to comprehend what things may have looked like. Similar challenges are faced by
both the person who is struck by psychotic illness and the clinician or the
anthropologist who is trying to help or relate to the patient's experience.
Without being carried away by this analogy, one point to consider is the
role of those building blocks of meaning systems, which we can think of
in terms of what Jacques Lacan (1993, pp. 267–268) has termed *points
de capiton*, or, as occasionally translated into English, "quilting points."
If we think of systems of meaning as highly complex structures that are
made around such basic blocks (*points de capiton*) and then expanded via
successive levels and layers of metaphoric and metonymic constellations
that are progressively more complex and less solid, then an examination
of that metaphoric earth quake scene shows us that while more complex
structures have mostly fallen apart, certain more basic structures have kept
their integrity. Just as in a city hit by earthquake these remaining structures
are usually foundational building blocks, in a mind hit by psychotic illness
certain foundational blocks or points of semiotic reference seem to remain
intact and continue to function as extremely important compasses for the
subject's desperate attempt at orienting its chaotic experience. As it were,
it is the simplicity, the solidity and the certitude with which these primary
blocks of meaning are vested that renders them most resilient to the vaga-
ries of psychotic illness. And significantly, the solidity and certitude of these
points de capiton is determined politically and historically – collectively.
They function as the turning points where private experience is determined

and held together by the collective systems of power and meaning, and by that same token, they also ensure the fundamental continuity of the private experience and collective systems. Psychotic constructions of meaning tend to deviate significantly from common sense. Yet, when it comes to the basic blocks, the case analyses have clearly shown that the basic points of reference to which psychotic patients adjust their semiotic and phenomenological compasses are generally the same as those used by their nonpsychotic neighbors. These points of reference are simple concepts, typically learned early, and almost without an exception signifiers associated with great amounts of power, such as God and his prophets or the Devil and his associates, political leaders, central mythical or historical figures, and so on. Coinciding directly with the Lacanian notion of *point de capiton*, these basic blocks of meaning consist of metaphoric bonds that hold chains of associations together and function as imaginary centers, though in reality they do not refer to any "real" signified (i.e., like all other signifiers, their reference is simply to other signifiers), and they are not centers of anything either. These locally evolved discursive tropes organize the systems of meaning and augment other metaphoric and metonymic connections.

As both theoretical discussions and case analyses have made quite clear here, as exotic, different, and anarchic as psychotic 'reality' might appear, it is 'analyzable,' at least to the extent that it corresponds to parts and fragments of the local collective system of cultural, political, and historical references. To begin with, psychotic content is continuous with the collective system of references insofar as the psychotic subject is able and willing to use comprehensible utterances including words, sounds, gestures, and other expressions that make sense within the dominant linguistic, semantic, and semiotic systems of sense and order. Furthermore, what may originally appear as a disorganized and incomprehensible heap of 'broken chains of associations' may be shown, as I have done here, to bear sense through levels of meaning not immediately accessible. If it is possible to systematically uncover patterns of associations that coincide with those of the psychotic subject's surrounding systems of associations, then it is only reasonable to attribute 'continuity' to the psychotic and the nonpsychotic individuals who, in a final analysis, use a shared local pool of semiotic resources to experience, live, and express their states of subjectivity. These findings resonate strongly also with Jenkins's (2004) findings that "the subjective experience of persons with schizophrenia is forged at the nexus of culture and agency, desire and attachment, none of which are annulled by disease process," and that "the study of schizophrenia casts a bright light on our understanding of culture and subjectivity more generally" (p. 30). In addition to the obvious clinical implications of these findings, which would urge psychiatrists to reconsider the traditional trend of automatically disregarding psychotic content as purely pathological nonsense, they also have powerful implications in terms of the study of subjectivity as such, as Jenkins has also pointed out. The metaphor of a post-quake city might once again be useful in understanding the unique occasion the study of psychotic experience offers for the investigation of subjectivity as such. Since schizophrenia has a direct impact on the associative processes through severe disruption of the regular capacity of organization of symbolic content, one of the primary struggles of the psychotic subject becomes re-construction and perpetuation of basic working structures of meaning and associative patterns. These structures and patterns, as we have seen in all cases and discussed above, are constructed around the same basic blocks or semiotic anchors that also serve the function of holding together local orders of power and legitimacy. In a sense then, the psychotic moment gives the observer the occasion of observing the human subject involved in fundamental processes that normally take place at early developmental stages (associated with language acquisition and ego formation, primarily between the ages 6 to 24 months) and are thenceforward forgotten, hidden beneath layer after layers of semiotic processes and symbolic content. Close examination of the psychotic moment, in other words, makes possible an observation of very early processes associated with construction of ego and the formation of the subject of meaning and power, which play unequaled roles in our understanding of the emergence of subjectivity in its collective and political context.

It is my hope that future studies will specifically address the central statement of this work, that the human subject is always a crossroads, not only of private agency and collective meaning/power systems but also of forgotten genealogies of meaning systems in time and historic trajectories of power systems. The basic findings and discussions of this book are obviously not bound within the cultural or political borders of Turkey or the Islamic world, but, insofar as they capture basic dynamics of human experience in its private and collective forms, I expect them to be applicable to all humans and all cultures. The line of relevance of these findings also crosses disciplinary borders across cultural psychiatry through cultural and medical anthropology and reaches those areas of social psychology and political theory concerned with the nature of subjective experience and its significance for larger collective phenomena, such as political processes, or the relationship of the state and the subject. Such concepts as power, resistance, or collective memory and change, which we have found to be of central significance throughout this book, have important reverberations in contemporary political theory, not simply as general and abstract notions but also, indeed, in terms quite similar to those that have emerged in this book. Most notably, writers on power and politicality such as Ernesto Laclau and Chantal Mouffe or Yanis Stavrakakis seem to have worked their way from within the field of political theory to precisely where this book has led us, namely the location of the political within the subjective, and the subjective within the political. In their book, *Hegemony and Socialist Strategy*, Laclau and Mouffe (2001) incorporate a fundamentally semiotic analysis of subjectivity into their theories of the political. They propose, for instance, the two notions ("the logics") of equivalence versus difference, respectively representing metaphor, identity, and exclusion versus metonymy, plurality, and inclusion, as basic principles where the political can be recognized in the formation of meaning and the logical (see, e.g., p. 63f.). Stavrakakis (1999), a political theorist, applies a similar strategy in his work on the political nature of subjectivity in his *Lacan and the Political*. One common basic theme across new theorists of subjectivity and power, from Derrida to Laclau and Mouffe, and from Philippe Lacoue-Labarth and Jean-Luc Nancy to Judith Butler and Slavoj Zizek, is that, like meaning and like a subject's identity, and for much the same reasons, power is always incomplete, never final, and always subject to slippage – hegemony in its traditional sense, in other words, is an impossible idea. One basic implication of this is that in order to understand the process of assertion of power, and the process of resistance against that assertion, one needs to focus not just on the macro-political world of social and historical facts but also, if not more so, on the micro level of subjective experiences and the subject simultaneously thriving within and struggling against that world – and thence also the reverse, which holds as strongly: if one wants to develop an accurate understanding of the micro processes of subjectivity, the political world inhabited by the subject needs to be understood as fundamentally relevant. This in many ways is the significant corollary of the notion of political subjectivity: just as it would be misguided to try to understand the subject and its various dimensions (behavior, affect, psychology) independent of local political and historical processes of meaning and power, any theory of the political would be fun-damentally flawed if it does not include mechanisms that would account for the subjective and the semiotic.

Finally, I would like to close this concluding discussion by opening another door for research and turning the case for continuity and the inter-generational transmission of political affect on its head with the argument that the diachronic framework deployed here may be helpful in explaining how change can happen despite the hegemony of 'powerful' groups. Power changes hands, not only because systems of meaning are susceptible to slip-pages, shifts, and mutations within the natural order of affairs but also, perhaps even more significantly, because that which a specific group knows in a conscious manner of what they want and what upholds their interests is never all that there is – there is always more. And that 'more' is typically rid-dled with paradoxes and complications, so much so that it remains literally impossible for any group to stop the system they are invested in from liter-ally 'slipping' away from their hands and transforming in the process. This then has implications in terms of change: not only personal change, as in the question of psychotherapy that grows immediately out of the case analyses here, but also social and political change, which is another way of saying it is perfectly reasonable, in fact imperative, to study sociopolitical change in its historic dimensions through individual realities and articulations of pri-vate experiences, precisely because the individual is the seat of power. 'The subject' is where configurations of power and meaning are instantiated, the very same configurations that shape a society's political order.

The challenge of creating political change then needs to be formulated as the question of how to change configurations of meaning in a society so that a specific idea (anywhere from experience of psychosis, to stigma toward mental illnesses, to attitudes toward slavery and women's rights, or regime change and democratization) no longer holds a privileged position in the local logical system. As the three cases of psychosis and the deep analysis of the structures of affect and subjectivity in Turkey's cultural, political, and historical context have shown us, if a system of symbols as vastly complex and intricate as a society is to change, the place to seek and observe such changes reflected is first and foremost at the level of the symbolic system as a manifestation of meaning and power. Cultural logics and structures of power and meaning unfold within the frame of history to serve as conduits for the transmission of political affect and implicit memories across generations, and in doing so they prefigure patterns of individual and collective experience, and anticipate modalities of power, affect and subjective interaction in a society, which I have termed political subjectivity.

Note

1 I have addressed this topic in greater detail in a paper titled "Haunted Metaphor, Transmitted Affect: The Pantemporality of Subjective Experience" (submitted for publication).

Bibliography

Adams Leeming, D., Adams Leeming, M. (1994). *A Dictionary of Creation Myths*, Oxford, UK: Oxford University Press.

Addas, C. (1993). *Quest for the Red Sulphur: The Life of Ibn Arabi*. Trans. Peter Kingsley. Cambridge, UK: The Islamic Texts Society.

Aktar, A. (2000). *Varlık Vergisi ve Türkles, tirme Politikaları [Capital Levy and the politics of Turcification]*. Istanbul, TR: Iletis,im.

Alangu, T. (1965). *Cumhuriyetten Sonra Hikâye ve Roman: Antoloji; Hayatlar, Eserler, Değerler Üzerinde Açıklamalar ve Örnekler [Post-Republican Stories and Novels: Anthology, Lives, Works, Critical Reviews and Samples]*. İstanbul, TR: İstanbul Matbaası.

Alexander, F. G., Selesnick, S. T. (1966). *The History of Psychiatry: An Evaluation of Psychiatric Thought and Practice from Prehistoric Times to the Present*. New York, US: Harper & Row

Alexandrov, V. E. (2000). Biology, Semiosis, and Cultural Difference in Lotman's Semiosphere. *Comparative Literature*, 52, 339–362.

Al Hariri-Wendel, T. (2002). *Symbols of Islam*. New York, US: Sterling.

Al-Issa, I. (2000). Mental Illness in Medieval Islamic Society. In Ihsan Al-Issa (Ed.), *Al-Jonun: Mental Illness in the Islamic World*, pp. 43–70. Madison, US: International Universities Press.

Amnesty International (2004). *Turkey: Women Confronting Family Violence*. London, UK: Amnesty International.

Andreasen, N. (2001). *Brave New Brain: Conquering Mental Illness in the Era of the Genome*. New York, US: Oxford University Press.

Angrist, B. M., Gershon, S. (1974). Proceedings: Dopamine and Psychiatric States: Preliminary Remarks. *Psychopharmacology Bulletin*, 10(3), 15.

Apel, K. O. (1995). Transcendental Semeiotic and Hypothetical Metaphysics of Evolution: A Peircean or quasi-Peircean Answer to a Recurrent Problem of Post-Kantian Philosophy. In K. Laine Ketner (Ed.), *Peirce and Contemporary Thought: Philosophical Inquiries*, pp. 366–397. New York, US: Fordham University Press.

Arieti, S. (1959). Schizophrenia: The Manifest Symptomatology, the Psychodynamic and Formal Mechanisms. In S. Arieti (Ed.), *American Handbook of Psychiatry*, pp. 455–484. New York, US: Basic Books.

Aristotle (1979). *Categories*. Trans. J. Ackrill. Oxford, UK: Clarendon Press.

Aristotle (1995). *Poetics*. Trans. S. Halliwell. Cambridge, US: Harvard University Press.

Armstrong, H.C. (1932). *Grey Wolf, Mustafa Kemal: An Intimate Study of a Dictator*. London, UK: A. Barker Ltd.

Ataturk, M.K. (1929). *A Speech Delivered by Ghazi Mustapha Kemal, President of the Turkish Republic*. Leipzig, DE: K.F. Koehler.

Atiş, S.M. (1983). *Semantic Structuring in the Modern Turkish Short Story: An Analysis of* The Dreams of Abdullah Efendi and Other Short Stories *by Ahmet Hamdi Tanpinar*. Leiden, NL: E.J. Brill.

Augustine, St. (389/1995). *The Teacher*. Trans. P. King. Indianapolis, US: Hackett.

Augustine, St. (396–426/1947). *On Christian Instruction*. Trans. J.J. Gavigan. Washington, DC, US: Catholic University of America.

Augustine, St. (401/1991). *Confessions*. Trans. H. Chadwick. Oxford, UK: Oxford University Press.

Awn, P.J. (1983). *Satan's Tragedy and Redemption: Iblīs in Sufi Psychology*. Leiden, Netherlands: E.J. Brill.

Baker, M., Malmkjaer, K. (1998). *Routledge Encyclopedia of Translation Studies*. London, UK: Routledge.

Bakhtin, M. (1935/1981). Discourse in the Novel (Trans. C. Emerson and M. Holquist Austin). In M. Bakhtin, *The Dialogic Imagination*, pp. 259–422. Austin, US: University of Texas Press.

Bakhtin, M. (1953/1986). The Problem of Speech Genres (Trans. V.W. McGee). In M. Bakhtin, *Speech Genres and Other Late Essays*, pp. 60–102. Austin, US: University of Texas Press.

Bakhtin, M. (1994). Social Heteroglossia. In P. Morris (Ed.), *The Bakhtin Reader: Selected Readings of Bakhtin, Medvedev, Voloshinov*, pp. 73–80. London, UK: Edward Arnold.

Baldwin, J.M. (1913). *History of Psychology: A Sketch and Interpretation*. London, UK: Watts.

Barrett, R. (1996). *The Psychiatric Team and the Social Definition of Schizophrenia: An Anthropological Study of Person and Illness*. Cambridge, UK: Cambridge University Press.

Barthes, R. (1957). *Mythologies*. Paris, FR: Seuil.

Barthes, R. (1968). *Elements of Semiology*. Trans. Annette Lavers and Colin Smith. New York, US: Hill and Wang.

Barton, J.L. (1908). *Daybreak in Turkey*. Boston, US: The Pilgrim Press.

Bates, D. (1973). *Nomads and Farmers: A Study of the Yörük of Southeastern Turkey*. Ann Arbor, US: University of Michigan Press.

Bateson, G. (1972). *Steps to an Ecology of Mind*. New York, US: Ballantine.

Bateson, G., Jackson, D., Haley, J., Weakland J. (1956). Toward a theory of schizophrenia. *Behavioral Science*, 1(4), 251–264.

Bayar, C. (1998). *Atatürk Gibi Düsünmek [To Think Like Ataturk]*. Istanbul, TR: Tekin Yayinevi.

Bayülkem, F. (2002). *Türkiye'de Psikiyatri, Nöroloji ve Nöroflirurji'nin Tarihi Geliflimi [Historical Development of Psychiatry, Neurology and Neurosurgery in Turkey]*. Istanbul, TR: Pentamed Ltd.

British Broadcasting Corporation Online (2003). Turkish Synagogue Bombers Named. Available online: http://news.bbc.co.uk/2/hi/europe/3283251.stm.

Bennington, G. (2004). Saussure and Derrida. In C. Sanders (Ed.), *The Cambridge Companion to Saussure*, pp. 186–204. Cambridge, UK: Cambridge University Press.

Benson, R. L., Constable, G., Lanham, C. (1982). *Renaissance and Renewal in the Twelfth Century*. Cambridge, US: Harvard University Press.

Bentall, R. P. (Ed.) (1990). *Reconstructing Schizophrenia*. London, UK: Routledge.

Bentall, R. P. (1996). From Cognitive Studies of Psychosis to Cognitive Behaviour Therapy for Psychotic Symptoms. In G. Haddok and P. D. Slade (Eds.), *Cognitive Behavioural Interventions with Psychotic Disorders*, pp. 3–27. London, UK: Routledge.

Berman, H. J. (1983). *Law and Revolution: The Formation of the Western Legal Tradition*, Cambridge US: Harvard University Press.

Bernal, M. (1991). *Black Athena*. New Brunswick, US: Rutgers University Press.

Berrios, G. (1991). Delusions as 'Wrong Beliefs': A Conceptual History. *British Journal of Psychiatry*, 159(suppl. 14), 6–13.

Berthold-Bond, D. (1995). *Hegel's Theory of Madness*. Albany, US: State University of New York Press.

Bezertinov, R. (2000). *Tengrianizm: Religions of Turks and Mongols*. Naberezhnye Chelny, RU: n.p. [See chapter III: 'Old Turkic Deities' published in *The Tatar Gazette*, available online: http://tatar.yuldash.com/eng_174.html.]

Bleuler, E. (1924). *Textbook of Psychiatry*. New York, US: Macmillan.

Bloch, M.L.B. (1961). *Feudal Society*. Trans. L. A. Manyon. Chicago, US: University of Chicago Press.

Bobula, I. (1982). *Sumer-magyar rokonsag*. Buenos Aires, AR: Esda.

Bowen, M. (1960). A Family Concept of Schizophrenia. In D. Jackson (Ed.), *The Etiology of Schizophrenia*, pp. 346–372. New York, US: Basic Books.

Boyle, M. (1990). The Non-Discovery of Schizophrenia? Kraepelin and Bleuler Reconsidered. In R. P. Bentall (Ed.), *Reconstructing schizophrenia*, pp. 3–22. London, UK: Routledge.

Brentano, F. (1874) *Psychology from an Empirical Standpoint*. Trans. A. C. Rancurello, D. B. Terrell, and L. L. McAlister. London, UK: Routledge & Kegan Paul.

Breuillard, J. (2001). Review of Boris A. Uspenskii's *Selected Works*. *Russian Linguistics*, 25(1), 105–110.

Brown, G. W., Birley J.L.T., Wing J. K. (1972). Influence of Family Life on the Course of Schizophrenic Disorders. *British Journal of Psychiatry*, 121, 241–258.

Bryant, R. (2002). The Purity of Spirit, and the Power of Blood: A Comparative Perspective on Nation, Kinship and Gender in Cyprus. *Journal of Royal Anthropology Institute*, 8, 509–530.

Bulloch, A., Gruen, E. S., Long, A. A., Stewart, A. (1993). *Images and Ideologies: Self-Definition in the Hellenistic World*. Berkeley, US: University of California Press.

Burkhardt, J. (1878/1990). *The Civilization of the Renaissance in Italy*. Trans. S.G.C. Middlemore. London, UK: Penguin Books.

Burckhardt, T. (1970). *An Introduction to Sufi Doctrine*. Wellingborough, UK: Thorstons.

Burge, T. (1978). Buridan and Epistemic Paradox. *Philosophical Studies*, 34, 21–35.

Bynum, C. (1982). *Jesus as Mother: Studies in the Spirituality of the High Middle Ages*. Berkeley, US: University of California Press.

Caceres Sanchez, M. (1995). *Within Lotman's Semiotic Sphere*. Paper presented at International Meeting in Memoriam Juri M. Lotman, Granada, Spain. Available online: http://www.uni-ak.ac.at/culture/withalm/semiotics//AIS/con-ausp/95-gran/95gra-rep.html.

Cahen, C. (2001). *The Formation of Turkey: The Seljukid Sultanate of Rum, Eleventh to Fourteenth Century*. Harlow, UK: Longman.

Cardini, F. (2001). *Europe and Islam*. Malden, US: Blackwell Publishing.

Carlson, E. (1985). Medicine and Degeneration: Theory and Praxis. In J. E. Chamberlin and S. L. Gilman (Eds.), *Degeneration: The Dark Side of Progress*, pp. 121–144. New York, US: Columbia University Press.

Carras, C. (2000). Identity. In G. Speake (Ed.), *Encyclopedia of Greece & the Hellenic Tradition*. London, UK: Fitzroy Dearborn.

Cartledge, P. (1993). *The Greeks: A Portrait of Self and Others*. Oxford, UK: Oxford University Press.

Çelik, H. (2005). *Bediuzzaman Said Nursi and the Ideal of Islamic Unity*. Paper presented at Nursi Symposium, Istanbul, Turkey, September 24–26. Available online: http://www.saidnursi.com/symposium/s12.html. [See also similar document at www.risale-inur.com.tr/rnk/eng/tarihce/3.html.]

Chevalier, J., Gheerbrant, A. (1994). *The Penguin Dictionary of Symbols*. Trans. John Buchanan-Brown. London, UK: Penguin.

Chomsky, N. (1975). *Reflections on Language*. New York, US: Pantheon.

Chomsky, N. (1986). *Knowledge of Language: Its Nature, Origin, and Use*. New York, US: Praeger.

Çırakman, A. (2002). *From The "Terror of The World" to The "Sick Man of Europe": European Images of Ottoman Empire and Society from The Sixteenth Century to The Nineteenth*. New York, US: Peter Lang.

Clanchy, M. (1979). *From Memory to Written Record: England, 1066 to 1307*. London, UK: Arnold.

Corin, E. (1980). Vers une réappropriation de la dimension individuelle en psychologie africaine. *Canadian Journal of African Studies*, 14(1), 135–156.

Corin, E. (1990). Facts and Meaning in Psychiatry: An Anthropological Approach to the Lifeworld of Schizophrenics. *Culture, Medicine and Psychiatry*, 14, 153–188.

Corin, E. (1998). The Thickness of Being: Intentional Worlds, Strategies of Identity, and Experience among Schizophrenics. *Psychiatry*, 61, 133–146.

Corin, E. (2012). Interdisciplinary Dialogue: A Site of Estrangement. *Ethos*, 40(1), 104–112.

Corin, E., Lauzon, G. (1992). Positive Withdrawal and the Quest for Meaning: The Reconstruction of Experience among Schizophrenics. *Psychiatry*, 55, 266–278.

Corin, E., Lauzon, G. (1994). From Symptoms to Phenomena: The Articulation of Experience in Schizophrenia. *Journal of Phenomenological Psychology*, 25(1), 3–50.

Corin, E., Thara, R., Padmavati, R. (2004). Living through a Staggering World: The Play of Signifiers in Early Psychosis in South India. In J. H. Jenkins and R. J. Barrett (Eds.), *Schizophrenia, Culture, and Subjectivity: The Edge of Experience*, pp. 110–145. Cambridge, UK: Cambridge University Press.

Corrigan, K. (1980). Body and Soul in Ancient Religious Experience. In A. H. Armstrong, (Ed.) *Classical Mediterranean Spirituality: Egyptian, Greek and Roman*, pp. 360–383. New York, US: Crossroads.

Corrington, R. S. (1993). *An Introduction to C.S. Peirce, Philosopher, Semiotician, and Ecstatic Naturalist*. Lanham, US: Rowman & Littlefield.

Crapanzano, V. (1992). Hermes' Dilemma. In *Hermes' Dilemma & Hamlet's Desire: On the Epistemology of Interpretation*, pp. 43–69. Cambridge, US: Harvard University Press.

Creasy, E. S. (1877). *History of the Ottoman Turks: From the Beginning of Their Empire to the Present Time.* London, UK: R. Bentley and Son.

Crow, T. J. (1984). A Re-Evaluation of the Viral Hypothesis: Is Psychosis the Result of Retroviral Integration at a Site Close to the Cerebral Dominance Gene? *British Journal of Psychiatry*, 145, 243–253.

Csikszentmihalyi, M. (1977). *Creativity: Flow and the Psychology of Discovery and Invention.* New York, US: HarperCollins.

Culler, J. (1976). *Saussure.* Glasgow, UK: Fontana-Colins.

Dalrymple, W. (1997). *From the Holy Mountain: A Journey among the Christians of the Middle East.* New York, US: Henry Holt.

Danesi, M. (1998). *Sign, Thought, & Culture: A Basic Course in Semiotics.* Toronto, CA: Canadian Scholars' Press.

Danesi, M., Perron, P. (1999). *Analyzing Cultures: An Introduction and Handbook.* Bloomington, US: Indiana University Press.

Davis, J. M. (1975). Overview: Maintenance Therapy in Psychiatry, I. Schizophrenia. *American Journal of Psychiatry*, 132, 1237–1245.

Davison, R. H. (1988). *Turkey: A Short History.* Huntingdon, UK: The Eothen Press.

de Lamartine, A. (1855). *History of Turkey.* New York, US: D. Appleton & Company.

Derrida, J. (1974). *Of Grammatology.* Trans. G. C. Spivak. Chicago, US: University of Chicago Press.

Derrida, J. (1978). *Writing and Difference.* Trans. A. Bass. Chicago, US: University of Chicago Press.

Derrida, J. (2001). Cogito and the History of Madness. In *Writing and Difference*, pp. 36–76. London, UK: Routledge.

de Saussure, F. (1959). *Course in General Linguistics.* New York, US: McGraw-Hill.

Diamond, D. B. (1997). The Fate of the Ego in Contemporary Psychiatry with Particular Reference to Etiologic Theories of Schizophrenia. *Psychiatry*, 60, 67–88.

Diderot, D., d'Alembert, J.L.R. (1751–1772/1996). *Encyclopédie ou Dictionnaire raisonné des sciences, des arts et des métiers, par une Société de Gens de letters.* Stuttgart-Bad Cannstatt, DE: Frommann.

Dodds, E. R. (1971). *The Greeks and the Irrational.* Berkeley, US: University of California Press.

Doerner, K. (1981). *Madmen and the Bourgeoisie.* Oxford, UK: Basil Blackwell.

Dols, M. W. (1992). *Majnun: The Madman in Medieval Islamic Society.* Oxford, UK: Clarendon Press.

Durbin, P. T. (1968). *St Thomas Aquinas: Summa Theologiae.* Blackfriars ed. and trans., vol. XII. New York, US: McGraw-Hill.

Eigen, M. (1986). *The Psychotic Core.* Northvale, US: Aronson.

Eliot, C. N. [Odysseus]. (1900). *Turkey in Europe.* London, UK: Edward Arnold.

Ellenberger, H. F. (1970). *The Discovery of the Unconscious.* New York, US: Basic Books.

Elver, H. (2005). Gender Equality from a Constitutional Perspective: The Case of Turkey. In R. Rubio-Marin and B. Baines (Eds.), *Constituting Women: The Gender of Constitutional Jurisprudence*, pp. 278–305. Cambridge, UK: Cambridge University Press.

Esin, E. (1980). *A History of Pre-Islamic and Early-Islamic Turkish Culture.* Istanbul, TR: Unal Matbaasi

Estroff, S. E. (1989). Self, Identity and Subjective Experiences of Schizophrenia: In Search of the Subject. *Schizophrenia Bulletin*, 15(2), 189–196.

Ewing, K. P. (1998). A *Majzub* and His Mother: The Place of Sainthood in a Family's Emotional Memory. In P. Werbner and H. Basu (Eds.), *Embodying Charisma: Saints, Cults and Muslim Shrines in South Asia*, pp. 160–183. London, UK: Routledge.

Fabrega, H. (1989). The Self and Schizophrenia: A Cultural Perspective. *Schizophrenia Bulletin*, 15(2), 277–290.

Fediman, J. (1997). *Essential Sufism*. New York, US: Harper Collins.

Feighner, J. P., Robins, E., Guze, S. B., Woodruff, R. Jr., Winokur, G., Munoz, R. (1972). Diagnostic Criteria for Use in Psychiatric Research. *Archives of General Psychiatry*, 26, 57–63.

Feigl, E. (1999). *A Myth of Error: Turkey, Europe and Public Opinion*. Vienna, AU: Amalthea. [Note: citations in this volume were taken in September 2002, from online version of the book provided by the Turkish Ministry of Foreign Affairs at http://www.mfa.gov.tr/grupe/eg/eg35. The online document was no longer provided, however, when access was attempted in December 2005.]

Fenichel, O. (1945). *The Psychoanalytic Theory of Neurosis*. New York, US: Norton.

Feuerbach, L. (1841/1957). *The Essence of Christianity*. Trans. M. Evans. New York, US: Harper & Row.

Feuerbach, L. (1843/1966). *Principles of the Philosophy of the Future*. Trans. M. Vogel. Indianapolis, US: Bobbs-Merrill.

Fink, B. (1996). The Subject and the Other's Desire. In R. Feldstein, B. Fink, and M. Jaanus (Eds.), *Reading Seminars I and II: Lacan's Return to Freud*, pp. 76–97. Albany, US: State University of New York.

Foucault, M. (1965). *Madness and Civilization: A History of Insanity in the Age of Reason*. New York, US: Random House.

Frembgen, J. W. (1998). The *Majzub* Mama Ji Sarkar: 'A Friend of God Moves From One House to Another. In P. Werbner and H. Basu (Eds.) *Embodying Charisma: Saints, Cults and Muslim Shrines in South Asia*. London, UK: Routledge.

Freud, S. (1911/1958). Pschyo-Analytic Notes on an Autobiographical Account of a Case of Paranoia. In J. Strachey (Trans. and Ed.), *Standard Edition of the Complete Psychological Works of Sigmund Freud*, vol. 12, pp. 1–82. London, UK: Hogarth Press.

Friedmann, H. (1955). *The Honey-Guides*. U.S. National Museum Bulletin, 208. Washington DC, US: Smithsonian.

Fromm, E. (1941). *Escape from Freedom*. New York, US: Holt, Reinhardt and Winston.

Gara, M. A., Rosenberg, S., Cohen, B. D. (1987). Personal Identity and the Schizophrenic Process: An Integration. *Psychiatry*, 50, 267–279.

Garmezy, N. (1996). A Paradoxical Partnership: Some Historical and Contemporary Referents Linking Adult Schizophreniform Disorder and Resilient Children under Stress. In S. Matthyse, D. Levy, J. Kagan, and F. Benes (Eds.), *Psychopathology: The Evolving Science of Mental Disorder*, pp. 200–228. New York, US: Cambridge University Press.

Geertz, C. (1973). *The Interpretation of Culture*. New York, US: Basic Books.

Gelb, I. (1963). *A Study of Writing*. Chicago, US: University of Chicago Press.

Goldschmidt, A. (2002). *A Concise History of the Middle East*. Boulder, US: Westview Press.

Good, B. J. (1977). The Heart of What's the Matter: The Semantics of Illness in Iran. *Culture, Medicine and Psychiatry*, 1, 25–58.

Good, B.J. (1994). *Medicine, Rationality, and Experience: An Anthropological Perspective*. Cambridge, UK: Cambridge University Press.

Good, B.J. (2012). Theorizing the 'Subject' of Medical and Psychiatric Anthropology. *Journal of the Royal Anthropological Institute*, 18(3), 515–535.

Good, B.J., DelVecchio Good, M.J. (1981). The Meaning of Symptoms: A Cultural Hermeneutic Model for Clinical Practice. In L. Eisenberg and A. Kleinman (Eds.), *The Relevance of Social Science for Medicine*, pp. 165–196. Dordrecht, NL: D. Reidel.

Good, B.J., Subandi, M.A. (2004). Experiences of Psychosis in Javanese Cultures: Reflections on a Case of Acute, Recurrent Psychosis in Contemporary Yogyakarta, Indonesia. In J.H. Jenkins and R.J. Barrett (Eds.), *Schizophrenia, Culture, and Subjectivity: The Edge of Experience*, pp. 167–195. Cambridge, UK: Cambridge University Press.

Goodwin, J. (1998). *Lords of the Horizons: The History of the Ottoman Empire*. New York, US: Henry Holt.

Gould, J.B. (1970). *The Philosophy of Chrysippus*. Albany, US: State University of New York Press.

Gow, P. (2001). *An Amazonian Myth and Its History*. Oxford, UK: Oxford University Press.

Grant, E. (2001). *God and Reason in the Middle Ages*. Cambridge, UK: Cambridge University Press.

Greenblatt, S. (1980). *Renaissance Self-Fashioning: From More to Shakespeare*. Chicago, US: University of Chicago Press.

Guntrip, H. (1968). *Schizoid Phenomena, Object Relations, and the Self*. New York, US: International Universities Press.

Hale, W. (1994). *Turkish Politics and the Military*. London, UK: Routledge.

Haley, J. (1959). The Family of the Schizophrenic: A Model System. *Journal of Nervous and Mental Disease*, 129, 357–374.

Hall, E. (1989). *Inventing the Barbarian: Greek Self-Definition through Tragedy*. Oxford, UK: Oxford University Press.

Hamori, F. (2004). The Goddess of Birth and Fertility: Based on the Work of Dr Ida Bobula 'A Magyar ösvallás istenasszonya.' Available online: http://users.cwnet.com/millenia/BAU.htm.

Hardwick, C.S. (Ed.) (1977). *Semiotic and Significs: The Correspondence between Charles S. Peirce and Victoria Lady Wellby*. Bloomington, US: Indiana University Press.

Haskins, C.H. (1979). *The Renaissance of the Twelfth Century*. Cambridge, US: Harvard University Press.

Haslip, J. (1958). *The Sultan: The Life of Abdul Hamid*. London, UK: Cassell.

Hawkes, T. (1977). *Structuralism and Semiotics*. Berkeley, US: University of California Press.

Hegel, F.W. (1807). *Phenomenology of Mind*. Trans. J.B. Baillie. Available online: http://www.class.uidaho.edu/mickelsen/ToC/Hegel%20Phen%20ToC.htm.

Hegel, F.W. (1827/2001). *The Philosophy of History*. Trans. J. Sibree. Kitchner, CA: Batoche Books.

Heisenberg, W. (1952). *Philosophic Problems of Nuclear Science*. London, UK: Faber & Faber.

Helminski, K. (1998). *The Rumi Collection: An Anthology of Translations of Mevlana Jalaluddin Rumi*. Boston, US: Shambhala.

Heper, M., Criss, N. B. (2009). *Historical Dictionary of Turkey*. Lanham, US: Scarecrow Press.

Hitti, P. K. (1961). *The Near East in History, a 5000 Year Story*. Princeton, US: Van Nostrand.

Hoffmeyer, J. (1997). The Global Semiosphere. In I. Rauch and G. F. Carr (Eds.), *Semiotics Around the World. Proceedings of the Fifth Congress of the International Association for Semiotic Studies*, pp. 933–936. New York, US: Mouton de Gruyter. [Note: Quotations in this text are from an online version of this paper provided by Jesper Hoffmeyer, available at http://www.molbio.ku.dk/MolBioPages/abk/PersonalPages/Jesper/Semiosphere.html.]

Holdcroft, D. (1991). *Saussure: Signs, System, and Arbitrariness*. Cambridge, UK: Cambridge University Press.

Hollingdale, R. J. (1982). Introduction. In A. Hoffmann, *Tales of Hoffmann*, pp. 7–15. London, UK: Penguin Books.

Hookway, C. (1992). *Peirce*. London, UK: Routledge.

Hookway, C. (1995). Metaphysics, Science, and Self-Control: A Response to Apel. In K. L. Ketner (Ed.), *Peirce and Contemporary Thought: Philosophical Inquiries*, pp. 398–416. New York, US: Fordham University Press.

Horton, R. (1993). *Patterns of Thought in Africa and the West: Essays on Magic, Religion and Science*. New York, US: Cambridge University Press.

Howard, D. A. (2001). *The History of Turkey*. London, UK: Greenwood Press.

Howe, M. (2000). *Turkey Today: A Nation Divided Over Islam's Revival*. Boulder, US: Westview Press.

Howells, J. G. (1991). Introduction. In J. G. Howells (Ed.), *The Concept of Schizophrenia: Historical Perspectives*. Washington DC, US: American Psychiatric Press.

Howells, J. G., Guirguis, W. R. (1980). Schizophrenia and Family Psychopathology. *International Journal of Family Psychiatry*, 1, 113–126.

Howells, J. G., Osborn, M. (1984). *A Reference Companion to the History of Abnormal Psychology*. Westport, US: Greenwood Press.

Hughes, P., Brecht, G. (1975). *Vicious Circles and Infinity: A Panoply of Paradoxes*. Garden City, US: Doubleday

Hume, D. (1751/1978). *Enquiries Concerning Human Understanding and Concerning the Principles of Morals*. Oxford, UK: Clarendon Press.

Hutchings, S. C. (2004). The Russian Critique of Saussure. In C. Sanders (Ed.), *The Cambridge Companion to Saussure*, pp. 139–156. Cambridge, UK: Cambridge University Press.

Ibn Alawi, S. M. (1999). *The Prophets in Barzakh and the Hadith of Isra and Miraj Followed by the Immense Merits of Al-Sham and the Vision of Allah*. Fenton, US: As-Sunnah Foundation of America.

Ibn Arabi, M. (1197/1993). *Kitab al-Isra ila al-Maqam al-Asra*. Tehran, IR: Ketabkhane-ye Tahuri.

Ibn Arabi, M. (1238/1972). *Futuhat al-Makkiyah*. Cairo, EG: Maktabah al-Arabiyah.

Inalcik, H. (1973). *The Ottoman Empire: The Classical Age 1300–1600*. London, UK: Weidenfeld & Nicolson.

Isikli, A. (1987). Wage Labor and Unionization. In I. C. Schick and E. A. Tonak (Eds.), *Turkey in Transition: New Perspectives*. Oxford, UK: Oxford University Press.

Istanbul Teknik Üniversitesi. (2002). Discover Turkey: Ancient Anatolia. Available online: http://www.turkishnews.com/DiscoverTurkey/anatolia/history.html

Jackson, H. F. (1990). Are There Biological Markers of Schizophrenia? In R. P. Bentall (Ed.), *Reconstructing Schizophrenia*, pp. 118–156. London, UK: Routledge.

Jakobson, R. (1990). *On Language*. Cambridge, US: Harvard University Press.

Jameson, F. (1983).*The Political Unconscious: Narrative as a Socially Symbolic Act.* London: Routledge.

Jaspers, K. (1963). *General Psychopathology*. Trans. J. Hoenig and Marian Hamilton. Chicago, US: University of Chicago Press.

Jenkins, J. H. (1988). Ethnopsychiatric Interpretations of Schizophrenic Illness: The Problem of *Nervios* within Mexican-American Families. *Culture, Medicine and Psychiatry*, 12, 301–329.

Jenkins, J. H. (2004). Schizophrenia as a Paradigm Case for Understanding Fundamental Human Processes. In J. H. Jenkins and R. J. Barrett (Eds.), *Schizophrenia, Culture, and Subjectivity: The Edge of Experience*, pp. 29–61. Cambridge, UK: Cambridge University Press.

Jeste, D., del Carmen, R., Lohr, B., Wyatt, R. J. (1985). Did Schizophrenia Exist before the Eighteenth Century? *Comprehensive Psychiatry*, 26(6), 493–503.

Jones, K. (1955). *Lunacy, Law, and Conscience 1744–1845*. London, UK: Routledge & Kegan Paul.

Jones, K. (1960). *Mental Health and Social Policy*. London, UK: Routledge & Kegan Paul.

Kahn, M. (1980). *Children of the Jinn: In Search of the Kurds and their Country*. New York, US: Seaview Books.

Kallman, F. (1938). *The Genetics of Schizophrenia*. New York, US: J. J. Augustin.

Kant, E. (1781/1998). *Critique of Pure Reason*. Trans. N. K. Smith. London, UK: McMillan.

Kavanagh D. J. (1992). Recent Developments in Expressed Emotion and Schizophrenia. *British Journal of Psychiatry*, 160, 601–620.

Kedourie, S. (1999). *Turkey before and after Ataturk: Internal and External Affair*. London, UK: Frank Cass.

Keeling, S. V. (1968). *Descartes*. London, UK: Oxford University Press.

Kennedy, J. L., Giuffra, L. A., Moises, H. W., Cavalli-Sforza, L. L., Pakstis, A. J., Kidd, J. R., Castiglione, C. M., Sjogren, B., Wetterberg, L., Kidd, K. K. (1988). Evidence against Linkage of Schizophrenia to Markers on Chromosome 5 in a Northern Swedish Pedigree. *Nature*, 336, 167–170.

Kenny, A. (1994). *The Oxford Illustrated History of Western Philosophy*. New York, US: Oxford University Press.

Khairallah, A. E. (1980). *Love, Madness and Poetry: An Interpretation of the Magnun Legend*. Beirut, LB: Orient-Institut der Deutschen Morgenländischen Gesellschaft.

Killoran, M. (1998). Nationalism and Embodied Memory in Northern Cyprus. In V. Calotychos (Ed.), *Cyprus and Its People: Nation, Identity, and Experience in an Unimaginable Community, 1955–1997*, pp. 159–170. Boulder, US: Westview.

Kinross, L. (1977). *The Ottoman Centuries*. New York, US: Morrow.

Kinzer, S. (2001). *Crescent and Star: Turkey between Two Worlds*. New York, US: Farrar, Straus and Groux.

Kirmayer, L. J. (2001). Sapir's Vision of Culture and Psychiatry. *Psychiatry*, 64, 23–31.

Kleinman, A. (1973). Medicine's Symbolic Reality: On a Central Problem in the Philosophy of Medicine. *Inquiry*, 16, 206–213.

Kleinman, A. (1975). Medical and Psychiatric Anthropology and the Study of Traditional Forms of Medicine in Modern Chinese Culture. *Bulletin of the Institute of Ethnology, Academia Sinica*, 39, 107–123.

Kleinman, A. (1980). *Patients and Healers in the Context of Culture*. Berkeley, US: University of California Press.

Kleinman, A. (1995). *Writing at the Margin: Discourse between Anthropology and Medicine*. Berkeley, US: University of California Press.

Kleinman, A. (1999). Experience and Its Moral Modes: Culture, Human Conditions, and Disorder. In G. B. Peterson (Ed.), *The Tanner Lectures on Human Values*, pp. 357–420. Salt Lake City, US: University of Utah Press.

Kneale, W., Kneale, M. (1962). *The Development of Logic*. Oxford, UK: Clarendon Press.

Knollenberg, J. (2000). Statement Regarding the Armenian Genocide. Available online: http://www.house.gov/knollenberg/mediacenter/speeches/2000/12.15.00.htm.

Knudsen, C. (1982). Intentions and Impositions. In N. Kretzmann, A. Kenny and J. Pinborg (Eds.), *The Cambridge History of Later Medieval Philosophy*, pp. 479–495. Cambridge, UK: Cambridge University Press.

Knysh, A. D. (1999). *Ibn Arabi in the Later Islamic Tradition: The Making of a Polemical Image in Medieval Islam*. Albany, US: State University of New York Press.

Kohler, K., Malter, H. (2005). Shabbethai Zebi B. Mordecai. *Jewish Encyclopedia*. Available online: http://jewishencyclopedia.com/view_friendly.jsp?artid=531& letter=S.

Kristeva, J. (1989). *Black Sun: Depression and Melancholia*. New York, US: Columbia University Press.

Kristeva, J. (1994). On Yuri Lotman. *Publications of the Modern Language Association*, 109, 375–376.

Kroll, J, Bacharch, B. (1982). Medieval Visions and Contemporary Hallucinations. *Psychological Medicine*, 12, 709–721.

Kundera, M. (1980). *The Book of Laughter and Forgetting*. New York, US: Alfred A. Knopf.

Lacan J. (1949/2006). The Mirror Stage as Formative of the I Function. In B. Fink (Trans.), *Ecrit: The First Complete Translation in English*, pp. 75–81. New York, US: Norton.

Lacan, J. (1968). *The Language of the Self: The Function of Language in Psychoanalysis*. Trans. Anthony Wilden. New York, US: Dell.

Lacan, J. (1993). *The Seminars of Jacques Lacan Book III: The Psychoses 1955–1956*. CITY, New York, US: W. W. Norton.

Laclau, E., Mouffe, C. (2001). *Hegemony and Socialist Strategy: Towards a Radical Democratic Politics*. London: Verso.

Leff, J. P., Wing, J. K. (1971). Trial of Maintenance Therapy in Schizophrenia. *British Medical Journal*, 3, 599–604.

Lévi-Strauss, C. (1966). *The Savage Mind*. Chicago, US: University of Chicago Press.

Lewis, B. (1975). *The Emergence of Modern Turkey*. London, UK: Oxford University Press.

Lewis, B. (2001). *Music of a Distant Drum: Classical Arabic, Persian, Turkish and Hebrew Poems*. Princeton, US: Princeton University Press.

Lewisohn, L. (1995). *Beyond Faith and Infidelity: The Sufi Poetry and Teachings of Mahmud Shabistari*. Surrey, UK: Curzon Press.

Lewy, H. (1956). *Chaldean Oracles and Theurgy: Mysticism, Magic and Platonism in the Later Roman Empire*. Cairo, EG: Impremerie De L'institut Francais D'Archeologie Orientale.

Lidz, T. (1958). Schizophrenia and the Family. *Psychiatry*, 21, 21–27.

Linke, L. (1937). *Allah Dethroned: A Journey through Modern Turkey*. London, UK: Knopf.

Little, L. K. (1978). *Religious Poverty and the Profit Economy in Medieval Europe*. Ithaca, US: Cornell University.

Lopez, R. (1971). *The Commercial Revolution of the Middle Ages: 950–1350*. Englewood Cliffs, US: Prentice Hall.

Loriedo, C., Vella, G. (1992). *Paradox and the Family System*. New York, US: Bruner/Mazel.

Lotman, J. (1966/1988). Problems in the Typology of Texts. In D. Lucid (Ed.), *Soviet Semiotics: An Anthology*, pp. 119–124. Baltimore, US: Johns Hopkins University Press.

Lotman, J. (1973). The Origin of Plot in the Light of Typology. *Stat'i po tipologii kul'tury*, 2, 9–41. [Note that quotations are from the online version, trans. Julian Graffy, http://www.tau.ac.il/humanities/publications/poetics/art/ori10.html.]

Lotman, J. (1977). Problems in the Typology of Texts. In D. Lucid (Ed.), *Soviet Semiotics*, pp. 119–124. Baltimore, US: Johns Hopkins University Press.

Lotman, J. (1984). O Semiosfere [On Semiosphere]. *Sémeiótiké*, 17, 5–23.

Lotman, J. (1990). *Universe of the Mind: A Semiotic Theory of Culture*. Trans. Ann Shukman. Bloomington, US: Indiana University Press.

Lotman, J., Uspensky, B. (1978). On the Semiotic Mechanism of Culture. *New Literary History*, 9(2), 211–232.

Love, A. M. (2002). Timelines of Ancient History. Available online: http://www.sarissa.org.

Lovelock, J. E. (1979). *Gaia: A New Look at Life on Earth*. Oxford, UK: Oxford University Press.

Luhrmann, T. M. (2001). *Of Two Minds: An Anthropologist Looks at American Psychiatry*. New York, US: Vintage Books.

Lyons, J. (1977). *Semantics*. New York, US: Cambridge University Press.

Lysaker, P. H., Lysaker, J. T. (2002). Narrative Structure in Psychosis: Schizophrenia and Disruptions in the Dialogical Self. *Theory and Psychology*, 12, 207–220.

MacDonald, S. (1993). Theory of Knowledge. In N. Kretzmann and E. Stump (Eds.), *The Cambridge Companion to Aquinas*, pp. 160–195. Cambridge, UK: Cambridge University Press.

Madigan, D. (2001). *Qur'an's Self-Image: Writing and Authority in Islam's Scripture*. Princeton, US: Princeton University Press.

Mahler, M. S. (1952). On Child Psychosis and Schizophrenia. *Psychoanalytic Study of the Child*, 14, 314–382.

Mardin, Ş. (1989). *Religion and Social Change in Modern Turkey: The Case of Bediuzzaman Said Nursi*. Albany, US: SUNY Press.

Marsella, A. J., White, G. M. (1982). *Cultural Conceptions of Mental Health and Therapy*. Boston, US: D. Reidel.

Marshall, R. (1990). The Genetics of Schizophrenia: Axiom or Hypothesis? In R. P. Bentall (Ed.), *Reconstructing Schizophrenia*, pp. 89–117. London, UK: Routledge.

Marx, K. (1867–1894/1977). *Capital*. 3 vols. Trans. B. Foulkes. Harmondsworth, UK: Penguin.

Marx, K., Engels, F. (1975) *Collected Works*. New York, US: International Publishing Co.

Mason, H. W. (1995). *Al-Hallaj*. Surrey, UK: Curzon Press.

Massignon, L. (1922). *Passion d'al-Hosayn-Ibn-Mansour al-Hallaj : martyr mystique de l'Islam, exécuté a Bagdad le 26 Mars 922*. Paris, FR: Geuthner.

McCarthy, J. (1997). *The Ottoman Turks: An Introductory History to 1923*. London, UK: Longman.

Mears, E. G. (1924). *Modern Turkey: A Politico-Economic Interpretation, 1908–1923 Inclusive, with Selected Chapters by Representative Authorities*. New York, US: Macmillan.

Meeker, M. (2002). *Nation of Empire: The Ottoman Legacy of Turkish Modernity*. Berkeley, US: University of California Press.

Melchert, N. (1991). *The Great Conversation: A Historical Introduction to Philosophy*. Mountain View, US: Mayfield Publishing Company.

Mellor, C. S. (1970). First Rank Symptoms of Schizophrenia. *British Journal of Psychiatry*, 117, 15–23.

Meltzer, H. Y., Stahl, S. M. (1976). The Dopamine Hypothesis of Schizophrenia: A Review. *Schizophrenia Bulletin*, 2, 19–76.

Mercier, L. S. (1783). *Tableau de Paris*. Amsterdam, NL: Publisher unknown.

Merton, R. (1938) *Science, Technology and Society in Seventeenth-Century England*. New York, US: Harper & Row.

Mitchell, S. (1993). *Anatolia: Land, Men, and Gods in Asia Minor*. 2 vols. Oxford, UK: Clarendon.

Monfasani, J. (1998). Humanism: Renaissance. In E. Craig (Ed.), *Routledge Encyclopedia of Philosophy* [CD-ROM, Version 1.0]. London, UK: Routledge.

Moore, G. H. (1998). Paradoxes of set and property. In E. Craig (Ed.), *Routledge Encyclopedia of Philosophy* [CD-ROM, Version 1.0]. London, UK: Routledge.

Moris, Z. (1997). Rumi's View of Evil. *Sufi: A Journal of Sufism*, 36(Winter), 21–25. Available online: http://www.sufism.ru/eng/txts/rumi.htm.

Morris, C. (1972/1987). *The Discovery of the Individual 1050–1200*. Toronto, CA: University of Toronto Press.

Morris, P. (1994). *The Bakhtin Reader: Selected Readings of Bakhtin, Medvedev, Voloshinov*. London, UK: Edward Arnold.

Morrison, K. (1995). *Marx, Durkheim, Weber: Formations of Modern Social Thought*. London, UK: Sage.

Mulle, J. G. (2012). Schizophrenia Genetics: Progress, at Last. *Current Opinion in Genetics & Development*, 22(3), 238–244.

Murray, A. (1978). *Reason and Society in the Middle Ages*. Oxford, UK: Clarendon Press.

Nesim, A. (1987). *Batmayan Egitimguneslerimiz: Kibris Turk egitimi hakkinda bir arastirma* [*Our Unsetting Educational Suns: A Research on Cypriot Turkish Education*]. Nicosia, CY: K.K.T.C. Milli Egitim ve Kultur Bakanligi.

Nettle, D. (2001). *Strong Imagination: Madness, Creativity and Human Nature*. New York, US: Oxford University Press.

Neyzi, L. (2002). Remembering to Forget: Sabbateanism, National Identity and Subjectivity in Turkey. *Comparative Studies in Society and History*, 44(1), 137–158.

Ng, V., Barker, G. J., Hendler, T. (2003). *Psychiatric Neuroimaging*. Amsterdam, NL: IOS Press.

Nicolle, D. (1995). *The Janissaries*. London, UK: Osprey Publishing.

Nisbet, W. (1815). *Two Letters to the Right Honourable George Rose, M.P. on the Reports at Present before the Honourable House of Commons on the State of Madhouses*. London, UK: Cox.

Obeyesekere, G. (1976). The Impact of Ayurvedic Ideas on the Culture and the Individual in Sri Lanka. In M. Leslie (Ed.), *Asian Medical Systems*, pp. 201–226. Berkeley, US: University of California Press.

Obeyesekere, G. (1985). Depression, Buddhism, and the Work of Culture in Sri Lanka. In A. Kleinman and B. Good (Eds.), *Culture and Depression*, pp. 134–152. Berkeley, US: University of California Press.

Obeyesekere, G. (1990). *The Work of Culture: Symbolic Transformation in Psychoanalysis and Anthropology*. Chicago, US: The University of Chicago Press.

O'Neil, Patrick H. (2013). *The Deep State: An Emerging Concept in Comparative Politics*. Available online at the SSRN website: http://dx.doi.org/10.2139/ssrn.2313375.

Özal, T. (1991). *Turkey in Europe and Europe in Turkey*. Nicosia, CY: K. Rustem and Brothers. [Citations in this paper are from the online version of this book, provided by the Government of the Turkish Republic, Ministry of Foreign Affairs. Access URL: http://www.mfa.gov.tr/grupe/eg/eg05/default.htm.]

Pao, P. (1979). *Schizophrenic Disorders: Theory and Treatment from a Psychodynamic Point of View*. New York, US: International Universities Press.

Parmentier, R.J. (1994). *Signs in Society: Studies in Semiotic Anthropology*. Bloomington, US: Indiana University Press.

Parviz, A. (1972). *Tarikh-eh Salajegheh va Kharazmshahan* [History of the Seljuks and the Khwarazms]. Tehran, IR: Elmi Publications.

Patterson, J.C., Kotrla, K.J. (2004). Functional Neuroimaging in Psychiatry. In R.J. Leo, S.C. Yudofsky, and R.E. Hales (Eds.), *Essentials of Neuropsychiatry and Clinical Neurosciences*. Washington DC, US: American Psychiatric Publishing.

Peirce, C.S. (1931–1958). *Collected Papers of Charles Sanders Peirce*, vols. 1–8. Ed. C. Hartshorne, P. Weiss, and A. Burks. Cambridge, US: Harvard University Press.

Peirce, C.S. (1982–1986). *Writings of Charles Sanders Peirce: A Chronological Edition*, vols. 1–4. Ed. Max Fisch. Bloomington, US: Indiana University Press.

Peters, U.H. (1991). Concepts of Schizophrenia after Kraepelin and Bleuler. In J.G. Howells (Ed.), *The Concept of Schizophrenia: Historical Perspectives*, pp. 93–108. Washington DC, US: American Psychiatric Press.

Pettifer, J. (1998). *The Turkish Labyrinth: Ataturk and the New Islam*. London, UK: Penguin Books.

Petrovic, G. (1991). Alienation. In T. Bottomore (Ed.), *The Dictionary of Marxist Thought*, pp. 11–16. Malden, US: Blackwell Publishing.

Phillips, W.A., Silverstein, S.M. (2003) Convergence of Biological and Psychological Perspectives on Cognitive Coordination in Schizophrenia. *Behavioral and Brain Sciences*, 26(1), 65–82.

Pilgrim, D. (1990). Competing Histories of Madness. In R. Bentall (Ed.) *Reconstructing Schizophrenia*, pp. 211–233. London, UK: Routledge.

Pinch, G. (1994) *Magic in Ancient Egypt*. Austin, US: University of Texas Press.

Pinker, S. (1994). *The Language Instinct: How the Mind Creates Language*. New York, US: William Morrow.

Piontelli, A. (2002). *Twins: From Fetus to Child*. London, UK: Routledge.

Plato (370 bc/1974). *Republic*. Trans. G.M.A. Grube. Indianapolis, US: Hackett.

Plato (2000). *Laws*. Trans. Benjamin Jowett. Amherst, US: Prometheus Books.

Ponzio, A. (1984). Semiotics between Peirce and Bakhtin. *Recherche Sémiotic*, 4, 273–292.

Pope, N. (1997). *Turkey Unveiled: A History of Modern Turkey*. Woodstock, US: The Overlook Press.

Porter, R. (1991). *The Faber Book of Madness*. London, UK: Faber and Faber.

Porter, R. (2002). *Madness: A Brief History*. New York, US: Oxford University Press.

Poulton, H. (1997). *Top Hat, Grey Wolf, and Crescent: Turkish Nationalism and the Turkish Republic*. New York, US: New York University Press.

Priest, G.G. (1994). The Structure of the Paradoxes of Self-Reference. *Mind*, 103, 25–34.

Rahimi, S. (2002). Is Cultural Logic an Appropriate Concept? A Semiotic Perspective on the Study of Culture and Logic. *Sign System Studies*, 30(2), 455–464.

Rahimi, S. (2007). Intimate Exteriority: Sufi Space as Sanctuary for Injured Subjectivities in Turkey. *Journal of Religion and Health*, 46(3), 409–421.

Rahimi, S. (2013). The Ego, the Ocular, and the Uncanny: Why Are Metaphors of Vision Central in Accounts of the Uncanny? *International Journal of Psychoanalysis*, 94(3), 453–476.

Rajai-Bokharai, A.A. (1986). *Farhangeh Ash'areh Hafez* [*Dictionary of Hafiz' Poetry*]. Tehran, IR: Elmi Publications.

Ramsay, W.M. (1897). *Impressions of Turkey during Twelve Years' Wanderings*. London, UK: Hodder & Stoughton.

Raspe, R.E. (ca. 1800). *The Travels and Surprising Adventures of Baron Munchausen Illustrated with Thirty Seven Curious Engravings From the Baron's Own Designs and Five Illustrations by G. Gruikshank*. Available online: http://www.ffutures.demon.co.uk/munch/munch.htm.

Rawandi, M. bin A. bin S. (1238/1954). *Rahat-us-Sudur wa Ayat-us-Surur fi Tarikh al-Dawlat al-Saljuqiyah* [*Ease of the Heart and Signs of Joy: On the History of the Seljuks*]. Tehran, IR: Amir Kabir Publications.

Restivo, G. (1998). The Enlightenment Code of Yuri Lotman's Theory of Culture. *Interlitteraria* (Annual Publication of Tartu University), 3, 11–37.

Rhode, E. (1994). *Psychotic Metaphysics*. London, UK: H. Karnac.

Rice, M. (2003). *Egypt's Making: The Origins of Ancient Egypt*. New York, US: Routledge.

Rice, T.T. (1961). *The Seljuks in Asia Minor*. New York, US: Praeger.

Robbins, M. (1993). *Experience of Schizophrenia: An Integration of the Personal, Scientific, and Therapeutic*. New York, US: Guilford.

Roberts, D. (1960). *Victorian Origins of the British Welfare State*. New Haven, US: Yale University Press.

Roberts, G. (1994). A Glossary of Key Terms. In P. Morris (Ed.), *The Bakhtin Reader: Selected Readings of Bakhtin, Medvedev, Voloshinov*, pp. 245–252. London, UK: Edward Arnold.

Robins, K, Aksoy, A. (2000). Deep Nation: The National Question and Turkish Cinema Culture. In M. Hjort and S. McKenzie (Eds.), *Cinema and Nation*, pp. 203–221. London, UK: Routledge.

Robinson, N. (1729). *A New System of the Spleen, Vapors, and Hypochondriack Melancholy*. . . . London, UK: Printed for A. Bettesworth, W. Innys, and C. Rivington.

Roccatagliata, G. (1991). Classical Concepts of Schizophrenia. In J. G. Howells (Ed.) *The Concept of Schizophrenia: Historical Perspectives*, pp. 1–28. Washington DC, US: American Psychiatric Press.

Rorty, A. O. (Ed.) (1992). *Essays on Aristotle's Poetics*. Princeton, US: Princeton University Press.

Rose, N. (1996). Power and Subjectivity: Critical History and Psychology. In C. F. Graumann and K. J. Gergon (Eds.), *Historical Dimensions of Psychological Discourse*, pp. 103–124. New York, US: Cambridge University Press.

Ross, K. L. (2001). Islam: 622 AD to Present. Available online: http://www.friesian.com/islam.htm.

Rumi, J. M. (1984). *Kolliaat-eh Shams-eh Tabrizi [Collected Poems on Shams of Tabriz]*. Tehran, IR: Amir Kabir Publications.

Rümke, H. C. (1990/1941). The Nuclear Symptom of Schizophrenia and the Praecox Feeling (Trans. J. Neeleman). *History of Psychiatry*, 1, 331–341.

Rush, B. (1948). *The Autobiography of Benjamin Rush: His "Travels through Life" Together with His "Commonplace Book for 1789–1813."* Ed. George W. Corner. Princeton, US: Princeton University Press.

Russell, B. (1903). *The Principles of Mathematics*. Cambridge, UK: Cambridge University.

Russell, B. (1906). Les paradoxes de la logique. *Revue de Métaphysique et de Morale*, 14, 627–650.

St. Clair, D., Blackwood, D., Muir, W., Baillie, D., Hubbard, A., Wright, A., Evans, J. (1989). No Linkage of Chromosome 5q11-q13 Markers to Schizophrenia in Scottish Families. *Nature*, 339, 305–309.

Sainsbury, R. M. (1995). *Paradoxes*. Cambridge, UK: University of Cambridge Press.

Sardar, Z., Nandy, A., Wyn Davies, M. (1993). *Barbaric Others: A Manifesto on Western Racism*. London, UK: Pluto Press.

Sass, L. (1994). *Madness and Modernism: Insanity in the Light of Modern Art, Literature, and Thought*. Cambridge, US: Harvard University Press.

Sass, L. (1999). Schizophrenia, Self-Consciousness, and the Modern Mind. In S. Gallagher and J. Shear (Eds.), *Models of the Self*, pp. 319–341. Thorverton, UK: Imprint Academic.

Sass, L. (2004). 'Negative Symptoms', Common Sense and Cultural Disembedding in Modern Age. In J. H. Jenkins and R. J. Barrett (Eds.), *Schizophrenia, Culture and Subjectivity: The Edge of Experience*, pp. 303–328. Cambridge, UK: Cambridge University.

Saylan, T., Karadeniz, A., Iyier, N., Soydan, M., Pamuk, D. (2000). A Scholarship Project for the Children of Leprosy Patients in Turkey. *Leprosy Review*, 71, 212–216.

Scheper Hughes, N. (2001). *Saints, Scholars and Schizophrenics: Mental Illness*. Berkeley, US: University of California Press.

Schick, I. C., Tonak, E. A. (1987). *Turkey in Transition: New Perspectives*. New York, US: Oxford University Press.

Schimmel, A. (1992). *Rumi's World: The Life and Works of the Greatest Sufi Poet*. Boston, US: Shambala.

Schneider, K. (1959). *Clinical Psychopathology*. New York, US: Grune and Stratton.

Scott, T. K. (1966). *John Buridan: Sophisms on Meaning and Truth*. New York, US: Appleton-Century-Crofts.

Scull, A. (1993). *The Most Solitary of Afflictions: Madness and Society in Britain 1700–1900*. New Haven, US: Yale University Press.

Searles, H. F. (1963). *Collected Papers on Schizophrenia and Related Subjects*. New York, US: International Universities Press.

Sebeok, T. A. (1963). Communication among Social Bees; Porpoises and Sonar; Man and Dolphin. *Language*, 39, 448–466.

Sebeok, T. A. (1972). *Perspectives in Zoosemiotics*. The Hague, NL: Mouton.

Sebeok, T. A. (1984). Signs of Life. *International Semiotic Spectrum*, 2, 1–2.

Sebeok, T. A. (1994). *Signs: An Introduction to Semiotics*. Toronto, CA: University of Toronto Press.

Sebeok, T. A. (1998). The Estonian Connection. *Sign Systems Studies*, 26, 20–41.

Sells, M. A. (1996). *Early Islamic Mysticism: Sufi, Quran, Miraj, Poetic and Theological Writings*. Mahwah, US: Paulist Press.

Sewell, W. H. (2005). *Logics of History: Social Theory and Social Transformation*. Chicago, US: University of Chicago Press.

Seyed-Gohrab, A. A. (2003). *Layli And Majnun: Love, Madness and Mystic Longing in Nizami's Epic Romance*. Leiden, NL: Brill.

Shaftesbury, A.A.C. (1711/1977). Inquiry Concerning Virtue and Merit. In D. Walford (Ed.), *Characteristics of Men, Manners, Opinions, and Times*, pp. 163–230. Manchester, UK: Manchester University Press.

Shaner, R. (2000). *Psychiatry*. Baltimore, US: Lippincott Williams & Wilkins.

Shaw, S. J. (1971). *Between Old and New: The Ottoman Empire under Sultan Selim III, 1789–1807*. Cambridge, US: Harvard University Press.

Shaw, S. J. (1976). *History of the Ottoman Empire and Modern Turkey: Volume 1, Empire of the Gazis: The Rise and Decline of the Ottoman Empire 1280–1808*. Cambridge, UK: Cambridge University Press.

Sheriff, J. K. (1989). *The Fate of Meaning: Charles Peirce, Structuralism, and Literature*. Princeton, US: Princeton University Press.

Sherington, R., Brynjolfsson, J., Pertursson, H., Potter, M., Dudleston, K., Barraclough, B., Wasmuth, J., Dobbs, M., Gurling, H. (1988). Localization of a Susceptibility Locus for Schizophrenia on Chromosome 5. *Nature*, 336, 164–167.

Shimizu, K. (1979). *Bibliography on Saljuq Studies*. Tokyo, JP: Institute for the Study of Languages and Cultures of Asia and Africa.

Short, T. L. (1981). Semiosis and Intentionality. *Transactions of the Charles S. Peirce Society*, 17(3), 197–223.

Shukman, A. (1977). *Literature and Semiotics. A Study of the Writings of Yu M. Lotman*. Amsterdam, NL: North Holland.

Shukman, A. (1994). Modeling System. In Thomas A. Sebeok (Ed.), *Encyclopedic Dictionary of Semiotics*, 2nd ed., vol. 1, pp. 558–560. Berlin, DE: Mouton de Gruyter.

Sicker, M. (2001). *The Islamic World in Decline: From the Treaty of Karlowitz to the Disintegration of the Ottoman Empire*. Westport, US: Praeger.

Silverman, K. (1983). *The Subject of Semiotics*. Oxford, UK: Oxford University Press.

Simon, R. I., Gold, L. H. (2004). *The American Psychiatric Publishing Textbook of Forensic Psychiatry*. Arlington, US: American Psychiatric Publishing.

Sivan, E. (1990). *Radical Islam*. New Haven, US: Yale University Press.

Siorvanes, L. (1998). Neoplatonism. In E. Craig (Ed.), *Routledge Encyclopedia of Philosophy* [CD-ROM, Version 1.0]. London, UK: Routledge.

Slater, B. H. (2001). Logical Paradoxes. *The Internet Encyclopedia of Philosophy.* Available online: http://www.utm.edu/research/iep.

Smith, A. (1759/1976) *The Theory of Moral Sentiments.* Ed. D.D. Raphael and A. L. Mackie. Oxford, UK: Clarendon Press.

Smith, H., Freely, M. (1999). Greek Missions of Mercy Melt Ancient Hatred. *The Observer,* Sunday, August 29. Available online: http://www.guardian.co.uk/quaketurkey/Story/0,2763,201835,00.html.

Solomon, R. (1996). *A Short History of Philosophy.* New York, US: Oxford University Press.

Sönesson, G. (1998). The Concept of Text in Cultural Semiotics. *Sign System Studies,* 26, 83–114. Available online: http://www.arthist.lu.se/kultsem/sonesson/TextTartu3.html.

Sönesson, G. (2001). Bridging Nature and Culture in Cultural Semiotics. In *Bridging Nature and Culture. Proceedings of the Sixth International Congress of the IASS, Guadalajara, Mexico, July, 13–19, 1997.* Mexico City, DF: Porrua. Available online: http://www.arthist.lu.se/kultsem/sonesson/CultureNature.html

Sörensen, D. (1987). *Theory Formation and the Study of Literature.* Amsterdam, NL: Rodopi.

Southern, R. W. (1953). *The Making of the Middle Ages.* London, UK: Hutchison's University Library.

Stanton, J. L. (2003). *The Alchemy Reader: From Hermes Trismegistus to Isaac Newton.* Cambridge, UK: Cambridge University Press.

Starr, J. (1978). *Dispute and Settlement in Rural Turkey: An Ethnography of Law.* Leiden, NL: E. J. Brill.

Stavrakakis, Y. (1999). *Lacan and the Political.* London, UK: Routledge.

Steiner, P. (1981). In Defense of Semiotics: The Dual Asymmetry of Cultural Signs. *New Literary History,* 12, 415–435.

Stierlin, H. (1974). Karl Jaspers' Psychiatry in the Light of His Basic Philosophical Position. *Journal of the History of the Behavioral Sciences,* 10, 213–226.

Stronach, D. (2004). On the Antiquity of the Yurt: Evidence from Arjan and Elsewhere. *Silk Road Newsletter,* 2(1), 9–18. Available online: http://www.silkroadfoundation.org/toc/newsletter.html.

Swallow, C. (1973). *The Sick Man of Europe: Ottoman Empire to Turkish Republic, 1789–1923.* London, UK: E. Benn.

Tanpınar, A. H. (1943). *Abdullah Efendinin Rüyaları: Hikâyeler [The Dreams of Abdullah Efendi: Stories].* Istanbul, TR: A. Halit Kitabevi.

Tanpınar, A. H. (1970). *Ya adığım Gibi [As I Lived].* Istanbul, TR: Birol Emil.

Teilhard de Chardin, P. (1955). *Le Phenomene Humain.* Paris, FR: Seuil.

Teilhard de Chardin, P. (1959). *The Phenomenon of Man.* New York, US: Harper & Row.

Thibault, P. J. (1997). The Time Dependant Nature of Language: The Dialectic of Synchrony and Diachrony. In *Re-Reading Saussure: The Dynamics of Signs in Social Life,* pp. 80–112. London, UK: Routledge.

Timur, T. (1987). The Ottoman Heritage. In I. C. Schick and E. A. Tonak (Eds.), *Turkey in Transition: New Perspectives,* pp. 3–26. Oxford, UK: Oxford University Press.

Tissot, S. A. (1778–1780) *Traité des nerfs et de leurs maladies.* Paris. [Note: An item with the same title, but authored by Saint August David Tissot (rather than Simon-André Tissot, as Foucault documents), is also available. In writing this bibliography I gave priority to Foucault's version, because I am quoting his text and because I do not have access to the original.]

Todd, W. M. (1998). Moscow-Tartu School. *Routledge Encyclopedia of Philosophy*, vol. 6, pp. 583–588. London, UK: Routledge.

Torrey, E. F. (1980). *Schizophrenia and Civilization*. Northvale, US: Jason Aronson.

Turk, O. (2004). Personal Homepage. Available online: http://www.geocities.com/Pentagon/Bunker/6066/kurt.html.

Turkic Peoples. (2014). In *Encyclopaedia Britannica*. Available online: http://www.britannica.com/EBchecked/topic/609972/Turkic-peoples.

Tynianov, Y., Jakobson, R. (1928/1971). Problems in the Study of Literature and Language. In L. Matejka and K. Pomorska (Eds.), *Readings in Russian Poetics: Formalist and Structuralist Views*, pp. 66–79. Ann Arbor, US: University of Michigan Press.

Tyrrell, D. A. J., Crow, J. J., Parry, R. P., Johnson, E., Ferrier, I. N. (1979). Possible Virus in Schizophrenia and Some Neurological Disorders. *The Lancet*, 21, 839–841.

Uexkül, J. V. (1940/1982). The Theory of Meaning. *Semiotica*, 42, 25–82.

Unver, H. A. (2009). *Turkey's "Deep-State" and the Ergenekon Conundrum*. Middle East Institute Policy Brief, 23. Washington, DC, US: Middle East Institute.

Uspenskij, B. A. (1996–1997). *Selected Works*, vol. I–III. Moscow, RU: n.p.

Uzuner, B. (2000). *Mediterranean Waltz*. Istanbul, TR: Remzi Kitabevi.

Van Eck, C. (2003). *Purified by Blood: Honour Killings amongst Turks in the Netherlands*. Amsterdam, NL: Amsterdam University Press.

Van Horne, J. D., Berman, K. F., Weinberger, D. R. (1996). Pathophysiology of Schizophrenia: Insights from Neuroimaging. In S. J. Watson (Ed.), *Biology of Schizophrenia and Affective Disease*, pp. 393–420. Washington, DC, US: American Psychiatric Publishing.

Vaner, S. (1987). The army. In I. C. Schick and E. A. Tonak (Eds.), *Turkey in Transition: New Perspectives*, pp. 236–268. Oxford, UK: Oxford University Press.

Vaughn C. E., Snyder, K. S., Jones, S., Freeman, W. B., Falloon, I. R. (1984). Family Factors in Schizophrenic Relapse: Replication in California of the British Research on Expressed Emotion. *Archives of General Psychiatry*, 41, 1169–1177.

Vernadsky, V. I. (1926). *Biosfera*. Leningrad, RU: Nauka.

Voigt, V. (1995). In Memoriam of "Lotmanosphere." *Semiotica*, 105, 191–206.

Voloshinov, V. (1994). Critique of Saussurian Linguistics. In P. Morris (Ed.), *The Bakhtin Reader: Selected Readings of Bakhtin, Medvedev, Voloshinov*, pp. 25–37. London, UK: Edward Arnold.

Von Hammer, J. F. (1844). *Histoire de L'Empire Ottoman depuis Son Origine jusqu'a Nos Jours* [*History of the Ottoman Empire from its Origin to Our Time*]. Paris, FR: Bethune et Plon.

Walker, C. (1991). Delusion: What Did Jaspers Really Say? *British Journal of Psychiatry*, 159(suppl. 14), 94–103.

Watt, W. C. (1998). Semiotics. In *Routledge Encyclopedia of Philosophy*, vol. 8, pp. 675–679. London, UK: Routledge.

Weber, M. (1930). *The Protestant Ethic and the Spirit of Capitalism*. New York, US: Charles Scribner's Sons.

Werbner, P. (2003). *Pilgrims of Love: The Anthropology of a Sufi Cult*. Bloomington, US: Indiana University Press.

Whinfield, E. H. (1898/1975). *Teachings of Rumi: The Mathnawi of Maulana Jalalu-d-din Muhammad Rumi*. New York, US: Dutton.

Wiley, N. (1994). *The Semiotic Self*. Chicago, US: University of Chicago Press.

Wittgenstein, L. (1953). *Philosophical Investigations*. Trans. G.E.M. Anscombe. Oxford, UK: Basil Blackwell.

World Health Organization. (2003). Schizophrenia: Youth's Greatest Disabler. Available online: http://w3.whosea.org/schizophrenia/history.htm

Willis, T. (1684). *Two Discourses Concerning the Soul of Brutes, Which Is That of the Vital and Sensitive Man*. Trans. S. Pordage. London, UK: Thomas Dring, Ch. Harper, and John Leigh.

Wilson, J.V.K. (1967). Mental Diseases of Ancient Mesopotamia. In D. Brothwell and A.T. Sandison (Eds.), *Diseases of Antiquity*, pp. 723–733. Springfield, US: Charles C Thomas.

Yağcioğlu, H. (2005). Mustafa Kemals Will Never End. Available from the Turkish Ministry of Culture and Tourism website: http://www.kulturturizm.gov.tr/portal/tarih_en.asp?belgeno=5504.

Yahya, H. (1999a). *Maryam [Mary] An Exemplary Muslim Woman*. Istanbul, TR: Global Publishing.

Yahya, H. (1999b). *The Glad Tidings of the Messiah*. Istanbul, TR: Global Publishing.

Yasamee, F.A.K. (1996). *Ottoman Diplomacy: Abdulhamid II and the Great Powers*. Istanbul, TR: Isis Press.

Yildiz, M. (2014). *Turkish-English Dictionary*. Available online: http://translation.babylon.com/turkish/to-english/Turkish-English-Dictionary-(M.-Yildiz).

Yilmaz, I. (2005). State, Law, Civil Society and Islam in Contemporary Turkey. *The Muslim World*, 95, 385–411.

Zeman, J.J. (1988). Peirce on the Indeterminate and on the Object: Initial Reflections. *Grazer Philosophische Studien*, 32, 37–49.

Index

Note: Page numbers with *f* indicate figures.

Printed in Poland
by Amazon Fulfillment
Poland Sp. z o.o., Wrocław

93434199R00141